V I E W P O I N T S

from

Outdoor
PHOTOGRAPHY

VIEWPOINTS

from

Outdoor PHOTOGRAPHY

GUILD OF MASTER CRAFTSMAN PUBLICATIONS

First published 2001 by
Guild of Master Craftsman Publications Ltd
166 High Street, Lewes, East Sussex, BN7 1XU

© GMC Publications Ltd

ISBN 1 86108 232 0

British Cataloguing in Publication Data.
A catalogue record for this book is available from the British Library.

Front cover photograph: Glen Affric, by Niall Benvie
Back cover photographs, from left: Corfe Castle, by Steve Day;
Ashness Bridge, by Lee Frost; Rumps Peninsula, by Joe Cornish;
Alnwick Castle, by Chris Weston

Cover design by Ian Smith, GMC Studio
Original design, Ed Le Froy

Colour separation by Viscan Graphics Pte Ltd (Singapore)
Printed and bound by Kyodo Prinding (Singapore) under the supervision
of MRM Graphics, Winslow, Buckinghamshire, UK

C O N T E N T S

INTRODUCTION

View (vju:) n 1. the act of seeing or observing; an inspection. 2. vision or sight, esp. range of vision. 3. a scene, esp. of a fine tract of countryside. 4. a pictorial representation of a scene, such as a photograph.

Although the above dictionary definition takes 39 words to link a view with a photograph, most of us know that the relationship between the two is much closer. For readers of *Outdoor Photography* magazine, views and photography are inseparable partners. The view inspires and challenges the photographer, while the photograph immortalises the view. Once formed, this perfect circle is difficult to break.

This book is a compilation of 67 perfect circles, each is a different view from somewhere in the British Isles, faithfully captured on film by photographers who know these locations intimately. Some views you will recognise immediately – Derwent Water, the New Forest, Salisbury Cathedral, the Giant's Causeway. These are popular locations visited by tens of thousands of people each year. Others are known only to a handful of people, a lone photographer's favourite location, such as Lewesdon Hill, Feall Bay, or Kingcombe.

The Viewpoints section has quickly established itself as the most popular part of *Outdoor Photography* magazine. Its appeal lies in introducing readers to specific locations that have been photographed at the same time of year as the cover date of that particular issue. It is this seasonality - of text, photography and planning information - that makes Viewpoints such a vital reference for anyone who feels inspired enough to take the trouble of getting to the featured destination for themselves.

Of course, there is more to photographing these places than just turning up. Photographers should always respect the countryside, the flora and fauna that live there, and the interests of the local community. After all, there is surprisingly little public land in the UK, so making yourself aware of any restrictions on trespass or photography is advisable. The biggest landowners in the UK are the Ministry of Defence, the National Trust, the Forestry Commission and the Crown. Then, of course, there are thousands of farms and private estates. Quite often, a courteous introduction or polite request is all that's needed, especially as far as farmers are concerned.

It's important to remember too that most of the pictures taken for this book were the result of more than one visit. Landscape photographers swear by the need to reconnoitre an area. They study local maps in detail, find out the sunrise and sunset times, learn about the seasonal changes to the landscape, and take into account any number of factors that only local knowledge can bring.

My deepest gratitude and thanks go to all the photographers who have contributed to this book. Your efforts have been rewarded by the result and now your results can be enjoyed by all who hold this book.

Keith Wilson
Editor, *Outdoor Photography* magazine

Despite **Joe Cornish**'s relative lack of large format experience when he took this picture, it still remains a firm favourite – no little thanks to the National Trust

WITH A NAME LIKE MINE you might imagine I have more than a passing acquaintance with the People's Republic of Cornwall. In fact, I was born and raised in Devon, but we always took family holidays in Polzeath on the north Cornish coast. I have never been able to break the habit, for I still return there year after year. And in spite of 20 years of work and worldwide travel, I still consider it one of the best locations for landscape photography on the planet. Certainly it's been one of my most fruitful destinations.

One of the finest cliff walks in Cornwall is around the National Trust property of Pentire Farm, just north of Polzeath. Its outstanding feature is the Rumps Peninsula, an ancient defensive site whose western profile looks uncannily like a sleeping dragon. At least, that's what the grown-ups used to tell us when we were kids. Now I'm a bit older I know they were lying. It is, in fact, a fossilised stegosaurus...

In the summer of 1993 I had recently bought an Ebony 5x4in field camera. Having very little experience of shooting large format out on location, I decided to load the dice in my favour by trying it out somewhere very familiar and photogenic, so Rumps was selected. Although it was a fine afternoon when I set off, I readily admit I got better conditions than I had bargained for. That I was able to exploit those conditions fairly successfully was as much down to luck as good judgement, for my technique at the time was primitive. Having found a viewpoint with the foreground forms and textures I prefer, I initially set up a horizontal composition framed with a 90mm wideangle lens. But as the sun dropped, the colours improved, and the sky became more beautiful, I decided a vertical composition would allow me to make more of the clouds. To 'contain' the elements correctly now involved switching to a super-wideangle 58mm lens. A polariser helped emphasise the clouds, but when mounted in front of this lens, the corners were heavily vignetted. So I took the camera back off and wedged the polariser up against the rear element, using the camera bellows as an impromptu filter holder. I've used this method quite successfully ever since! A graduated ND filter was also needed to bring the sky exposure down overall. Super-wideangle large format lenses need extreme care in focusing and

because of my inexperience at the time, the distant parts of the scene are not as sharp as they could have been. Nevertheless, large format is also relatively forgiving of such minor imperfections because it rarely needs to be enlarged to an enormous scale, so I have probably got away with it.

I put a couple of transparencies into the National Trust photo library, and it was a source of huge satisfaction to me that the trust chose this image for a poster entitled *A Priceless View* to promote membership recruitment. It also serves to remind us that without the Trust's ownership, the Rumps, for instance, might now be a clifftop caravan park. Like any large organisation, the Trust gets its share of flak whenever it does anything unpopular. Yet most of the time while it successfully balances the conflicting demands of conservation and access for all, we take it for granted. So let's hear it for the National Trust, an organisation to whom landscape photographers should gratefully show their appreciation. ❖

Right The mackerel sky provided the perfect foil for the sprawling peninsula as it juts out into the sea
Ebony 45s with Schneider 58mm lens, Velvia, one second at f/11²/₃, polariser and 0.6 ND grad

Below Polzeath beach is worth a visit in its own right, even if your eventual aim is to reach Rumps Peninsula

RUMPS PENINSULA

Planning

How to get there New Polzeath is the nearest village to Rumps Peninsula, and makes a good base from which to start. The nearest parking is actually at Pentire Farm, but even then you will still have to walk nearly a mile or so to reach it.
Where to stay Camping and caravan sites abound on this part of the Cornish coast, as do B&Bs and hotels. Polzeath is very popular in the height of season, and booking ahead for accommodation is probably essential.

Best time of day Tide makes little or no difference. Early morning or late afternoon sunlight is probably best.
Other subjects Polzeath beach is magical at twilight, especially on a low tide. The tiny cove of Lundy Bay is rich in metamorphic rock details. Clifftop wildflowers are spectacular in May.
Ordnance survey map Landranger 200 or Explorer 106. Grid ref 934 812
Culinary delights The area is not renowned for its pubs, but at Padstow on the west side of the Camel Estuary is Rick Stein's world-famous The Seafood Restaurant

(01841 532485). You may need to book a table several weeks in advance though...

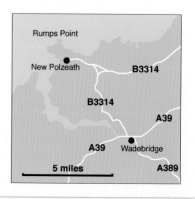

GIANT'S CAUSEWAY

 The mysterious basalt columns of the Giant's Causeway have been attracting visitors for many centuries – photographers, too. **Derek Croucher** is just one of them

OCCASIONALLY, a photographer's life is easy. You turn up at a location, the light is perfect, and you get what you want in no time, moving swiftly to the next target. More often than not, though, it requires patience and perseverance to achieve the result you want. That was certainly the case with this shot of eroded basalt columns at the Giant's Causeway in Northern Ireland.

I was part way through a three-week circuit of Ireland, and had a number of locations to photograph in this area of the north coast, but didn't want to move on until I had something special of the Causeway. So I waited for the light. Five days later I was still waiting. It wasn't until then that the sun was actually shining during the late afternoon to give low, cross lighting. In the meantime I had made sure I had shots of the other highlights in the area, including White Park Bay, Dunluce Castle, Carrickarade Rope Bridge and Glenariff waterfall. Plus at each dawn and evening, if the forecast mentioned any chance of sunshine, I would take a walk down to the Causeway to check out the conditions.

This is a fascinating area and deserves plenty of time to explore. The shapes were formed 60 million years ago when volcanic lava flowed on to the earth's surface. As it cooled, the rock arranged itself into the great polygonal section columns that remain today. There is a twin sister landscape – formed at the same time – in surprisingly nearby Scotland, at Fingal's Cave on the island of Staffa. This proximity of such a similar area gave rise to the popular legend that it was the work of the Irish giant Finn McCool who built it to get across to Scotland to fight with another giant. Certainly you can see how they would make ideal stepping stones.

Photographically speaking, on the Irish side you have the advantage of being able to take as much time as you like, whereas on Staffa the regular boat trips only give a limited stay on the island. And with the weather conditions I was experiencing, I was certainly in for a long wait. In the end, though, I got a good bag of shots, and this close-up detail was one of the last frames as the sun dipped down below the horizon. I chose my position so the fading light highlighted the wet rocks, and included some waves on the left so the eight second exposure would create a misty effect.

Once the films were processed I was pleased with the variety of different shots. It seems the lesson for me was the old one about turning a threat into an opportunity. Thinking about it, I often get my best shots when initially things don't go according to the original plan. The key is to be adaptable and not to give up when all seems lost. ❖

Left Also taken on the fifth evening just before the main shot. I spotted the elusive sunlight highlighting the shapes of the columns and had to work quickly before it was gone *Linhof Technikardan with 210mm lens, Velvia, 4 sec at f/45, neutral density graduate*

Below left The long exposure required for this shot after sunset has caused the waves to look more like low lying fog. Also note the coolness of the colour balance. Just before sunset, direct sunlight creates a very warm light, but by this time the conditions have given an obvious blue cast *Mamiya RZ67 with 50mm lens, Velvia, 16 sec at f/22, neutral density graduate*

Planning

Location The Giant's Causeway is on the north Antrim coast, near Bushmills.
How to get there By car take the B146 north of Bushmills. By bus use Ulsterbus 138 from Coleraine or 172 Ballycastle-Portrush.
What to shoot There is no end of ways to shoot the Causeway. Evening or dawn are both good (though at this time of year dawn light will be hidden behind the hill). Try catching the breaking waves in windy weather, short or long exposure; close-ups of the columns; views looking out to sea or back inland from the rocks; plus the view from above looking down.
What to take Plenty of film! If it's windy, a decent lens cloth – salt spray can build up surprisingly quickly. Occasionally I have had to clean the lens between every shot.
Nearest pub Causeway Hotel, (028207 31226). Also tea room at visitor centre.
Other times of year I would be happy to shoot here at any time of year. Thrift grows on the rocks in late spring and early summer.
Ordnance Survey map Discovery Series No 4 or 5 (overlapping)
Essential reading *The Giant's Causeway* by Philip Watson, The O'Brien Press, ISBN 0 8627 8675 4.

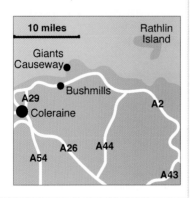

SANDYMOUTH AND DUCKPOOL

 Tourists love the Cornish beaches, but **Ross Hoddinott**, prefers to visit these two small beaches in the winter when there is better light and fewer people

SANDYMOUTH AND DUCKPOOL form just a small part of the impressive Cornish coastline. The two join in the middle and, when walking, it is difficult to know when one beach becomes the other.

Although Cornwall has been well photographed over the years, many places like Sandymouth and Duckpool remain relatively unknown. Some of the best photographs can be taken in winter, when you usually find yourself alone. In contrast, summer brings thousands of tourists to this area, which often makes photography impossible. I also prefer the light in winter, especially when it is cold and clarity is perfect. The sunsets can be spectacular.

One such day – having checked the tide was going to be out – I decided to head for Sandymouth. I nearly always prefer Sandymouth to Duckpool when the beach is exposed. Although the two beaches – cared for by the National Trust – are only separated by approximately one mile, they are quite different. Sandymouth, as its name suggests, is a large open sandy beach – at low tide – and has curious and colourful cliffs. Duckpool is smaller, sheltered and rugged, and the beach is quite rocky.

It is easy to take our coastline for granted when you live so close to it. Tourists probably see more of the beach in a fortnight's holiday than many locals do in the whole year. I try to visit my local beaches as regularly as possible, especially during winter. The seasonal changes in the landscape can be striking and alter from day to day – depending on the climate. As a photographer

Facts about Sandymouth and Duckpool

Tradition suggests Duckpool's name is the result of the medieval practice of ducking suspected witches in ponds. But mallard ducks can often be seen on the pond near the car park at Duckpool and offer a more likely – if less interesting – explanation. Sandymouth and Duckpool are both rich in shore life, but when the tide is in, the coast path that links them is worth walking. The views are beautiful from the cliff path and you may see ravens, kestrels hovering and buzzards. You are also increasingly likely to glimpse peregrine falcons here. This impressive bird stoops on its prey at speeds in excess of 120mph, so don't expect to take too many photographs! The National Trust cares for this stretch of north Cornwall. Help them maintain it by keeping to the paths and respecting the natural history found there. Take nothing but photographs. Close to Duckpool is a government communications site. Huge satellite dishes form part of NATO's early warning defence. Do not attempt to photograph them if you drive near the perimeter fence – they don't like it!

Left The tide was going out and the light fading. The smooth rocks were wet and reflective, and made an eyecatching foreground. The sky was colourless so I tried using a sepia filter, which I rarely employ. The resulting shutter speed was slow enough to blur the water effectively
Nikon F90x with Sigma 28mm lens, Sensia 100, 8 seconds at f/22, tripod

you can never be sure what you are going to find to photograph on a particular day.

Having parked my car and walked the short path to the beach, it was obvious I was going to enjoy a rewarding afternoon. The tide was fully out and had revealed dozens of shallow pools in the sandy beach. The pools were also reflecting the cliffs and the clear blue sky. When presented with such a beautiful natural landscape, photographs can seem easy. The greatest difficulty was selecting a view which showed the reflections at their best. I decided a low viewpoint would prove the most striking. Not only did it show the colours mirrored in the water, but it also emphasised the wavy patterns in the sand and the shadows they created. With the camera mounted on my faithful Benbo tripod, I composed the picture then added an 81C warm-up filter to add extra warmth to the sand and cliffs. I chose a small aperture of f/22 to keep the whole scene in sharp focus. Having taken a couple of pictures using the exposure recommended by the camera's lightmeter, I increased the shutter speed to underexpose the shot and further saturate the colours.

Conditions were so perfect, there were few signs anyone had visited the beach all day. Footprints can be one of the biggest problems when photographing sand. In the past I have composed a picture only for a surfer or dog to kindly run through the scene leaving distracting and ugly prints. You also need to watch where you walk.

The warmth and comfort of home grew more appealing as the feeling in my toes disappeared with the cold. And with the light fading, I returned to the car and promised myself a small whisky on my return home; purely to warm myself up, you understand. ❖

Above The patterns these molluscs create can be very photogenic. A Benbo tripod was essential as its versatility meant I could set it up securely on the awkward rocks. I used a macro lens to compose the picture and a small Lastolite reflector to angle some light into the shadows
Nikon F90x with Sigma 90mm lens, Sensia 100, 1/30sec at f/16

Planning

Location Sandymouth bay and Duckpool can be found near Bude on the north coast of Cornwall.

How to get there The neighbouring beaches can be found a few miles from Bude and are signposted. Take the Stibb road from the A39 on the Bude side of Kilkhampton. After one mile take second left turning to Sandymouth bay or follow the road for a further mile and turn left – immediately after crossing old stone bridge – to Duckpool.

What to shoot Beautiful beaches and coastline. A good and varied shore life. Rock pools. Mussels, limpets and whelks make interesting patterns when seen in the numbers found here.

What to take Wellington boots are a good idea. Also warm clothing as the wind can be bitter in winter. A plastic bag can prove useful to put your camera bag down on to stop it getting damp and sandy. A tripod is a necessity for landscape and macro work.

Nearest pub The New Inn in Kilkhampton (01288 321488) provides good pub grub and drink.

Nearest accommodation Plenty of good and reasonably priced B&Bs in Bude and Kilkhampton village. Ring the Bude TIC (01288 354240)

Other times of year In spring the coast path is home to an array of flowers and insects.

Ordnance Survey map Landranger 190

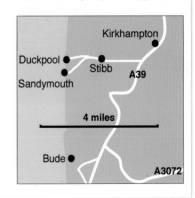

Right In difficult exposure conditions such as this I decide which particular part of the scene I want correctly exposed. In order to render the rocks and cliffs as dark silhouettes, I exposed off the whole scene and opened up a stop *Nikon FE2 with Nikkor 70mm lens, Velvia, 1/500sec at f/11, tripod*

KIMMERIDGE BAY

In the winter months **Colin Varndell** often heads to a little known bay on the Purbeck coast for the afterglow of a sunset at low tide

Facts about the Kimmeridge Bay

The bay is an established marine nature reserve and, due to its proximity of halfway along the English Channel, supports several species of marine life that are at or near their normal distribution limits. An information centre for the reserve has recently opened at Kimmeridge. For more information about the reserve, contact the warden on 01929 481044.

THE PURBECK COASTLINE in east Dorset is famous for its geology and magnificent scenery where a succession of bays and coves attract huge numbers of visitors throughout the year. Kimmeridge Bay does not act quite like many of the other honeypots along this stretch of coast, due to the inhospitable rocky shore. The shallow beach at low tide is covered with large rocks which are unusually rounded due to the constant pounding of the sea. These big, pebble shaped stones are difficult to negotiate, but can be highly photogenic.

The land immediately west of Kimmeridge Bay is controlled by the Ministry of Defence, and the coast path is closed except for weekends and the month of August. The path is steep and tortuous in places but the walk west towards Worbarrow Bay offers spectacular views of Kimmeridge and the dramatic Purbeck coastline beyond.

The best conditions for photography occur at low tide when the famous Kimmeridge ledges are exposed. The rock pools and beds of rock to the west side of the bay offer enormous potential for textures, patterns and close-ups of seaweed, shells and other life forms. From November to February the sun sets over the sea and although waiting for a sunset is something of a lottery, it is well worth making the effort, especially at low tide when the afterglow is reflected in the rock pools.

On this day, the sky was clear in the afternoon and having already checked the sunset would coincide with low tide at Kimmeridge, I made my way to the Purbeck coast. From the steep winding lane that leads down through Kimmeridge village and to the bay beyond, I could see the sunlight already glistening on the water. At the shoreline the effect of strong sunlight glistening on the rounded rocks and sparkling in the shallow pools was sheer magic, begging to be photographed.

This almost monochrome view of Kimmeridge Bay was taken by shooting directly towards the sun during its final descent about one hour before sunset. I had climbed up to the cliff top car park to maximise the depth of light on the water. The portrait format suited the width of the band of shimmering water and I felt it was important to include a strip of silhouetted rock at the base of the picture to give the image a solid foundation. In difficult exposure conditions such as

this I tend to look at a scene and decide what particular part I want correctly exposed. My first thoughts were that the brightness of the shimmer might trick my meter into gross underexposure so I was tempted to ignore this and expose for the sky. But after further consideration I wanted the rocks and cliffs to block up into dark silhouettes so I eventually exposed straight off the scene and opened up by one full stop. To prevent flare I held an A4 card above and in front of the lens so that its shadow fell across the front element. ❖

Left This was one of those cold January days when the sky remained clear. The sunset was not spectacular because there were no clouds in the sky but around 20 minutes after the sun had gone this golden glow developed on the horizon. The exposure reading was taken off the sky without including the glow at the moment of reading
Nikon FE2 with Nikkor 105mm macro lens, Velvia, 15 sec at f/11, tripod

Above This was taken in fairly rough weather with waves constantly crashing off these rocks. The long exposure has prevented these waves from being recorded
Nikon FE2 with Nikkor 200mm lens, Velvia, 4 sec at f/22, tripod

Planning

Location Kimmeridge Bay is situated on the south coast of Purbeck in east Dorset approximately halfway between Swanage and Weymouth.

How to get there There are no public transport facilities but Kimmeridge Bay is accessible by car. Travelling south from Wareham on the A351, take a turning right approximately 1½ miles from the town signposted Church Knowle. Turn right at Church Knowle and the road to Kimmeridge is signposted to the left just over one mile along this road.

What to shoot The best opportunities for sunsets occur at this time of year at low tide. Before sunset there are abundant opportunities along the shoreline for pebbles, patterns and textures.

What to take There is no actual tide table for Kimmeridge. Locals use the tide times for Portland, for which first water is the same but for second water 3½ hours are added for the time at Kimmeridge. Tide tables are available from Dorchester Tourist Information Centre, 11 Antelope Walk, Dorchester, Dorset DT1 1BE and cost £1 plus 27p stamp.

Nearest pub The New Inn, Church Knowle, Near Wareham

(01929 480936)

Where to stay Kimmeridge Farmhouse B&B (01929 480990), Chaldecotts B&B (01929 480936).

Other times of year The rock pools and the Kimmeridge ledges are always interesting throughout the year at low tide. Kimmeridge Bay is located on the Purbeck coast path which covers some of the most photogenic coastal landscapes in England. During spring and summer there is a wealth of interesting flowers along this stretch of coast.

Ordnance Survey map Purbeck and south Dorset, Outdoor Leisure Series No 15

Essential reading *Isle of Purbeck* by Paul Hyland, published by Dovecot Press, Stanbridge, Wimborne, Dorset BH21 4JD.

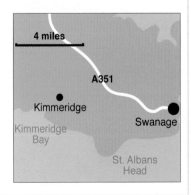

Right Taken near Queen Bess Rock. It was quite a low contrast scene, and so was easy to meter for. I think the sky only needed a one-stop ND grad, plus a polarising filter to deepen the blue areas a little. Being a distant scene, an aperture of f/11 or f/16 was sufficient, but I can't for the life of me remember the time exposure! *Cambo 58XL Wide with Cambo 6x9 back, Velvia*

BEDRUTHAN STEPS

These intriguing rock stacks on the north Cornwall coast make a great subject whatever the weather, but **Philip Askew** particularly likes them in moody, misty conditions

Facts about Bedruthan

Bedruthan Steps became a popular place to visit more than 100 years ago, when nearby Newquay had developed as a holiday resort. I've read that Victorian visitors found it a convenient attraction to visit, and would arrive in their horse-drawn carriages, paying a toll to the local farm of the time. Six Bronze Age barrows, two Iron Age cliff castles, and a 19th century iron mine are along two miles of this coastline. North Cornwall Heritage Coast and the Southwest Coast path runs along the cliffs.

Access to the beach (not NT) is made by a cliff staircase, which is the probable origination of the name Bedruthan Steps, and not the rock stacks which were supposed to be the stepping stones for the legendary giant. Be aware of the risk of being cut off by the tide. Pathway access to the cliff views commences from the National Trust car park at Carnewas, where there is a shop, visitor centre and very pleasant tea room. Opening times are limited during the colder months of the year.

BEDRUTHAN STEPS, a popular National Trust Cornish beauty spot, with its dramatic, wave-swept rock stacks and long expanse of beach, is much visited and photographed in the warmer months of the year. However, autumn and winter also offer the possibility of some great atmospheric shots.

Just occasionally, here in Cornwall, amid the many grey and wintry days, we get what I call golden days. Those days with warm, low-angled sunshine and with it, just a hint of mist. It's during these diffused lighting conditions that I make my way to Bedruthan Steps for the last few hours of daylight.

I have always preferred to photograph this stretch of coastline from the northern end, towards Park Head, looking south rather than taking the more popular view from the car park area. On a day with the right degree of mist, a sense of depth can be brought to the scene. The famous stacks (or giant's stepping stones, as legend would have it) fade off into the distance, leaving nearby Newquay (thankfully) obscured. Wave patterns of a flooding tide onto a still partly uncovered beach greatly add to the aesthetics of the scene.

The day I took the main picture illustrated here was one such day – or at least to start with. The weather became very murky and grey in the late afternoon. Hope for a decent picture was rapidly diminishing but I decided to wait it out. Very close to the time of sunset, the sky began to clear, revealing a very pleasing cloud formation – a usually elusive but important part of the picture-making equation that keeps me returning to many locations time and again. The clouds were constantly moving, so when the patterns looked balanced within the scene being viewed on the ground glass screen of my camera, I quickly closed the lens, set the aperture and inserted my 6x9cm rollfilm back. A drawback with using view cameras on a constantly changing scene is that you don't always get exactly what you see on the ground glass, due to the short time delay in setting the lens etc.

Metering for the scene was straightforward. Using a spotmeter, I chose the reading given off the nearest stack towards the centre of the picture, this being a mid grey with some degree of texture. I took two pictures and then re-composed for a landscape format shot, as I wanted to include a slight glimmer from the setting sun which had appeared through the clouds to the right. The winter months bring the setting sun closest to this scene which increases picture possibilities, especially for anyone with a not-so-wide lens. Two more pictures and the scene was gone. A reasonably successful day, but not so good as to stop me returning on another occasion when, fingers crossed, the combination of conditions could be even better!

If you should ever end up at Bedruthan Steps in weather such as this, don't be surprised if, while you're standing there next to your tripod, a perplexed rambler stops to ask: 'What are you taking a picture of in the murk?' Such occasions make me glad that we are not all blessed with the ability to see a potential picture. ❖

Below Like the main shot, this picture was also taken in February. A bitingly cold breeze had blown away a previously attractive slight haze. With no visible fade off amid the rocks, a different viewpoint was needed to visibly break up the mass. There was a very distracting bright stone in the foreground being illuminated by the sun. Some grass torn from nearby and laid over the stone solved the problem. The inclusion of the foreground took away an over-empty looking beach and sky
Cambo 58XL wide camera with Horseman 6x12 back, Velvia, four seconds at f/22, 0.9 ND grad and 81B warm-up filters

To contact Philip Askew, telephone 01503 26 4235

Planning

Location Carnewas and Bedruthan Steps, four miles northeast of Newquay, in Cornwall.
How to get there Just off the B3276 from Newquay to Padstow, signposted Carnewas, immediately opposite Bedruthan House Hotel (not to be confused with Bedruthan Steps Hotel).
Best time of day Mid-afternoon to sunset for the colder months. Late afternoon onwards for the warmer months of the year. If you want to take the dramatic view looking north from the staircase area, then I would suggest the morning light.
What to shoot Dramatic coastline with long expanse of beach. When walking north to the area illustrated in this feature, keep a lookout for other stop-off points offering different views, some of which suit the morning light. There is also some old but attractive stonewalling around and about, which holds interesting plantlife in the warmer months.
What to take A tripod is essential for a quality picture. A moderate to wideangle lens, and also a macro for plantlife in the summer. If you are prepared to sit it out for a picture, then warm clothing, stout footwear and a flask are strongly recommended.
Nearest pub Tredea Inn, Porthcothan Bay (01841 520540)
Nearest accommodation Bedruthan House Hotel (01637 860346)
Ordnance Survey map Landranger 200, grid ref for the main picture, 850 690.
Website www.connexions.co.uk/areas /html/bedruthan.html

Right The post-sunset light provides some wonderfully subtle tones, and the long shutter speed required smooths the water completely
Horseman SW612 with Rodenstock Grandragon-N 65mm f/4.5 lens on Velvia at f/22 and 40 seconds; centre filter ND graduated and 0.9 ND grad

SALTWICK BAY

For renowned landscape photographer **Joe Cornish**, the north-east coast of England is both close to home and close to his heart. In this article, he explains why

I TRAVEL A LOT in my line of work but, photographically speaking, I find as much inspiration where I live in North Yorkshire as I can anywhere else in the world. This is important for two reasons. Firstly, I see photography itself as a journey where I try always to improve my skills and develop my style and ideas. To do this requires frequent practice and experimentation and, having family responsibilities, I need to practise close to home. Secondly, since lighting conditions are a central theme of my work, inspiring locations nearby allow me to take advantage of magical lighting possibilities as I see them start to unfold.

Saltwick bay is one of my favourite backyard locations. Although close to the popular tourist destination of Whitby, and in spite of the holiday camp on the cliff above it, it is a lovely, windswept spot which I often have to myself. Facing north north east, it is usually at its best at dawn with low tide. But, for a few

brief weeks either side of the summer solstice, the sun sets in the north west beyond the headland of Saltwick Nab. It was in early July that I took the picture here, at around 10pm. It had been a slightly frustrating evening with good late sunlight but a total absence of clouds, which I much prefer in any landscape photo that includes the sky. I had tried to photograph the silhouette of a wrecked boat near the sea stack of Black Nab, but excessive contrast put paid to that idea.

After the sun had set, I was on my way back to the clifftop when I saw the incoming tide begin to creep up around these large, flat boulders. The rippling of the water made the scene too busy, but I realised the long exposure required might well help me out in this respect. Working as quickly as I could in the fading afterglow, I found a composition which would flow through the foreground of the image to convey depth and movement, and also which took into account the

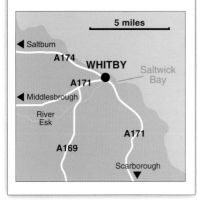

Planning

How to get there Start from Whitby Abbey. Take the minor road that goes south east towards Hawsker. A mile from the abbey is a left turn with a sign announcing Haven Holiday Camp. A paved single track road leads to the clifftop caravan and camping site. There is verge parking outside for non-residents. A steep track leads down to the (north east facing) bay, which is marked by the isolated headland of Saltwick Nab to the west, and the sea stack Black Nab to the east.

Where to stay There are plenty of camping and caravan sites in the surrounding areas, as well as B&Bs in nearby towns such as Whitby. Try the Northumbria Tourist Board (01913 753000), or visit www.travelengland.org.uk

Best time of day Low tide is best, although intermediate tides work well photographically, too. There is little beach at high tide, and beware of being cut off by an incoming tide at Black Nab. Although there is safe ground to retreat to, the cliff behind is steep and few would attempt climbing it. You might find yourself with a long cold wait until the tide retreated again!

Other subjects Whitby – beach, harbour, piers, abbey, rooftops, fishing boats and characters. Robin Hood's Bay – isolated smugglers' village, fossil rich foreshore, headland of Ravenscar. Sandsend – picturesque village; Runswick Bay – peaceful bay with village and fossil-rich foreshore. Staithes – dramatic fishing village; Scarborough – large traditional Yorkshire seaside resort, fine beach, castle, harbour.

Ordnance Survey map Landranger 94-921 107

Essential reading Northumbria & Hadrian's Wall by David Winpenny, £8.99, AA/Ordnance Survey (ISBN 0-7495-2057-4); and for photographic inspiration, take a look at Northumbria by Lee Frost, £20.00, Constable (ISBN 0-0947-7410-2)

reflective character of the foreground stones. I knew the fine weather sky and the water blurred by the long exposure would give a calm yet slightly mysterious atmosphere.

Low light – long exposure

Generally I work with a 5x4in camera, but on this occasion I had with me my Horseman SW612, which produces 6x12cm images on 120 roll film. I used the ground-glass screen to ensure a precise composition in which I kept the sky to a minimum. This was tricky with it being so dark, and of course viewing upside down. However, I feel the inversion of the image can be an advantage, provoking a more detached and balanced analysis of the elements. Having taken spotmeter readings off the foreground stones and the sky, I selected a 0.9 graduated filter (three stops) to help bridge the five stop gap between the two areas. I used the ground-glass to ensure correct positioning of the graduation zone.

Using a 65mm lens, I was fairly confident I could produce good sharpness throughout the image by stopping down to f/22, and I focussed on the middle section using an 8x magnifying loupe. To avoid a prominent hot spot in the centre of the image and the risk of

exposure fall-off at the edges (always more obvious with the panoramic formats) I used an ND graduated centre filter, matched to the 65mm. This takes 1^1/$_2$ stops out of incoming light. Since I normally rate Velvia at ISO 32, this meant my effective film speed was now ISO 10 or 12, before considering reciprocity failure! At 15 seconds, Fujifilm recommends opening up ^{2}/$_3$ of a stop with Velvia, and they don't recommend using it for longer exposures than this. Nonetheless, many photographers do, and I am one of them.

In this case I made exposures of 15 seconds, 25 seconds and 40 seconds, hoping to compensate both for reciprocity and the fading light. In the end, the longest exposure proved to be the best.

I was surprised, when I saw the processed film, that this shot worked as well as it did. The secret seems to be in the rich colour palette of film, tweaked, perhaps, by the distortions of reciprocity failure and the subtle intensity of fine weather twilight. The panoramic format suits the subject and the stunning quality of the Horseman lens does the rest. A 30x15in print will convince you that, when it comes to landscape, size does matter! ❖

MARLOES SANDS

If at first you don't get the light you want... wait. The last half hour before sunset might just be the answer to your prayers, as **Derek Croucher** discovered

A BEAUTIFUL STRETCH of beach, contrasting with great stacks of angled rock strata projecting up through the sand, combine to make Marloes Sands one of my favourite coastal locations. I spent a day there last autumn, but the presence of haze and cloud for much of the time made photography very difficult. Then – as is so often the case on a day like this – during the last half hour before sunset, the atmosphere softened the sunlight to a rich orange, while the clouds reflected this light onto one another, so that, even in the east, they were glowing yellow, orange and pink. For any photographer, it's times like this that make the waiting worthwhile.

Facts about Marloes Sands

Marloes lies within the Pembrokeshire Coast National Park, much of which is protected by the National Trust. There is plenty of public access, including from the Pembrokeshire Coast Path. There are two National Trust car parks, one just above the Sands, and one almost at the end of the peninsula, along with a small exhibition centre. In summer there is a ferry to Skomer Island with many opportunities for photographing nesting seabirds. Since the beach faces southwest, at this time of year there could also be good opportunities for shooting at dawn, but don't forget to check the tide tables, since a high tide would severely restrict your possibilities.

I had arrived mid morning, and planned to stay all day. At this time, the tide was high and the sand covered, so I took the path to the clifftop to take some general views of the rocks and waves. Luckily there was a strong westerly wind so this created some decent white water. I had a brief spell of blue sky before the cloud closed in and I returned to the car to have a quick coffee from the flask, then drove around for a while looking for any other good locations.

Footprints in the sand

About one and a half hours before sunset the tide had retreated, so I went to the beach, ready for any special lighting that might happen. One thing I was very careful to try and avoid was leaving any footprints in the sand, since I didn't yet know exactly where I would be shooting. As the light began to improve, I took a few shots, but still wasn't convinced I'd found a good composition. I checked my watch against the sunset time and decided I just had time to return to the clifftop. From there, due to the lighting and a few footprints I had not been able to avoid leaving, I was restricted to shooting towards the east, away from the most interesting rock strata. I quickly took a few shots, being forced to use a fast shutter speed due to the very high wind constantly shaking my camera on the tripod.

I scrambled back down to the beach, by now muttering obscenities because I felt I was missing the best of the light. Climbing onto one of the rock stacks, I finally found a spot I was happy with and began shooting, the light changing with every frame. I used a 50mm wideangle on my Mamiya RZ67 to take in the massive cumulous clouds overhead. An ND grad was needed to even out the sunlit area and the shadowed foreground, exposing for 1/4sec at f/16 on Velvia.

As the light faded I watched the clouds change colour and eventually turn grey. Only then, when I knew my work for that day was complete, could I go to the water's edge to dip my boots in and have the waves chase me up the beach. Some people never grow up! ❖

Planning

Location Marloes Sands is on the south side of a small peninsula, seven miles west of Milford Haven.

How to get there From Haverfordwest, take the B4327. After about 10 miles, turn right for the village of Marloes. Both car parks are beyond the village.

What to shoot Always try to visit at a low or mid tide. Take some from the clifftop and some from the beach, perhaps climbing on the rocks to gain extra height. If there is a good west wind try to capture the waves crashing on the rocks. If the tide is out, check out the low angle shot at the waters edge – there's often a good reflection, particularly after sunset.

What to take Wider lenses are the most useful in this area. ND grads and a polariser will probably be needed. Make sure you use a sturdy tripod if it's windy or for dawn/evening shooting.

Nearest pub There is a pub in the village of Marloes.

Other times of year Coasts show little change with the seasons. If possible, time your visit so the tide is low at dusk and dawn.

Ordnance Survey map Outdoor Leisure 36, South Pembrokeshire; grid reference 780075.

Essential reading *Pembrokeshire Coast Path* (Ordnance Survey National Trail Guide) by Brian John, Aurum Press, ISBN 1-85410-459-4, £10.99

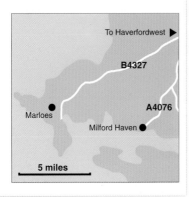

SEATON CLIFFS

Red rocks facing east? When better to photograph them than at sunrise? And, says **Niall Benvie**, you don't have to go to Arizona to find them...

MENTION 'Red Rock Country' to any photographer and there is a good chance that Arizona or the Colorado plateau will be the first places to spring to mind. However, Scotland has its own red rock formations – albeit on a more modest scale – on the coast north of Arbroath in Angus.

The most impressive features are found between Arbroath and Auchmithie (which appears as Musselcraig in Sir Walter Scott's *The Antiquary*). Here the rocks are mostly Lower Old Red Sandstone, although there is a rare section of Upper Old Red Sandstone, which has evaded erosion at Whiting Ness, the start of the Seaton Cliffs trail. The rock's relative softness makes it prone to sculpting by the sea and, in earlier epochs, the wind, too. This has resulted in a fine arch, the Needle's E'e, a substantial sea stack (now on dry land), the Deil's Heid, a series of fissure caves, and a gloup – or collapsed sea cave – known as the Gaylet Pot. Conglomerate or pudding stone features prominently in the geology and

at Auchmithie the cliffs have yielded a pebble beach rich in quartz and jasper, whose colours shine when an on-shore breeze glazes them with fine spray.

Most of the features on the Seaton Cliffs section are easily accessible from the trail, although getting to the seaward side of the Needle's E'e (the arch is much better viewed from here) involves a bit of climbing. This is not advisable in stormy weather or if there is a particularly high tide.

With its eastern aspect, the coastline here is best photographed at first light. This provides the option of warm light on the red sandstone cliffs or a striking sunrise silhouette of the Deil's Heid. The reddest light comes when the sun rises to meet a low cloud base and is reflected back; the colours at these times are as vivid as any from the American southwest.

When I took the main picture shown above, I had arrived at Whiting Ness at 7am, giving myself 40 minutes or so to find a composition and wait for sunrise.

Facts about Seaton Cliffs

Although the Seaton cliffs are nominally a nature reserve under the care of the Scottish Wildlife Trust, unfortunately the Trust is unable to support a full-time member of staff on site and, as a result, it suffers from the same abuses as any other under-appreciated location in the country. The botanically rich grassland of Carlingheugh Bay, at the northern end of the reserve, is annually churned up by trials bikes, while the soft, flat rock on the seaward side of the Needle's E'e allows 'Kenny' and his mates to play at being masons. Although it is possible to find compositions here which do not include defacement, they are more limited.

Left To avoid flare, I positioned myself so that the sun was hidden, but kept it as close to the edge of the rock as possible to imply it was just about to appear. Which, three minutes later, it did. Since I wanted the stack to be a solid silhouette, I went with a centre-weighted meter reading from the horizon just to the left of the rock *Nikon F4 with 20mm lens, Velvia, 1/60sec at f/11, tripod*

The sky was entirely cloudless so the sun was not going to be as red as I would have liked, so I set out to mitigate this by making a big block of the clear blue sky a key part of the composition. The sky is usually at its richest blue in the zenith – directly above us – so when I need to include it in frame, I shoot from as low an angle as possible. In this case, it meant going in close to the cliff with a 20mm lens. A bonus was the exaggeration of the dimensions of the low cliff, which now appeared to tower overhead.

Exposing directly-lit sandstone can be a bit tricky, particularly when some areas are in full sun and others are semi-shaded. I decided it was most important that the conglomerate comprising the upper part of the cliff wasn't burned out, so I took a spot reading off a mid-toned area – the plain sandstone at the far left of the picture – and closed down half a stop. I confirmed that this was a good mid tone by metering the zenith, itself

a reliable mid tone if the sky is cloudless.

It's always very pleasant when you are able to get the day's work done before breakfast. ❖

Below On the foreshore at Auchmithie pebbles worked free from the cliffs find their way into depressions in the sandstone, eroding it in a pestle and mortar fashion. This reveals the fabulous patterns of lamination on the sandstone. The colours are best when an easterly wind is blowing a fine spray on to the beach
Nikon F4 with 90mm lens, Velvia, 1/8sec at f/11, 81A warm-up filter, tripod

Planning

Location Arbroath is on the Scottish east coast, about 25km along the A92 from Dundee. The Seaton Cliffs trail begins at Whiting Ness, at the north end of Victoria Park. Auchmithie is another 6km up the coast.
Getting there Arbroath is easily accessible by train. Alternatively, take the A92 from Montrose (approaching from the north) or from Dundee (approaching from the south). For Auchmithie, follow the A92 through Arbroath and turn right at the Meadowbank Inn on the northern outskirts of the town. Take this minor road, turn left at the T-junction then follow the signs for Auchmithie.
Where to stay Farmhouse Kitchen, Grange of Conon (01241 860202).
What to shoot As well as the grand scenics, there are lots of interesting patterns within the sandstone, and the strand line at Auchmithie often has interesting objects. People fish for cod from the rocks below the Seaton trail; I have photographed both the fish and the fishermen.
What to take The location is bitterly cold when the wind is out of the east, so dress accordingly. A pair of boots with good treads (but nothing metallic that will score the sandstone) is recommended if you want to climb

round to the front of the Needle's E'e. A bike will save a lot of plod-time.
Nearest pub The Old Brew House, Arbroath (3 High Street) by the harbour. The But and Ben is a fine restaurant in Auchmithie which specialises in traditional Scottish cooking (*not* porridge and haggis) and seafood.
Other times The summer months bring a profusion of flowers along the coast here, enjoying the locally lime-rich soils. Auchmithie has a small colony of puffins as well as cliff-nesting house martins, but these are both relatively inaccessible.
Ordnance Survey map Landranger 54
Essential reading Info about the Seaton Cliffs nature reserve is available from the Scottish Wildlife Trust (0131 312 7765); Arbroath Tourist Information, Market Place, Arbroath (01241 872609).

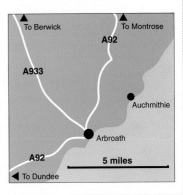

SOLWAY FIRTH

The Solway Firth is home to many a captivating sunset, says **David Herrod**. The hills of Dumfries to the north give you a choice of undulating backdrops, too

NOT BEING a bird photographer, which I consider to be a very specialised field, the Solway attracts me for its landscape potential. With its sparse population and lack of industrialisation, it has an appealing raw wildness. From the Cumbrian coast, the hills of Dumfries and Galloway can be seen across the water and can form an undulating backdrop to a beach composition, or the spectacular sunsets which can be seen from here.

Low tide is the best time. Rippled sand and rock pools make interesting subjects, but watch out for the tide

Facts about the Solway Firth

Situated on the west coast and separating England from Scotland, the Solway is an estuary with a boundary from the Mull of Galloway to St Bees Head. The coastline on the English side consists of sand flats, mud flats and salt marshes. On the Scottish side, the coastline is more rugged with sandy bays. The area is a haven for wildlife. Large numbers of birds feed on the flats and the salt marshes provide habitats for such rare creatures as natterjack toads and numerous species of flowers and plants.

The turf on the salt marshes is of such fine quality that it is harvested commercially and covers the greens of most of the bowling clubs in the country. The area has many historical sites and Sites of Special Scientific Interest and so, while providing a wealth of interest, care must be taken not to cause damage or disrupt the ecology.

Left Taken at low tide, a sand bar has trapped a lagoon, which curves nicely towards the sunset and the distant hill. The setting sun suffuses the scene with a warm glow which reflects from the water. Care has to be taken when photographing from sand bars, not to get cut off on a rising tide
Nikon FE2 with 28mm wideangle lens, Kodachrome 64

which, particularly in the upper reaches, can be fast moving. To quote Sir Walter Scott: 'Those that dream on the Solway, may wake up in another world.' While the shore can be rewarding, the Solway can be seen from inland, too. The foothills of the Lake District fells offer ideal viewpoints.

Given the right conditions and the time of day, the views can make you gasp. It was on the return from one of my fell walks that I took the shot shown left. I was coming off the fells to the west of Loweswater and had this view of the purple hills of Galloway with a shining sliver of gleaming pink sea in front. As the sun went down it reflected on the underside of the clouds, causing a colourful afterglow.

I have often watched this effect and know how fast it changes, so my camera was already on the tripod, focussed and roughly composed. I watched the rapidly spreading colours and continually spotmetered the bright colour on the underside of the cloud. It is important to keep this saturated and let the shadows find their own density. Washed out colours with shadow detail would be a disaster.

I used no filters. With Fuji Velvia, my favourite colour film, I find its natural colour perfect for this situation. When I thought the display was reaching its climax, I checked the composition, adjusted the exposure controls and fired. No matter how many sunsets I see, each fresh one fills me with awe. ❖

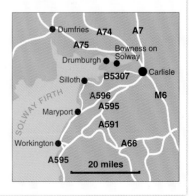

Above At Dubmill Point the receding sand ripples, combined with the stream and the reflection, draw attention to the farm building and its isolation. The distant shape of Criffel, on the Scottish coast forms the horizon to what would otherwise be an indiscernible merging of sea and sky
Nikon FE2 with Scotchchrome 1000

Planning

Location The northern coast of Cumbria and southern coast of Dumfries.

How to get there The Cumbrian coastline is accessible from the B5307 Carlisle-Silloth road, with unclassified roads leading from this to Drumburgh and Bowness on Solway, where there are good vantage points for bird watching. Burgh Marshes are also accessible. The B5300 Silloth-Maryport road runs along the coast and from this there are numerous car parking areas with access to the beach. Be warned: car thieves operate here, so, do not leave anything valuable in the car, or anything on display to tempt a break in.

What to shoot This is an ideal location for many types of outdoor photography – birds, plants, rock pools, seascapes and perhaps the most spectacular of all, sunsets.

What to take As well as your usual photographic equipment, warm and windproof clothing is essential. A cold wind blows off the sea and, especially if you are waiting for something to happen, you can soon find yourself shivering. Carlisle is the best place to stock up with film.

Best time of year Late summer to autumn. Check the weather forecast, tide tables and sunset times, before setting off.

Ordnance Survey map Landranger 85

Essential reading Try *The Solway Firth Review*, published by the Solway Firth Partnership in 1996, call 01387 260000 for details.

FEALL BAY, COLL

 Niall Benvie thinks he may be the only photographer to regularly visit Scotland's beautiful Isle of Coll. Not any more...

I'M NOT SURE if I should tell you about Feall Bay on the Isle of Coll. Of all the Scottish islands, Coll is the one I've enjoyed most. It has several fine beaches, but Feall (pronounced 'foil') is my favourite. And I have yet to meet another photographer working there. So far.

Coll lies with its neighbour, Tiree, in the Inner Hebrides, to the north west of Mull. It is not a big island, nor are there the rugged mountains which define the skyline of Rum or Jura. Instead, Coll's riches lie along its fringes where it meets the Atlantic. Long sandy beaches are slowly transformed by the prevailing wind and marram grass into sand dunes. Behind them is the fertile coastal plain, the machair, where wind-blown fragments of lime-rich shell sand sweeten the sour peat.

Here, are purple orchids and spring squill, yellow flag and purple loosestrife. A succession of species colours the machair from May to September, providing cover for breeding wading birds and the unsleeping corncrake.

Above Sand patterns in Feall Bay, Isle of Coll in the soft evening light of August *Nikon F4 with 20mm lens, Velvia, 1/4 second at f/11, -2 stop hard-edge ND filter, tripod*

Feall Bay beach looks north, its eastern flank guarded by an Iron Age fort below Ben Feall and ending 1.5km to the west at Port Mine. Feall is special because it is an empty stage where, without the distraction of a dramatic set, light and sand, wind and water come together to create their own dramatic dialogue. Coll and Tiree boast the longest hours of sunshine in the UK; their northerly latitude can mean sunshine from 4.30am to 9.30pm in summer and Atlantic weather tends to pass over these islands before falling as rain when it meets the mainland.

Evening shooting is usually a more relaxed business than rising for dawn. I knew I would be able to shoot until about 9pm on this August evening, so took time to look over the beach in advance. I settled on the most

Facts about Coll

Making a living from the land on Coll is not easy. Although most farmers are quite happy to have visitors around, some common sense should be exercised if you plan to bring a dog to the island, especially near the livestock which are central to the island's economy. Similarly, some will allow you to camp on their land if the simply courtesy of asking first is

shown. The RSPB has a sizeable nature reserve in the south west of Coll, with a visitors' centre at Totronald. Here, there are significant populations of the endangered corncrake as well as breeding waders and the warden, Charlie Self, is happy to advise on any sensitive areas which should be avoided at certain times of year.

Left By early August on Coll there are a lot of young twite, the upland counterpart of the linnet. I slowly followed a group along a fence line as they rose and fell to feed on weed seeds, eventually getting close enough for this portrait
Nikon F5 with 300mm lens plus x1.4 converter, Velvia, tripod

ripply sand I could find and framed up with a 20mm, to exaggerate the foreground. The light was streaming in from the left to highlight the edges of the ripples.

I routinely use a graduated ND filter for landscapes which include the sky; the contrast range is often just too great for slide film to accommodate detail in it and the foreground. Here, I fitted a -2 stop hard-edged Singh-Ray, sliding it in its holder so that only the sea, Ben Feall and the sky were held back.

Since I needed foreground to background sharpness, I used the lens's hyperfocal scale. This ensured the most efficient use of the depth of field available at the taking aperture of f/11. The focusing ring was moved to align the f/11 hyperfocal mark with infinity (for background sharpness); the other hyperfocal mark, indicating the closest point, showed 0.7m, close enough to keep the foreground sharp. Had I just focused on the foreground, 0.7m away, my depth of field would have extended only from 0.5m to 2m.

So now you know. And if I meet other photographers on my next visit to Coll, I've only myself to blame. ❖

Below While waiting for the best light for landscapes, take a look round for details such as these bird prints. If the sun falls too low in the sky, shadows showing relief start to merge and forms become ill-defined
Nikon F4 with 90mm lens, Velvia, tripod

Planning

Location Coll is in the Inner Hebrides, 2 hours and 40 minutes by Calmac ferry from Oban. If you sail on a Friday, the boat goes by Tiree first and the journey takes another couple of hours.

Getting there You can travel as either a foot passenger or take your vehicle to Coll with Calmac, leaving from Oban. From 21 April to 21 October, the MV Clansman leaves at 6.30am. There are no sailings on Thursdays or Sundays. Return fare, for driver and a vehicle up to 5m is £125.85. Confirm prices, timetables and all other information on 01475 650100/ www.calmac.co.uk.

Where to stay For B&B try Taigh-Solas (01879 230333) and others. If you prefer a hotel, The Coll Hotel (01879 230334) in Arinagour is a good option. In fact, it is the only option. There is a campsite at the Garden House (01879 230374).

What to shoot As well as the gorgeous beaches, the machair is rich in wildflowers and some lochs support a population of wild greylag geese. The corncrake is a Schedule One species and a licence must be obtained from Scottish Natural Heritage (0131 447 4784) to photograph it during the breeding season - which can last well into August. Otters are not uncommon around the coast.

What to take If you don't take a car,

you will definitely need a bike to get around. These can be hired at the pier (01879 230382). For campers, sources of clean wild water for drinking are very scarce. There is, however, a tap beside the phone box in Arinagour which seems to be for public use. I always take a week's supply in the camper with me since in some summers the island is prone to drought.

Nearest pub The Coll Hotel.

Other times of year Late April to late May sees the first flush of flowers over the machair and this is the time when you have the best chance of seeing a corncrake. Winter brings not only the risk of ferry sailings disrupted by bad weather but the sun sets too far to the south to be ideal for Feall Bay.

Ordnance Survey map Landranger Sheet 46. Conveniently, all on one map, with Tiree.

Essential reading Go to the excellent Coll website for full information about the island - www.collinfo.dircon.co.uk

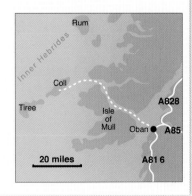

ASHNESS BRIDGE

 It may be one of the most photographed locations in the Lake District, but when he's in the area, **Lee Frost** just can't resist another visit to Ashness Bridge

THERE ARE CERTAIN scenes up and down the country that over the years have come to be regarded as classic examples of the English landscape at its very best.

Ashness Bridge is one of them. It may be cliched and over-photographed, but there's a very good reason for this – it's one of the most compositionally perfect and naturally beautiful scenes you're likely to find in the whole of Lakeland. From the tumbling Ashness Gill and 300-year-old stone bridge, to the furtive glimpse of distant Derwent Water and Bassenthwaite, and the magnificent fells of the Skiddaw range, it's got the lot.

Ashness Bridge is also close to my heart for more

sentimental reasons. As a boy scout I spent many memorable weekends bunking in the old slater's hut nearby which provided a base from which to hike into the hills. The routine of rising at dawn and taking a wake-up dip in the freezing waters of Ashness Gill will stay with me forever – as will the goosebumps!

Stormy warning

The main image shown here was taken during early November, on one of those frustrating autumnal days where the sky is laden with dark clouds, with frequent bursts of heavy rain. However, experience has taught me that such weather conditions are worth braving because if a break does appear, and light falls where you want it to – a tall order, but miracles do happen – the effect is always magnificent. Just make sure you're ready to capture it on film.

Arriving late morning with my wife (it was supposed to be a romantic break!), I found a convenient rock in the middle of the stream that was big enough for me and my tripod, then composed the scene through a 55mm wideangle lens on my trusty Pentax 67.

Front-to-back sharpness was achieved by stopping down to f/22 then using the depth-of-field scale on the lens barrel to determine the point of focus. An 81C warm-up filter enhanced the rich autumnal colours and a 0.6 neutral density grad exaggerated the stormy sky. The grad was angled to follow the bracken-clad ridge and line of trees running high right to low left.

All I had to do then was wait. I could see from the drifting clouds that a break was imminent, and after 30-40 minutes my prayers were answered – a brief burst of sunlight hit the foreground of the scene. It only lasted 30 seconds, but this was long enough for me to take a spot reading from the sunlit bridge to determine correct exposure – 1/2sec at f/22 – and fire off a few frames before cloud obscured the sun again.

The most annoying aspect of taking these pictures wasn't the unpredictable weather, but the tourists who would frequently stop their cars on or near the bridge then jump out to enjoy the view – oblivious to my shouts and frantically-waving arms.

Paranoid that the light would break while there was a bright red Ford Mondeo in the middle of my shot, my wife was duly dispatched to point out the car park no more than 100m away, and politely explain that if the vehicle wasn't moved post haste, she wouldn't be held responsible for my actions.

It did the trick. More importantly, I got the shot. ❖

Below left This is Barrow Beck flowing between mossy boulders in woodland near the Ashness Bridge car park. Grey, drizzly weather ruled out wider views, but such conditions bring soft, shadowless light that's ideal for recording the rich colours of autumnal woodland. Use a polariser to maximise colour saturation by reducing glare on the wet rocks and foliage. Its two-stop light loss will also give you a longer exposure to blur moving water *Pentax 67 with 55mm lens, Velvia, 2 seconds at f/16, polariser and 81B warm-up filters*

Planning

Location Ashness Bridge is located three miles south of Keswick in the Lake District, Cumbria.

How to get there By car come out of Keswick town centre heading south and pick up the B5289 signposted Borrowdale. After approx 2 1/2 miles watch out for a left turn onto a minor road signed for Watendlath and Ashness Bridge. Follow this road for 1/2 mile, cross the bridge and pull into car park approx 100m on right. By bus, take the 77 or the 79 from Keswick bus station, hop off at Ashness Gate then walk up the minor road to Ashness Bridge.

What to shoot The view to Ashness Bridge and beyond is the obvious highlight. A couple of miles up the road is Surprise View with superb panoramic views across Derwentwater – great at sunset. Grange village, a couple of miles beyond the Ashness Bridge turn-off, is highly photogenic, plus the B5289 gives great views of Derwent's shore as you head away from Keswick.

What to take Stout boots are advised for safe rock-hopping in Ashness Gill, plus waterproofs in dodgy weather if you walk rather than drive. A 28-70mm zoom will cover your needs for views and details, plus polariser, warm-up and neutral density grad filters, lots of slow-speed film and a solid tripod.

Nearest pub Try The Dog & Gun (01768 773463) or The Four-in-Hands (01768 772069), both on Lake Road.

Other times of year Ashness Bridge is a year-round classic, with every season adding its own magic. Strutta Wood and Ashness Woods come into their own in autumn for woodland views and details full of rich colours while Watendlath looks magnificent on a clear autumnal afternoon with its cottages and bracken-covered hills reflecting in the beck. Winter is a good time to photograph Derwent from the shore using fences and jetties as foreground interest.

Ordnance Survey map Outdoor Leisure 4, The English Lakes – North West; grid ref 2719

Essential reading Lakeland Landscapes by Rob Talbot & Robin Whiteman, Weidenfeld & Nicolson (ISBN 0-297-82204-7), £19.99.

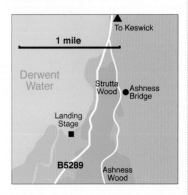

Right Like a sheet of opaque glass, Derwent Water is attractive from almost any viewpoint. This image was taken at the lake's southern end, where it often floods and becomes marshy
Horseman SW 612 with 65mm Grandagon-N f/4.5 lens, Velvia, four seconds at f/22, ND graduated centre filter, Gitzo tripod

Putting the cat firmly among the pigeons, **Joe Cornish** declares his love for Derwent Water – and his loathing for some of the other areas of the Lake District

IN GENERAL I think I'm quite easy going and tolerant, willing to see the other person's point of view, and happy to sit on the fence. But not when it comes to the Lake District. I loathe Windermere. I find Ullswater uninspiring. Thirlmere is a conifer plantation-dominated wasteland. Grasmere is a place for picnics.

Ditto Buttermere. Isolated in the southwest, Wast Water is mean, moody and magnificent, but photographically a struggle. For the landscape photographer, Derwent Water is by far the most beautiful of the Cumbrian Lakes. There, I'm off the fence!

The one place in England I could fantasise about

level is high. For the main shot here I was up before sunrise on a changeable autumn morning. From the road I could see reflections on the shallow water, so I donned my wellingtons and set off across the sodden fields. I found the foreground elements that I needed, but as the sun rose, so too did the breeze, blotting the reflection and undermining an image which intended to convey stillness and peace. I stayed, waiting and watching, making exposures at slacker moments in the wind. Before long, the sun disappeared into the building cloud, and my dawn shoot was over. Of the five exposures I made, only one was worth keeping. Here, the lack of reflection is compensated for by the subtle colouring, the shimmering light on the water, and the depth of shadow detail.

On another occasion I stood at Barrow Bay on the east side of the lake. Two fishermen stood on the end of the pier. The light was dull, but there was a total absence of wind and a curious timeless quality that inspired me to shoot in spite of the light. A large tree limb had collapsed into the lake, creating a compositional element which would never have worked in stronger lighting conditions. Whether the result really works is debatable, but I was glad to have tried something beyond my traditional 'comfort zone.'

The Derwent Water area has virtually unlimited potential, for as well as magnificent views it has beautiful broadleaf woodland fringes, rocky outcrops, picturesque farms and cascading waterfalls. It even has Casterigg stone circle, an ancient monument in an incomparable setting. If you can avoid school holidays and weekends, the northern lakes still provide peace and quiet, especially out on the fells. And if you can get up before dawn when the weather is fine, nowhere else in England will reward you like Derwent Water. ❖

Opposite page, bottom Sometimes even the blandest light conditions can provide something intriguing. At these times look for graphic shapes and textures in the landscape *Ebony 45SW with 58mm Super Angulon f/5.6 lens, Velvia, four seconds at f/11, 0.45 ND graduated centre filter*

living in is Keswick. With Derwent Water to the south and Skiddaw, Lonscale Fell and Blencathra as a mountain backdrop to the north, this is surely the most spectacular town setting in England. A healthy flow of tourists and day-trippers keeps the economy buoyant, but its more remote northerly location ensures that the traffic jams which blight Windermere and Ambleside are rare. The worst thing about Keswick is the Lake District weather. But when it is fine or changeable, nowhere else in the Lakes has so many viewpoints and such environmental variety to challenge your photographic skills.

The one location which (dare I suggest) you should avoid is Ashness Bridge on the Watendlath Road. It has been done to death, and like Vivaldi's *Four Seasons*, is devalued by overexposure. Yet from Ashness Bridge a path leads across the west-facing slopes of Castlerigg Fell to Falcon Crag, from which there are tremendous views across the lake and to the mountains beyond. I have taken this route on numerous occasions, but I have yet to see more than a couple of other walkers up there.

To the west side of the lake is the shapely ridge of Cat Bells, and here you will certainly see more people. This must be one of the most popular walks in the northern lakes, and erosion has taken a serious toll on the ridge itself. Its views will quickly explain its popularity, for once up onto the high part of the ridge, the outlook is truly panoramic, with photogenic possibilities to all points of the compass. This is the best place from which to photograph magical Newlands Valley, as well as Skiddaw, Derwent Water and Borrowdale.

At the south end of the lake, where the river flows in from its Borrowdale catchment area, is a flood plain with Grange-in-Borrowdale at its southernmost point. This rich grazing land is often inundated when the lake

Planning

How to get there Derwent Water is in the north of the Cumbrian Fells. It can be approached via the A591, which is picturesque but takes you through the often congested Windermere and Ambleside. From Scotland or the northeast, take the quieter A66 (which meets the M6 at Penrith).

Where to stay Most Derwent Water explorers stay in Keswick, but there are also hotels and guesthouses on the Borrowdale road. Caravan and camping sites can be found in Keswick, Braithwaite and Borrowdale.

What to take Landscape and nature photographers should take their usual photographic arsenal. A tripod is essential, and if you are going to hike any distance a carbon fibre model will lighten the load. Always get a weather forecast before venturing onto the fells, and take a waterproof whatever the weather. If you carry a lot of gear, hiking poles will ease the load on your knees. Always carry water and food on longer hikes. Wellingtons will help on lake edges, and by streams and waterfalls.

What to shoot Or what not to shoot – that is the question! When it's dull,

rock details, lichens, wildflowers, streams and waterfalls all make good subjects. When it is fine, enjoy the most scenic viewpoints in all England.

Best times of day For tranquillity and magical lighting, it has to be dawn.

Best time of year Early winter, with a dusting of snow on the mountains, and frost on the falling leaves. But any time of year will have something to offer if the light is good.

Ordnance Survey map Landranger 89 and 90; Outdoor Leisure sheet 4.

Essential reading For a good general background, including geographical and geological development, try *The Lake District: the official national park guide*, by Terry Marsh, £8.99, David & Charles, ISBN 1-898630-11-9.

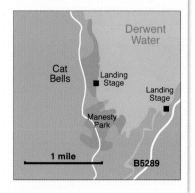

Right By waiting till all the tourists had left the shore, also meant having the advantage of soft early evening light for this shot
Horseman 45HD with 6x12 panoramic film back and 90mm lens, 1sec at f/16, Velvia, ND.06 graduated filter

Below It is always nice to be able to place a photograph in the season it was taken. The rowan tree does that perfectly here and adds colour contrast to the picture. The few clouds rolling around the sky complement the mood of the whole scene.
Horseman 45HD and 6x12 roll film back with 120mm lens, 1/2sec at f/22, Velvia, polarising filter and grad coral No1

WAST WATER

According to **David Tarn** Wast Water is 'the second best lake in the district', but it remains the most challenging to photograph. He reveals why

I WOULD LIKE to know who it was that said, 'If it is beauty you seek don't go to Wast Water, you will find no beauty there.'

It may have been a respected artist or poet, maybe even the great Wordsworth himself, but whoever it was would surely regret their statement now, especially as the Lake District National Park has adopted the view of Wast Water as its symbol.

For my taste Wast Water is the second best lake in the district and easily the most challenging to photograph. There seems to be only the one place from which to view and photograph the lake, this the classic

On the second attempt from my B&B I still drove through the Duddon Valley, but this time I drove straight through all the way to Wast Water. On arrival I was well pleased to see even from a distance that the deepest lake in England was reflecting the highest mountain perfectly on its surface.

On making my way down to the shore I was less pleased – the lake shore looked like the beach at Blackpool. Throngs of people had chosen to visit Wast Water and to sit about looking at it. I took a picture using the widest lens I had and composed so that as few people as possible would appear in the shot. The result wasn't bad at all. In fact, had I been able to preview the finished transparency I might have been satisfied with that and moved on. As it was I went in search of another view.

What I found was a view from a position just above the roadside using a wonderful rowan tree as foreground. The colours were rich and very indicative of the early autumn or late summer, and the viewpoint is just a little different from the one everybody has seen a hundred times before. This has undoubtedly helped the picture to sell for use on calendars, which it has done a couple of times already.

I took two versions of the picture, one on 645 and a panoramic version on 6x12. From a commercial point of view it can be useful to offer alternatives of the same basic picture. I did the same with the main picture. By waiting until late in the evening all the tourists had gone home. I think one of the great benefits of being a landscape photographer is the privilege of seeing places like this at their best, and on your own.

So if I rate Wast Water as the second best lake in the district, what is the best? Derwent Water. From every angle it is just wonderful. ❖

Below left Fast flowing water squeezed between rocks has always held an appeal for me as a photographer, and the water here in the Duddon Valley has a wonderful clean blue/green look to it. *Horseman 45HD with 6x12 roll film back and 90mm lens, 1/2sec at f/22, Velvia, polarising filter*

view with the well-known peaks of Yewbarrow, Great Gable and Lingmel forming the backdrop to the lake itself. So well known is the view that when I showed the resulting picture to my wife she said, 'That's an old one isn't it? We have a print of it somewhere.'

The print is a Heaton Cooper painting we bought years ago, but the view, even the angle of the sun are the same as my picture. Of course, there are other views to find and this is part of the challenge of Wast Water. The other part is to make this 'standard view' just that bit different from everyone else's version of it.

Wast Water is a remote lake and getting there from anywhere else in the Lake District can take quite a while. I took the route along Wrynose Pass and then turned left to traverse the Duddon Valley. It took me two days to get to Wast Water from the B&B I was staying at in Bowness.

The first day I didn't get past the Duddon Valley – I stopped there and took some photographs of Birks Rapids and Birks Bridge and the valley itself with the rowan trees. The Duddon Valley is an unknown corner of the Lake District, frequented by walkers and artists but very few tourists. This is because the Duddon Valley contains no lake!

Planning

Location The Lake District, Cumbria, in northwest England just below Scotland

How to get there The roads are narrow and winding and can be steep in places. When I first visited the Lake District I went to Wast Water via the Wrynose and Hardnott Passes. This is the direct route although I have never been this way again – the car I was using at the time needed an oil transfusion at the earliest opportunity. It is easier to take the longer route through the Duddon Valley, missing Hardnott Pass altogether.

Where to stay The Lake District is full of places to stay of every kind. However, if you plan to be at Wast Water first thing in the morning you have a more limited selection. There is the Wasdale Head Inn, which is a little pricey at £70-£90 per night for a double room. They also have a number of self-catering apartments available. For other places to stay, contact Whitehaven Tourist Information Centre: 01946 852939

What to Shoot As well as the lake, there are the screes on the far shore, the Scafell Pikes and some interesting field patterns at the top of the valley if

you feel like walking up the hills to gain some elevation.

What to take Walking boots and a good book to read until all the tourists go home.

Nearest pub The Wasdale Head Inn – it's the only pub there!

Other times of year Winter with snow on the three peaks can look great, if you can get to Wast Water at that time.

Ordnance Survey Map Outdoor Leisure 6

Essential Reading Rob Talbot and Robin Whitman's book *Lakeland Landscapes*. This has some stunning photographs and also serves as a very good location guide, it was this book that first alerted me to the beauty of the Duddon Valley.

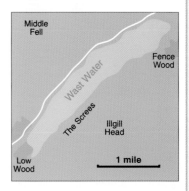

ULLSWATER

 The weather is the dominating factor in all landscape photography, but thankfully for **Derek Croucher**, Ullswater can be captured in many different conditions

PHOTOGRAPHY IN THE Lake District is all about mood. To plan a trip to the hills on a hot, hazy summer's day is great for a rewarding hike, but for photography it will probably be a disappointment. The sun is too high in the sky and the distant views are spoiled by the haze. What the photographer needs is something a little more interesting weather-wise, so with autumn approaching, things – as they say – can only get better. For me, the

excitement of landscape photography is all about the weather, and it's just a question of matching the prevailing weather to the location you choose. Have a variety of places in mind and only make a decision on where to head when you know what the weather will bring.

The area around Ullswater is ideal since there is a good choice of different subjects. If it is overcast, you could head for Glencoyne Wood near Glenridding and use the

Facts about Ullswater

Ullswater is the second largest of the Lakes, and its great attraction lies in the way it snakes through the hills. The best places are in the southern section, since the land flattens out to the north towards Penrith. There are many footpaths with just a few areas of private land to avoid. The

National Trust owns much of the land to the west of the lake, where it also provides a tearoom near Aira Force. A seasonal steamer makes its way up and down the lake, also calling at a halfway point on the east bank, providing a useful service for walkers planning a circular route.

trees to fill the frame and cover the white skies, or alternatively try Aira Force waterfall just north of here. Shooting in steep-sided, tree filled valleys is best under soft light, since sun would create contrast problems. If you have blue skies and no wind, head for the lake's edge where the reflection will turn an ordinary shot into a cracking one. If you wake up to heavy fog you could try climbing the hills. Just occasionally the fog lingers in the valley well into the day, while the tops are in clear sunshine – it's at times like these when you need to concentrate on your photography and not get carried away with just looking at the magical scenery.

It's another pattern of weather, though, that can often reveal the Lake District at its most dramatic. If the forecast says 'changeable,' 'sunshine and showers' or 'rain clearing from the west,' that's your cue to grab your camera and head for the hills as quickly as your

walking boots will carry you! Then you just have to wait for something to happen.

That was my plan when I took this shot of moody skies over the lake from the slopes of Gowbarrow Park. The walk to this spot is fairly easy. You can start from a choice of car parks by the Aira Force falls, one on the main lakeside road or one on the A5091 side turn. Cross the stream and follow the path as it climbs gently up the southern flank of the hill. Before long you have great views of the lake to the southwest with the hills neatly interlocking on either side. Then all you need is for the weather to do its stuff, and when something special does happen, it makes it all worthwhile. ❖

Above left Looking south from the lakeside just north of Glencoyne wood. This was one of those times when the cloud broke during an otherwise dull day *Mamiya RZ67 with 50mm lens, Velvia, 1/15sec at f/22, 81A warm-up filter*

Above right Autumn colours in Glencoyne wood are at their peak in late October or early November *Linhof Technikardan with 6x9cm back and 90mm lens, Velvia, 1 sec at f/22, 81A warm-up, polariser*

Below Glencoyne Wood in spring. The greens always look their best just after they have leafed out, so timing is all important *Mamiya RZ67 with 110mm lens, Velvia, 1/4sec at f/16, polariser*

Planning

Location Ullswater lies in the northeast Lakes.
How to get there Use the A592 from either Penrith to the north, or Windermere to the south. From Keswick take the A66 east, then turn right down the A5091. To access the east bank either use the ferry or turn off to Pooley Bridge at the north end of the lake and follow the lane south.
What to shoot Views along west shore, Aira Force waterfall, higher views from hills on both sides of lake.
What to take Pack a variety of lenses, warm-up and ND graduate filters, polariser and a sturdy tripod.
Nearest pub In Glenridding and Patterdale.
Other times of year Winter snow on the peaks looks great, but bear in mind that the days are short and the

sun very low – by February things begin to improve. Try to catch the beeches in Glencoyne Wood just as they leaf out in spring, usually in May.
Ordnance Survey map Outdoor Leisure 5, The English Lakes NE area.
Essential reading *On Foot in the Lake District, Southern and Eastern fells:* Vol II by Terry Marsh, David & Charles, £9.99, ISBN 0-7153-0944-7.

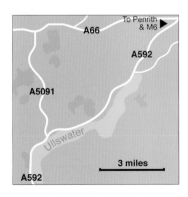

Loch Ness is famous mainly for its mythical monster, but, for photographers like **Steve Austin**, it's also popular for its winter sunsets

LOCH NESS

IT'S WORTH A VISIT to Loch Ness on an evening near the shortest day, because this is the only time of year when the sun sets far enough round to the southwest to be seen setting down the full length of the loch (about 20 miles). And this, combined with the fact that Loch Ness never freezes, gives a rare opportunity for sunset pictures, with reflections, colours and silhouettes.

All you need is a little settled weather in the two weeks either side of the shortest day, ideally with calm conditions and a scattering of clouds. Bear in mind that the weather can quickly change as dusk approaches (mid afternoon up here – so be prepared). The best viewpoint is from Dores, on the south shore. Just go into the Dores Inn car park and position yourself so that you are looking over Dores Bay and down the length of the loch, and watch the sunset develop.

Bring a selection of lenses, such as a 28-70mm zoom

Above The 30 minutes of light after the sun has set gives a variety of changing colours and the old pier posts in the water can be used for foreground interest. The fish cages can just be seen in the left of the picture
Ricoh XR-X with Tokina 28-70mm lens, Velvia, 1/2sec at f/11^{1}/$_{2}$

(ideal for general landscapes), plus another zoom going up to 200 or 300mm for close-ups of the distant hills and sky. Use a slow film and one with good colour saturation to boost the colours. Remember to stop well down, for maximum depth of field, especially when using telephoto lenses. To avoid any vibration when using a telephoto on a tripod, I place a small beanbag on top of the camera, or put the strap from a larger bean bag over the lens barrel, close to the camera mount. Alternatively, if you are parked in the pub car park, you can put a beanbag on the bonnet or the roof for a really

Facts about Loch Ness

Loch Ness is one of the world's most famous stretches of water and is home to the legendary monster, 'Nessie', of which there are usually several sightings a year. Loch Ness is 23 miles long and about a mile wide, and over 750 feet deep. This massive body of water never freezes and the yearly surface temperature ranges between 4°C and 17°C.

Loch Ness is open to both the North Sea and the Atlantic via the Caledonian Canal. There is a salmon farm just south of Dores, which rears fry and smelts in freshwater cages. The most famous view of Loch Ness is on the opposite bank by the ruined Castle Urquhart. This is situated on the main road south from Inverness to Fort William and is rarely free of tourists.

Above A general view of Dores, looking northwest into the bay. The line of brilliant white, puffy clouds drew me to this scene, particularly as they were balanced by the two white cottages in the foreground. A polariser makes them stand out even more
Ricoh XR-X with Tokina 28-70mm lens, Velvia, f/5.6 at 1/30sec, polarising filter

firm support. There are also some picnic tables which could be used for the same purpose.

A warm-up filter can be useful if the sky is a little pale, and also a neutral density graduated filter if the contrast between the sky and the water is high. To avoid flare when shooting directly into the sun, make sure the sun is diffused by cloud or partly hidden behind a hill. And after it has set, you have about 30 minutes of useful light to capture the changing colours before they fade away.

Above Be prepared to act fast and change lenses if necessary, to capture any action that occurs, such as ducks swimming by or kids playing by the water. Here some boys were trying their luck with a fishing net for sticklebacks
Ricoh XR-X with Tokina 28-70mm lens, Velvia, 1/45sec at f/8½

One of my most successful times at Loch Ness was Hogmanay a couple of years ago. It had been a mild day and people were gathering at the pub and enjoying drinks outside by the shore. Some kids had even brought their fishing nets and were trying their luck in the loch. I quickly took some pictures because the boys silhouetted against the light looked very evocative, and the old pier was adding to the foreground interest. There was just enough cloud around the sun to reduce lens flare. Then a gull landed on the old posts out in the bay: the reflected light was just in the right spot, so I switched to a telephoto lens for some close-ups. All through the sunset the clouds and light were changing, so there was plenty of opportunity to create variations of the main picture using different lens focal lengths. ❖

Above Use a telephoto zoom to crop tightly on parts, such as distant hills, patches of rich colour or interesting cloud
Ricoh XR-X with Tamron 80-210mm lens, Provia 100, 1/30sec at f/8, tripod

Planning

Location Dores is situated on the eastern shore of Loch Ness, about eight miles southwest of Inverness.
How to get there From Inverness, which is also the nearest railway station, take the B862 south to Dores. There are only a couple of buses a day from Inverness to Dores: check timetables with Highland Scottish Omnibuses (01463 233371).
What to shoot The rural landscape just outside Dores, with rolling fields and scattered trees can look good as the mist clears, or when covered in frost and the B862 south out of Dores soon gets you onto the moors and lochs for some snowy landscapes.
What to take Wideangle, standard and telephoto lenses, selected filters, tripod and bean bags. Take plenty of warm clothing, eg. thermals, gloves, balaclava and thick socks, boots and waterproof trousers (also very good at keeping the cold off your legs).
Nearest pub Dores Inn, 20 yards to your left! (01463 751203)
Other times of year The beach at the Dores Inn is popular in summer, and anytime with windsurfers when there is a good wind. There are plenty of parking and picnic areas along the B852 which follows the shore where you can get some monster shots (sorry) of Nessie. Urquhart castle, on the opposite shore, is one of Scotland's most popular attractions, along with the 'monster exhibitions' in Drumnadrochit.
Ordnance Survey map Landranger26.
Essential reading *The Complete Visitor's Guide to Loch Ness, Inverness and the Loch Ness Monster* by Andy Owens, £9.99, Mainstream Publishing, ISBN 1 840 1 8307 1. For tourist brochures of the area call 01463 234353.

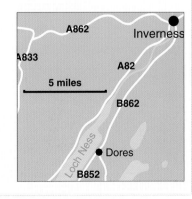

BUTTERMERE

The Lake District in winter is cold and wet. But it's often the best time for atmospheric – and people-free – photography, as **David Herrod** explains

BUTTERMERE IS on my doorstep. Well, not quite, but only 10 miles away. Living in the Lake District was a choice I made a long time ago, when I was 15. I fell in love with the area when I was on a cycling holiday and eventually found a job here. Now I can enjoy it along with my other passion, which also ensnared me around the same time – photography. First it was a hobby, but now it is a career, with Lake District landscapes being the core of my business.

Buttermere is in a complex geological area. Beyond the head of the valley are the volcanic rocks which form the roof of England. The valley containing Buttermere is

Facts about Buttermere

There is a circular walk all the way round Buttermere. Not all of it is public right of way. Part of it is by permission of the landowner, through the negotiation of the National Park Authority. The path should not be deviated from and the Countryside Code should be observed, especially where there are animals. There is a short length, at the south east of the lake, where the path is contiguous with the tarmac road and vehicles. Extra care should be taken here. During the lambing season, the shore path at the north end of the lake is closed, but the circular walk is maintained by a detour through the village. Remember that this is a living/working area, not a theme park. Amenities are limited and you can reduce the pressure on them by taking your rubbish home for disposal.

Above Taken from the top of Fleetwith Pike, looking down on Buttermere, with Crummock Water in the distance, one late evening in August. I have been to the same spot lots of times and it is never the same twice. Even when the sun is out, differing levels of atmospheric moisture change the colours. Remember when setting out on a shoot like this that time flies when you are engrossed in what you are doing, so be prepared to descend in the dark

Above This photograph is all about sky. It gives a terrific feeling of space and the almost explosive power of natural forces. This effect was very short lived and emphasises the need to work quickly and be decisive – even with landscapes. See the bright line on the water? That is the breeze stirring, and soon afterwards the placid surface of the lake had gone

steep sided and craggy, in hard slate. The lower valley changes to older, soft slate, with smoother contours. Between the two, just to complicate matters, is a volcanic intrusion of hard pink rock, which gives rise to the name of the peak overlooking Buttermere village – Red Pike. Also, separating the two, is a deposit of silt and glacial debris, splitting what was once one lake into two – Buttermere and Crummock Water.

I have spent a lot of time in and above this valley and use it for some of my guided walks. Needless to say, its variety provides me with a great deal of photographic inspiration.

At this point I must mention the weather. The rainfall in the Lake District is very high and to those who complain to me about this fact, I reply that without the rain we wouldn't have the lakes. After several weeks of a winter with incessant horizontal rain, however, even I find it hard to be positive.

It was after such a period, with a rare, sunny, mid winter day suddenly breaking up the gloom, that I went out to recharge my batteries and at the same time look for new pictures. At this time of year daylight hours are short, especially in the narrow valley, so it was a quick trip and I travelled light. I took a recent acquisition – a 1960s vintage, twin lens Rolleiflex with 75mm Tessar lens, which I had had restored, a Benbo tripod and a Minolta spotmeter. The camera was loaded with Ilford FP4 Plus.

There was no point in climbing high, so I decided to walk the lake shore. I like the north end in particular because, looking up the lake, the high fells rise above the water in a spectacular manner. On this day the water was placid, the sky was clear, but even though it was only just after noon, the sun was already dropping behind the fells. The atmosphere was slightly misty, suppressing detail in the distant fells and showing the sun's rays slanting across the valley. I came across a beautiful tree, bare of any foliage, so that its delicate tracery of branches stood out in a lacy silhouette. Because of all the rain, the water level was very high and the base of the tree was flooded. This provided a

perfect reflection of the trunk, enhancing its link with the earth. Unfortunately, the field of view of the Rollei's fixed lens included the shore, so the isolation of the tree was lost. I had to practise what I preach to those I give guidance to – the best zoom lens is your legs! Don't be lazy, move yourself. I only had walking boots on my feet. The water came over the tops and, what was worse, I had to stand and wait for the ripples I had caused to subside. Water is cold in winter. Anything for one's art! ❖

Planning

How to get there Junction 40/M6. A66 for Workington. At Keswick take the B5289 over Honister Pass, or at Braithwaite take the unclassified road over Newlands Pass. There is a National Trust car park and one run by the National Park in Buttermere. Pressure on these is great in the summer season. Double yellow lines have been put down on the road in recent years. Do not ignore them and do not try to circumvent them by finding your own space. Remember that working people need access. A far better solution is to use the bus service from Keswick. This operates throughout the summer.

What to shoot The opportunities are limitless. Use your eyes and respond to your feelings.

What to take Walking boots, waterproofs and dry socks. An umbrella, not for you, but to protect that valuable camera. Photographs in the rain can be very successful. All the film you will need.

Nearest pub Two in the village – The

Bridge Hotel (01768 770252) and The Fish (01768 770253).

Times of year Any time of year is good, but remember that in the depths of winter, daylight hours are short and the sun (ha ha) is low.

Ordnance Survey map Sheet 4, 1:25000 Leisure Series.

Essential reading There are so many books available on walking in the Lake District, that I couldn't recommend one. Wainwright is everybody's bible, but look for others. There's a lot of good stuff about. If you want a bit of dramatised history, read Melvyn Bragg's *Maid of Buttermere*.

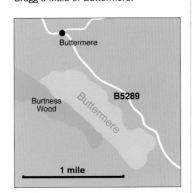

GLEN AFFRIC

You may have to rise exceedingly early to photograph the summer sunrise at Glen Affric, but it's usually well worth it, says **Niall Benvie**

GLEN AFFRIC is one of the most picturesque glens in Scotland. It has all the classical elements of old pine trees, impressive mountains and expansive lochs. But it can also be a frustrating place to photograph because many good viewpoints are marred by powerlines or other signs of human activity which diminish the sense of wilderness. Overnight stops in the glen are disallowed by Forestry Enterprise, who manage large parts of the glen. Nevertheless, with a little searching, the glen yields beautiful images at any time of year.

Cool summer mornings in the Highlands mean two things. Firstly (and most importantly), the midges will be inactive. Secondly, if the sky is clear there is a good chance of a misty dawn. I was aware of the coolness of the day as soon as my alarm work me at 3.30am and a glance at the blue-black sky above suggested that I'd see the sun that morning. Owing to the orientation of the glen, it is possible in summer to shoot the loch at first light as the sun is not blocked by mountains.

Creating character

The visual experience of Glen Affric, especially in good light, can be overwhelming and the photographer is challenged to find elements within the grand scene which encapsulate its character. The composition I settled for is explicitly about the natural forest in its loch-side setting. I wanted to hint that the pine forest is extensive (which, by Scottish standards, it is) by excluding reference to any boundaries, or even being clear about scale. Had I included the skyline, bare of trees, this suggestion would have been lost.

A 180mm lens gave me both the framing I needed and the foreshortening of perspective made the forest on the other side of the loch appear closer and compressed the perspective. I favour Fuji Velvia for all my landscape and close-up work, not only for its extremely fine grain and sharpness, but also its lively colour palette. In the days when I used Kodachrome, I would have automatically fitted an 81a filter to make up for being 10 minutes late for the best light. No need with Velvia.

Anyone who thinks landscape photography is a leisurely pursuit has never worked at the edges of the day when the light changes from minute to minute. It is essential, therefore, to identify the locations you want to shoot in advance; there is no time to be hunting around once the sun is up. In general, 35mm cameras are more suited to rapid reaction than larger formats, although modern 645 cameras have much of the convenience of the smaller format. There are a number of other good locations along the side of Loch Beinn a1 Mheadhoin, but some of them involve a bit of a climb. It's under these circumstances that the 35mm format really comes into its own. ❖

Left Scotch argus butterfly. This butterfly emerges in late July, appearing in grassy places in the glen. In the areas where it occurs, it tends to be abundant. Shooting butterflies demands a lot of mobility and often there is no option but to hand-hold the camera. If you use flash to light the picture, hold it as close to the subject as you possibly can for open, feathered shadows. *Nikon F4; 180mm with 52.5mm extension tube; Velvia; SB25 flash on TTL; 1/250sec at f/11*

Below left Old pinewoods are a stronghold of the red squirrel but you'll have to be quick to catch one on film. Away from bait sites, your best hope is to encounter an animal which has come to search for food on the forest floor. Keep your camera and lens mounted on the tripod ready for action. If you want to use fill-flash to brighten the scene, hold it off-camera to avoid 'eye-shine'. *Nikon F4; 300mm; Velvia rated at ISO 100; 1/60sec at f/2.8*

Planning

Location Glen Affric starts about 28 miles south west of Inverness, near the village of Cannich.

How to get there As in most of the Highlands, public transport services are infrequent and rarely timed to coincide with the prime time for photography. Take a car. To avoid Inverness, follow the A9 over the Kessock bridge as far as the Tore roundabout (watch out for red kites here). There, take the A832 then cut off before the Muir of Ord to join the A862 for Beauly. After Beauly, follow the A831 to Cannich. Go straight through the village (rather than following the main road round to the left) heading for Tomich then branch right at the power station. There are three main parking areas in the glen, but early in the morning you can get away with using some of the larger passing-places.

Where to stay In Tomich, Kerrow House (01456 415243/www.kerrow-house.demon.co.uk) provides good B&B in an elegant setting, or if you want to stay in Glen Cannich, the Mullardoch House Hotel (01456 415460) offers a bit of luxury, too. There are other bed and breakfasts in the area.

What to shoot Get out early and late for dramatic scenics, but also look out for red deer at this time, as well as buzzards, frogs and red squirrels.

What to take Midges are rampant at this time, especially in damp places which are sheltered from the wind. DEET (Jungle Formula) is effective but ruins film and contact lenses so you may want to try a midge net instead. Those for mosquitoes are ineffective. A thick book is recommended too since it can rain for days on end, even in summer.

Nearest Pub The Glen Affric Hotel, Cannich (01456 415214)

Other times of year The heather brings a welcome splash of colour in August then birch and bracken set the glen alight in late September.

Ordnance Survey map Landrangers 25 and 26

Essential reading Fire up your enthusiasm for the old pine forests with The Great Wood of Caledon, by Hugh Miles and Brian Jackman (Colin Baxter, 1991) (out of print). Further information from Forestry Enterprise Scotland, Inverness 01463 232811.

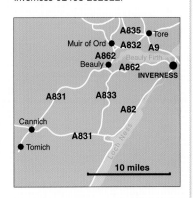

 No matter who owns it the Black Cuillin on the Isle of Skye is a challenge for photographers. **David Tarn** reveals how he captured this beautifully lit scene

BLACK CUILLIN

MY WORDS may sound slightly hollow, but unless you have the luxury of being able to follow the weather forecast and pick the time of your visit at short notice, the Isle of Skye can be a wash out. The west coast of Scotland is – quite rightly – renowned the world over for its outstanding beauty and for its bad weather. The Isle of Skye is outstanding in both, even by Scottish standards.

If you have the opportunity to visit the Isle of Skye on a good day, then it is well worth the effort. If you are planning a holiday in the area and have to take pot luck with the weather, it is more than worth the risk.

Perhaps the most famous sight on the island is the Cuillin Hills. These are divided in two, the smooth rounded slopes of the Red Cuillin, and the jagged sheer rocky faces of the Black Cuillin. It is at the valley of Sligachen that you can see both sides of this range of mountains.

The island, though, has many viewpoints to offer the photographer. The roads are often narrow with passing places, and it can take a while to get around to all the attractions. It would be a dream come true for me to have a whole fortnight of good weather on Skye so I could get to all the viewpoints I wanted in good light. But even this would be nowhere near

enough time to do the whole island justice. As it is, I have only spent a few days on Skye, and usually only one at a time, travelling from the mainland across from the Kyle of Lochalsh.

On the occasion I took the main picture shown

Above Keep an eye open for the unusual. This picture (inspired, I have to admit, by one I saw at The Picture House in Portree), looks to me like a plea to the world rather than a simple notice asking you not to drive along the dirt track it stands next to
Nikon FM2 with 35-70mm zoom lens and soft focus filter

Above This near silhouette of the bridge was taken from the Kyle of Lochalsh and shows the familiar shape of the Cullin behind the bridge. There was much opposition to the bridge being built at all, and now there is anger at the very high toll that is charged for using it. I therefore quite like the dark brooding nature of this picture
Mamiya 645 with 210mm Sekkor telephoto lens, 1/8sec at f/22, no filters

above, I had spent much of the day travelling around the island searching for more subjects. I had walked around the Quiraing and marvelled at this outrageous landscape with its rolling green hills, sheer cliffs and pinnacles of rock. The Quiraing always puts me in mind of Rivendale from Tolkein's Lord of the Rings.

This picture of the Black Cuillin from Sligachen was taken in the late afternoon/early evening sunlight, and

Below You don't have to be on the Isle of Skye to take photographs of it. This picture was taken from the tiny coastal village of Port An Eorna. It is full of colour thanks to the wonderful yellow lichen on the rocks, ever present at this time of year, but often a challenge for the landscape photographer. The natural colours of plants flowers and lichen provide a welcome break from the solid wall of green leaves and grass that can dominate the summer months

it was one of the quickest photographs I have ever taken. In contrast to my usual method of arriving at a location, finding a view and then waiting for an hour or two for the right light, on this occasion the right light was already there and fading fast! All I had to do was find the right view, set up the camera, frame and shoot. There wasn't even time to try for another lens or an alternative angle before the sun was lost behind cloud and all the life just drained from the scene. I was using a Mamiya 645 Pro SV with 55-110mm lens, and framed the scene at the 55mm wideangle end. I fitted a polariser and 81B filter to enhance the light.

Ironically, despite the short-lived lighting and my own hurried activity, there remains a feeling of timelessness in this scene, created by the lovely low directional sunlight on the hills. ❖

Left The Isle of Skye does not give up all of its gems easily. The Quiraing is found some 20 miles north of Portree; drive up the coast on the A855 to Staffin and there turn left along a narrow country road towards Uig. There are roadside car parks en route and from these you can explore this weird and wonderful landscape on foot

Planning

Location The Isle of Skye is situated just off the north west coast of Scotland. This means whatever route you take to get there you are likely to be distracted on the way by some of the most spectacular scenery this country has to offer.

How to get there The Isle of Skye ceased to be a proper island at all when they built that dreadful but very convenient bridge. Follow the A82 out of Fort William to Spean Bridge, continue along the shore of Loch Lochy and turn left at the A87 pass Loch Garry. Stop to see the loch from a roadside viewpoint where the loch is shaped just like the outline of Scotland itself. Stay on the A87 through Glen Sheil to Loch Duich; stop for the world famous picture of Eilean Donan Castle before continuing to the Kyle of Lochalsh and cross the bridge onto Skye.

Where to stay Go to the Picture House. As the name suggests, it is a bed and breakfast dedicated to photographers. The living room has a bookshelf full of wonderful tomes on all aspects of landscape photography. Your hosts Gill and Steve Terry also run photographic courses from there. Check out the website at www.skyepicturehouse.co.uk

What to shoot The Cullin hills

dominate the Isle of Skye, follow the B8083 from Broadford to Elgol for one of the classic views. The Sligachen Valley (main picture) is another classic. Neist Point lighthouse at the most westerly point is well worth a picture. Dunvegan Castle, The Storr, Portree harbour and The Quiraing are all worth photographing. Sunsets can be spectacular on Skye.

What to take A midge hood is a good idea all over Scotland during the summer, especially if you intend to take photographs in the early morning or late evening by the shore of lochs.

Nearest pub Go to the Sconcer Lodge Hotel on the road between Broadford and Sligachen for a pleasant evening meal. There are plenty of good pubs and hotels in Portree.

Ordnance Survey map Landrangers 23 and 32.

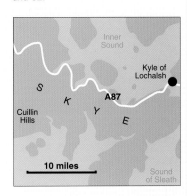

GREAT LANGDALE

The constantly changing light and conditions of Great Langdale are enough to tempt **Fred Hill** back time after time, sometimes with exhausting results!

BEFORE MOVING to the Lake District, one of my favourite corners of the lakes was Great Langdale. It still is today. I love its towering crags and ever-changing moods. It's a challenge, but rewarding to shoot when the elements come right. Northwest facing, it has good sidelighting for most of the day and can be photographed from vantage points such as Bow Fell, Pike of Blisco or Lingmoor.

Great Langdale is part of the western fells. It starts at Elterwater, cutting a broad swathe down the valley and eventually splitting in two by The Band. The valleys of Mickleden and Oxendale are then formed, like two giant fingers probing at the mountains beyond.

If you approach the valley along the B5343 you'll notice a steady change in the scenery from the little

Facts about Langdale Pikes

The National Trust has about 12,000 acres and 10 farms, including Langdale Pikes, under its protection. They also help maintain hundreds of miles of paths that crisscross the fells. Parts of Elterwater are private but Blea Tarn has free access and even a small car park. If you keep to the paths, which are usually well signposted, you won't go far wrong; but you can be sure that if you come across a sign that says, 'No right of way' it means it.

Also, all dogs must be kept on a lead, especially when going through a farm or on the fells where there are sheep.

hamlet of Elterwater – which was once known for its gunpowder works when mining was the main way of earning a crust – to the mainly farming community further down the valley.

The winter or autumn months are without doubt the best times to capture the beauty of the area; the contrast between the green of the valley floor and the colour of the bracken is a sight to savour. But you have to be there early as the shadows soon envelop the valley floor before creeping up the fell sides.

The photograph of Langdale Pikes was taken around 3pm on a winter's day. I was on the top of Lingmoor Fell hoping to get an overall view of Langdale, but was frustrated by the sun hiding behind dense cloud. After a long, fruitless wait I decided to call it a day and make my way down. You've guessed it. As soon as I reached the road, the sun started to break through the cloud. I realised then that I didn't have much time; the shadow on the valley had already reached the other side and was clawing its way up Langdale Fell. I needed some height to find a better viewpoint and some foreground interest. A tree clung to the fell side about three hundred feet up, on Side Pike. With some lung-bursting effort I knew I could get to it before the light disappeared altogether.

I eventually reached the tree. With no light falling onto the valley floor I decided to place the tree in this shadow area. It would help balance the picture, and at the same time the diagonal line of the fell across the frame would add a tension to it. I have also found in situations like this, where there is no obvious horizon line, a spirit level is an essential piece of kit. A slight blurring of the tree was inevitable due to the considerable breeze buffeting me at the time. However, this was a small consideration with the sun heading for the horizon and a large shadow creeping further up the far fell side. I used a Hasselblad 501CM mounted on a tripod, with a 50mm lens. Focusing on the tree gave me sufficient depth of field. A polarising filter enriched the colours and took off unwanted reflection on the tree trunk. A spot reading was also taken off the shadow area in the valley; then a stop more exposure was given to stop the tree from being swallowed up by the background. After just six exposures at f/16 and one second, the fading light forced me to call it a day. ❖

Below This is Blea Tarn House, which is found near the tarn of the same name, with snow-capped Bow Fell in the distance
Hasselblad 501CM with 80mm lens, Velvia, one second at f/22, polarising filter

Above Blea Tarn lies between the Great Langdale and Little Langdale valleys, just off the road that connects the two. It enjoys the sun, summer or winter, for most of the day and has one of the best backdrops in the Lakes – Langdale Pikes. The best side to photograph the tarn from is either the east or south shore; the west side is covered in conifers mingled with rhododendron bushes
Hasselblad 501CM with 80mm lens, Velvia, one second at f/22, polarising filter

Planning

Location Great Langdale is in what is known as the western fells, approximately six miles from Ambleside on the B5343.

How to get there By road from the south turn off the M6 at junction 36 on to the A590 (A591) to Ambleside. Then take the A593 to Coniston. About three miles outside Ambleside turn onto the B5343. From the northeast at Scotch Corner on the A1 take the A66 to just before Keswick, then A591 to Ambleside. Stagecoach Cumberland runs a bus service, the 516, down the valley to Dungeon Gill from Ambleside, until 28 October.

What to shoot Slater Bridge at Little Langdale Tarn and Loughrigg Tarn is in a perfect location. Grasmere, just two miles from Elterwater Village, offers plenty of scope.

What to take One very important consideration if you plan to go high on the fell tops, even on a summer's day, is to make sure you are well kitted out. Strong boots and good waterproofs are as important as your camera; it can get very cold at 3,000 feet. A tripod is a must, wideangle and a medium telephoto lens, polariser, and a set of graduated ND filters and a good stock of your favourite film.

Nearest pub Old Dungeon Gyll Hotel, Great Langdale (01539 437272) or Three Shires Inn at Little Langdale (01539 437215).

Other times of the year Any time of the year in the lakes, but July is particularly good, when the heathers start to appear.

Ordnance Survey map The English Lakes, southwestern number 6

Essential reading *Chris Bonington's Lake District*. It's not a mountaineers' book but a collection of photographs by four different photographers, £9.99, ISBN 1 8556 8144 7.

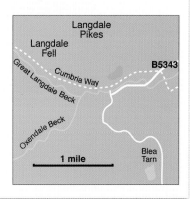

CAPEL CURIG

Snowdonia is renowned for its wonderful winter landscapes, but sometimes the most striking picture is frozen near your feet, as **Pierino Algieri** discovered

Facts about Capel Curig

Encircled by mountains, Capel Curig is one of the oldest and smallest resorts in Wales. It is ideal for both walkers and serious climbers alike. Centrally located in the northern area of Snowdonia (Eryri in Welsh) National Park, the changeable and atmospheric nature of the landscape makes it attractive to both photographers and artists.

Capel Curig has a long tradition of hospitality to travellers, being the last 'port of call' on the old London to Holyhead road before the mountain pass to Nant Ffrancon.

By the turn of the century there were four thriving hotels, including the Royal Hotel which was frequented by royalty including Queen Victoria. (Now called Plas y Brenin, it is the Sports Council's National Centre for Mountain Activities).

The Pen y Gwryd Hotel, at the foot of Snowdon, is where Mallory stayed before his ill-fated attempt to climb Everest.

Evidence of Roman settlements was found at Caer Llugwy and Pen y Gwryd. The Julita Chapel dates from the 14th Century. Disused slate quarries can still be seen on the eastern slopes of Moel Siabod.

HAVING HAD a spell of cold frosty weather I had been out at dawn every morning hoping to photograph snow capped mountain reflections in Llyn Mymbyr and Llyn Ogwen. The morning I took the main picture shown here, I was walking around the east side of Llyn Ogwen. I find it pays to go off the beaten track if you want to find the more unusual compositions. There are plenty of public footpaths in the area which can be identified on a detailed Ordnance Survey map.

There are endless opportunities for stunning photography in this part of Snowdonia: the majestic mountain, Tryfan, towers over Llyn Ogwen and can be very dramatic at this time of year. At the other end of the lake the mountain Y Garn can be seen reflected in the water if conditions are calm. During the winter months you can be out taking pictures all day. Sounds great but the short winter days soon draw in as it gets dark early. I'm usually out at dawn to get the best chance of the great morning light which makes a lot of difference to my pictures.

Living about 10 miles away from Capel Curig I can see most of Snowdonia from home, so I have a good idea of what the weather is going to be like and I can be there in about 15 minutes. Because the weather is so changeable in Snowdonia it pays to travel around: one part might have rain but another area not far away

could be bathed in sunshine. If you time it right you could use the dark clouds in the distance as a backdrop to the sunlit foreground. Consequently, I always check both the weather forecast and wind direction before setting off to take any photographs.

I do feel very lucky and privileged to be living in such a beautiful part of the country. Its sheer ruggedness merely adds to the beauty of the area. Being passionate about capturing the landscape on film, I get great pleasure from showing audiovisuals of the area to local groups, who then tend to appreciate even more the kind of landscape they have on their doorstep. ❖

Left Taken from the pinnacles above Capel Curig, the best time is early morning. Plas y Brenin dominates the middle ground and leads your eye up to the stunning Snowdon Horseshoe in the distance
Pentax Z1P with 28-70mm lens, Velvia, 1/15sec at f/22, Benbo MK I tripod with Velbon head

Above These swirling ice patterns contrasted stunningly with the brittle reeds which were poking through. The early morning light – just kissing the reeds from the side – completed the picture for me. It's always worth keeping an eye out for what's going on at your feet!
Pentax Z1P with 24-70mm Sigma lens, Velvia, 1/4sec at f/22, Benbo MK1 tripod with Velbon head

Planning

Location Capel Curig is situated in the heart of Snowdonia on the junction of the A5 and A4086, approximately five miles west of Betws y Coed.

How to get there By car on the A55 expressway take the A470 signposted to Betws y Coed for approximately 16 miles. Join the A5 and head for Bangor. The A5 passes through Capel Curig. Trains run to Betws y Coed and public transport is available.

What to Shoot Beautiful landscapes around every corner, mountains, lakes, and waterfalls.

Other times of year Autumn is great for broad leaf and conifer forests; wetlands

What to take Travel light, but wear good sturdy boots. Waterproofs are essential as the weather is very changeable; wideangle lens; sturdy tripod; cable release; plenty of film.

Nearest pub/accommodation There are three nearby: Bryn Tyrch (www.bryntyrch), Cobdens

(www.cobdens.co.utr) (hyperlinks to webcam on Snowdon), and Tyn y Coed, all popular with walkers and climbers.

Ordnance Survey map Landranger sheet 115.

Essential reading *Snowdonia: The Official National Park Guide*, by Merfyn Williams, photography by Jeremy Moore, Pevensey Press/David & Charles, £8.99. *Visions of Snowdonia – landscape & legend*, by Jim Perrin, photography by Ray Wood.

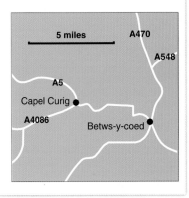

ELTERWATER

 Chocolate-box Lake District it may be, but few can resist the charms of Elterwater, least of all **Ann and Steve Toon**, who suggest including it on your lakes tour

ELTERWATER, AND the area surrounding it, truly is the Lake District in cameo. A reed-fringed lake, bracken-covered fells, and a stunning backdrop – the distant high peaks of the Langdale Pikes. Upstream, picturesque cottages cluster around a tiny green, sheltered by a sycamore. Downstream, the River Brathay meanders across gentle pastures before cascading through dense woodland to Skelwith Force.

On a bright, still September day the fells glow with early autumn colour and millpond-calm waters reflect perfect Lakeland views. Chocolate-boxy perhaps, but impossible to resist. If it's drama you're after, return on a blustery winter's day. Clamber up the slopes of Little Loughrigg for a marvellous panorama and wait for fleeting shafts of light to burst through storm cloud and illuminate the valley floor below.

Elterwater derives its name from the Norse for swan, and whooper swans still overwinter here occasionally. It's a small lake, and gradually is becoming smaller still, as silt from the Little and Great Langdale valleys builds up and reeds encroach.

The walk from Skelwith Bridge to Elterwater village, following the River Brathay and skirting the north shore of the lake, is very popular with ramblers, not least because of the Kirkstone Galleries and tearoom at one end and the welcoming Britannia Inn at the other. This footpath offers some wonderfully photogenic views and is well worth exploring. Land on the opposite bank is not accessible to the public, which is actually a plus point for photographers – you won't spend hours waiting for a crowd of Day-Glo cagoules to walk out of your frame, your lovely light diminishing all the time!

Our image of trees reflected in the still, quiet water of the Brathay was taken a few hundred yards downstream of where the river flows out of Elterwater, and only a short stroll from the National Trust car park at

Facts about Elterwater

Elterwater was once a much larger lake, but alluvial deposits carried down from the Great and Little Langdale valleys have created an increasingly reed-fringed and marshy lake which one day will disappear entirely. It is one of the few lakes to be privately owned, but much of the eastern and northern shores are National Trust land. The Langdales are classic examples of glacial U-shaped valleys, while the Wrynose and Hardknott passes between Little Langdale and the western Lake District are simply spectacular and not for the faint-hearted (see page 58).

Above Keep a look out for the little details as well as the big landscapes. A hard, early frost accentuated the beautiful natural pattern of this bracken frond
Canon EOS 1n with 50mm macro lens, Velvia, 1/15sec at f/22, tripod

Above We liked the interplay of strong dark verticals and feathery bright foliage against the blue sky. The wide end of a 35-80mm zoom was needed to encompass enough of the early autumn trees at Little Loughrigg
Canon EOS 1n with 35-80mm zoom, Velvia, tripod

Silverthwaite. It was getting towards lunchtime, but the sun was still low enough in the sky to give a pleasing light, enhancing the warm autumnal colours of bracken on the fells. Our choice of film, Fuji Velvia, helped saturate the colours.

Choosing a viewpoint wasn't difficult – stepping backwards would have introduced unwanted riverbank in the immediate foreground, stepping forwards would have meant a soaking! A 70-200mm zoom, set at about 150mm, allowed us to frame what we wanted. The sky wasn't particularly exciting, so we left in just enough to frame top and bottom of the picture and no more.

We stopped down to ensure the background fells were reasonably sharp. Part of the attraction of this scene was its clarity and stillness. This frame was taken on 1/60sec at f/11, the camera securely mounted on a tripod. Conventional wisdom has it that you shouldn't split your picture in half in this way, but some shots – particularly reflections like this – sometimes prove an exception.

Given the unhelpful lack of clouds most of that day, our best shot came when, out of nowhere, cloud shadow darkened the hillside immediately behind the trees. This had the double advantage of helping to throw the trees into relief while giving some depth to the hills in the distance.

Waterfall enthusiasts could head downstream from here, to find Skelwith Force. The force is only about 20

feet high, but has the greatest volume of water of any Lakeland waterfall, and turns into a raging white water torrent after rain.

Less committed souls might prefer a stroll in the opposite direction, up past the lake to the picturesque village of Elterwater. This was once an important centre for the Lake District's gunpowder industry and works remained until 1920. Today Elterwater's chief attraction is the Britannia Inn, where a pint of Jennings and a prawn sandwich make a worthy reward for a hard morning's photography. ❖

Below A standard zoom gave more depth and sense of perspective to this image of a reed bed at Elterwater, compared with the reflection shot in which a telephoto flattened the scene
Canon EOS 1n with 35-80mm zoom, Velvia, tripod

Planning

Location Elterwater lies in the heart of the Lake District, near the mouths of the Great and Little Langdale valleys.

How to get there Take the A593 Coniston road from Ambleside, turn right on the B5343 at the Skelwith Bridge Hotel, and look for the National Trust Silverthwaite car park after half a mile. Or carry on to the left turn to Elterwater village. The Langdale Rambler bus, number 516 from Ambleside, calls at Elterwater on its way up to the Old Dungeon Ghyll Hotel in Great Langdale.

What to shoot Autumn colours can be stunning. On still days look for reflections. Overcast conditions favour detail shots – look for fungi in the woods. Don't discount rainy weather – stormy lighting can be dramatic, if fleeting. Loughrigg Tarn, a 20 minute uphill walk from the Silverthwaite car park, is also very picturesque.

What to take Your usual landscape gear and wellington boots – it can be pretty boggy around the lake and river!

Nearest pub The Britannia in

Elterwater (01539 437210), a traditional country pub serving lunch and dinner.

Other times of year Every season has something to offer the landscape photographer. On still, wintry days climb a little for panoramic shots, with smoke from Elterwater's cottages drifting down the valley. In summer, rise early to catch the best light and avoid the tourist hordes.

Ordnance Survey map Outdoor Leisure Map 7 – southeast area.

Further information Cumbria Tourist Board (01539 444444); website: www.cumbria-the-lake-district.co.uk

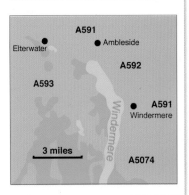

 In the bleak midwinter... there's always a photograph to be had. **Ruth Eastham** and **Max Paoli** venture into Scotland to make the most of the atmospheric light

THE EXTREME WEATHER and short days often associated with the Scottish Highlands in winter can create unique opportunities for the landscape photographer. In this season, the sun follows a shallow arc across the sky, so the quality of light can be special throughout the day.

Loch Cluanie, and the area surrounding it, has a quiet magic of its own. Few people stop as they drive by in wintertime. Its shores are unspoilt by buildings and its mountain setting gives the place a feeling of wild remoteness. The mixed weather can bring a rich variety of photographic possibilities, if you are prepared to look for them. Breaks in the clouds and pauses between storms can be even more inspiring than the still, clear days.

On several occasions, our visits around Loch Cluanie in early January have coincided with snowfall. We wanted to capture the wild beauty of this winter landscape. The dark shapes of a cluster of pines stood out from their snowy background. The inclusion of too much white, however, seemed to overpower the image, so we chose to use a long lens to select details from the view. This strengthened the composition by

Above Winter light and stormy weather create mood in this image of pine trees. The distant backdrop – compressed by the long focal length – appears almost like a film set, while the pines stand out in sharp relief
Canon EOS 3 with 80-200mm lens, Velvia, 1/2sec at f/11, Uniloc tripod

concentrating on its key elements. The monochrome quality of the scene shifted the emphasis onto shape and form. There had just been a storm and the lifting low cloud helped to isolate the trees further, giving the scene extra depth and mood. The muted light also enhanced the atmosphere. Since pale tones dominated the image, it was necessary to overexpose, and this was checked by spotmetering on a mid-tone within the frame. We shifted our position to optimise the viewpoint by adjusting the perspective of the trees against the mist. In addition, altering the focal length of the zoom lens allowed quick and versatile framing. Working fast is important when conditions are so changeable as an image can be lost within seconds.

A light drizzle in the air didn't prevent us from taking

Facts about Loch Cluanie

Loch Cluanie lies in an outstanding area of mountains, lochs and forest in the steep-sided Glen Moriston valley. The loch can be easily viewed from the road itself, and there are one or two lay-bys you can use to stop. There is little access to the loch's southern side, but on the north side a couple of footpaths climb along an old military road to give more elevated views over the water. Just beyond the west end of the loch, the rugged Glen Shiel valley begins, and is fringed by the Five Sisters of Kintail, mountain peaks that can rise above 3,000 feet.

LOCH CLUANIE

Left A view of Loch Cluanie just after a snowfall. The break in the clouds let light through onto the landscape, giving reflections in the water *Contax RX with 25mm Carl Zeiss lens, Ektachrome Elite II 50, 1/4sec at f/19, Manfrotto tripod*

Below left Overcast conditions give even tones for close-up photography. Look for details and move around them to find the most pleasing composition *Canon EOS 3 with 100mm macro lens, Velvia, 1/4sec at f/19, Uniloc tripod*

Bottom left Deer can be seen more easily as they move down into valleys over winter to feed. Although they are usually wary of humans, we were able to observe this stag using the car as a hide. Snow had begun to fall and the bluish evening tinge adds a sense of coldness *Canon EOS 3 with 400mm Sigma lens, Velvia, 1/90sec at f/5.6, beanbag*

the snow pines pictures. We had to take care, though, to avoid speckles on the lens, which would have led to a loss of definition. One advantage of photography in pairs is that one person can hold the umbrella over the tripod, while the other takes the shot! It is also useful to have a soft, dry cloth and a plastic bag to dry and protect equipment. All too often, camera gear is packed away at the slightest sign of rain, but being ready for breaks in the weather can lead to some dramatic images. The cold might be biting, but you can be confident that the infamous Scottish midge won't be. You can overcome some of the discomfort of chilly days by being well-dressed, carrying a hot drink or, even better (if you're not the driver), a hip flask of something stronger. Self-heating foot pads can be slipped into boots to overcome the numb-toe syndrome, and can be bought from outdoor shops. Remember to protect your hands, too, especially because the tripod can get very cold to the touch. We wear a thin pair of gloves underneath a main pair, so we can take off the outer layer and handle the camera more easily.

Having said all this, one of the best ways to keep warm is to focus your attention on picture-taking. Take time to walk. Observe and feel the landscape. Let the winter light inspire your photography. ❖

Planning

How to get there Loch Cluanie is 40 miles north of Fort William, along the A87, and about 30 miles east of the Kyle of Lochalsh.
What to shoot Winter light landscapes, moody skies, reflections in the water, close-ups, mountain views. The Glen Shiel and Five Sisters valley, six miles from Loch Cluanie, is also well worth a visit.
What to take Waterproof boots and clothing, energy-rich snacks and a flask; wideangle lenses for views, telephoto/zoom lenses to extract landscape details, macro lens for close-ups, tripod.
Nearest pub The Cluanie Inn, just to the west of the loch.
Nearest accommodation The Cluanie

Inn (01320 340238)
Other times of year Heather flowering on the loch shore in late summer.
Ordnance Survey map Landranger sheets 33 and 34.
Further information Scottish Tourist Board (08705 511511); www.visitscotland.com

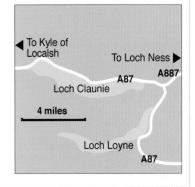

To Kyle of Localsh
To Loch Ness ▶
A887
A87
Loch Claunie
4 miles
Loch Loyne
A87

ROTHIEMURCHUS

Just when you think a wideangle view is all you need for landscapes, along comes a scene which compresses perfectly into telephoto, as **Geoff Simpson** explains

IF YOU IMAGINE the Scottish Highlands as a region of pine forests, with golden flecked birches adorning the fringes of a mist covered loch, nestling below the foothills of the snow capped mountains, then the reality won't disappoint. This vision is surely encapsulated in the Rothiemurchus Estate, in the Strathspey Valley.

The estate comprises several diverse forms of habitat, from open pine woodland, wet and dry heathland, raised bog, streams with cascading waterfalls and the impressive Loch an Eilein. This unique estate is a classic example of how most of the Scottish Highlands would have looked centuries ago without the intervention of man and the destruction of vast areas of the Caledonia pine forest, of which only 1% remains.

The Rothiemurchus estate is set against the majestic

backdrop of the Cairngorms. There can be no more spectacular site than the great glacial valley that is Lairig Ghru, situated at the southern end of the estate, where Britain's highest treeline eventually gives way to a harsh and often unforgiving alpine habitat. Carving its way through the Cairngorm granite, this steep sided glacial valley is hemmed in by some of Britain's highest mountains – Ben Macdui, Braeriach and Cairn Toul.

Having spent the previous three days actually on the Cairngorm plateau, with mixed results due to the low visibility, I decided to search for a classic mountain scene and at the same time incorporate the treeline as an additional feature. I tried various lenses, from my 24mm wideangle to a 200mm telephoto, but none really gave me the composition I had in mind. Determined not to

Facts about Rothiemurchus Forest

In the late 1500s, John Grant of Freachie acquired the lease of the estate for his second son Patrick, who became the first Grant Laird of Rothiemurchus. The Grant family has held the stewardship for over 400 years to the present day. The island castle ruins are thought to be at least 600 years old and was used as a refuge in troubled times. In the 1700s the castle was used to detain Jacobite prisoners but as Scotland became

a more peaceful country the castle fell into disuse. Many generations of breeding pairs of Osprey have nested on the castle ruins before their temporary extinction from Britain in 1916. Maybe one day they will return to nest here again as the population steadily increases. Today the estate is managed by Scottish Heritage, in partnership with the Forestry Enterprise, in an effort to preserve the estate for future generations.

give up, I decided to view the mountains with my long 500mm lens and 1.4x extender attached. To my amazement, the elements came together with comparative ease. The use of a longer lens reduced the image to its simplest components of treeline with snow-covered valley and mountains. The effect of using this long lens combination helps in terms of isolating a scene to its simplest form and is a technique I have used frequently, with satisfying results.

To compose this image, I searched for a relatively high viewpoint above the forest canopy in order to obtain a clear view of the distant Lairig Ghru, some six miles away. Eventually I found a large, flat boulder on which to rest my 740mm-lens combination and camera body. A beanbag comes into its own in such situations, allowing me to compose quickly. In order to keep the horizon straight I always use a hot-shoe mounted spirit level, which I find invaluable.

Having framed the image I used my tried and trusted Canon EOS 1N's spotmetering facility and took several readings from both the shaded snow and highlighted areas. The resulting spot readings ranged between 1/10sec to 1/4sec at f/11. Having opened up one full stop in order to compensate for the brightness of the scene, I decided to make several exposures in increments of a third, as the light was constantly changing due to snow flurries, which cascaded down the slopes of the valley.

We often see images in which an 81 series warm-up filter has been used to reduce the bluish cast, but I think this image benefits from the cold blue cast as it conveys a feeling of a remote wilderness in the depths of winter. ❖

Above Loch an Eilein is the epitome of a Scottish Highland loch, perfect for capturing those evocative misty morning scenes. The abundance of mature Scots pines that fringe the shoreline only add to the ambience. Ospreys are regularly observed diving for fish throughout the summer months, although they no longer breed on the ruined island castle *Canon EOS 1N with 24mm lens, Velvia, 1/8sec at f/16, spotmetered from green strip of grass in the foreground, Gitzo tripod*

Above Caledonian Scots pines in late evening light. In order to capture the texture of the flaking bark of these mature pines, I waited for the last rays of soft warm sunlight just before the sun descended below the Cairngorm Mountains
Canon EOS 1N with 80-200mm lens, Velvia, 1/60sec at f/11

Planning

Location Rothiemurchus Forest is situated in the Strathspey Valley, approximately two miles southeast of Aviemore, Inverness-shire, Scotland.
How to get there An infrequent local bus service operates from Aviemore town centre. By car, leave the A9 heading north immediately before entering Aviemore. Take a right turn sign posted for Inverdruie and Coylumbridge. After half a mile take a right turn (B970) signed posted Feshiebridge, Rothiemurchus Forest and Loch an Eilein. After approximately two miles turn left sign posted Loch an Eilein. Park in the visitors' car park where a small parking fee is payable.
Where to stay There are many hotels and guesthouses in Aviemore catering for all needs. Take a look at www.smoothound.co.uk/aviemore
What to shoot Loch an Eilein with its backdrop of Caledonian Scots pines and golden flecked birches. Wideangles to capture the pine forest interior. 300mm to 500mm lenses mounted on a tripod or beanbag should allow frame filling images of the red deer. Macro workers will be drawn to the lichens that encrust almost every boulder and tree trunk.
What to take Although Rothiemurchus Forest is somewhat sheltered from the bitterly cold gales that plague the nearby Cairngorm plateau, appropriate clothing is still necessary. In summer a fly repellent is advisable.
Nearest pub Many of the hotels in Aviemore have non-resident bars.

Other times Spring and summer are good for flowers, including the rare and diminutive twinflower species confined to this region of Scotland. The rich tapestry of purple heather and cranberry form a carpeted understorey laced with lichens of all descriptions. However, any time of the year can produce evocative images.
Ordnance Survey map Outdoor Leisure 3 – The Cairngorms (Aviemore and Glen Avon).
Essential reading *The Nature of the Land*, by Colin Baxter and Rawdon Goodier, published by Colin Baxter Photography Ltd and Scottish Heritage, ISBN 1 9004 5572 2. Out of print but well worth locating is a copy of the classic *The Cairngorms*, by Desmond Nethersole-Thompson and Adam Watson, (first published by Collins in 1974), an enlarged second edition by The Melven Press in 1981, ISBN 0 9066 6412 8. A free guide is available at the Loch an Eilein Visitor Centre or contact the Rothiemurchus Information Desk, on 01479 812345.

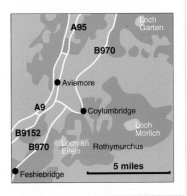

FALLING FOSS

 The lure of running water combined with long shutter speeds is a strong one for the landscape photographer. It's great fun, too. Well, **Joe Cornish** thinks so!

REGULAR READERS of *Outdoor Photography* may already be starting to wonder whether the Yorkshire Tourist Board sponsors the magazine, so frequently does this county feature in Viewpoints. Rest assured that no such conspiracy exists. The county has natural advantages that have blessed it with photogenic landscape, including several distinctive areas of high moorland which cannot be intensively farmed, many beautiful rivers, a geologically varied coast and – perhaps surprisingly – a climate which (in the east of the county at any rate) produces a lot of clear air and sunlight. Oh yes, and it is also home to a couple of the landscape photographers who write for the magazine!

My featured subject this month is not one of Yorkshire's well known tourist attractions. It is not even known by many people who live near to it. It is on the map, but barely marked from the road, and is truly tucked away, making it a real journey to reach, even if you happen to live elsewhere on the North York Moors. And if you should happen to go, expecting some moorland Niagara, you are likely to be disappointed. May Beck is more of a stream than a river, and Falling Foss merely a 20 metre shelf where May Beck drops to its next level. And yet, should you go in the height of autumn, the broadleaf setting for this modest waterfall provides a breathtaking backdrop of colour.

Not that I knew that when I went there one October day last year. I'd seen a picture of it in a guidebook and, having a desire to see anything and everything of note in what is now my home patch, I went in search of it. A nearby car park means that Falling Foss is easily reached, but viewpoints of the waterfall are quite limited from the footpath due to the abundance of trees. Only the extremely agile could negotiate the descent to the river below the falls, and carrying heavy camera gear would possibly involve ropes and a team effort! Certainly, I did not try it.

Anyway, on this particular day, the sun was shining from a cloudless sky on what should have been an idyllic scene. Yet I knew this sunlight was likely to scupper my chances of producing a good view shot, so extreme was the contrast it produced. I felt frustrated, but decided not to worry, and instead put my brain into neutral, before going for a wander. And there, in the stream above the waterfall, was the solution. Shaded from the direct rays of the sun, the clear water of the stream was glowing with reflected colour: blue from the sky, yellow and gold from the sunlit trees in the valley beyond. And many fallen leaves, some clustered together in eddy currents, others perched artlessly on boulders where they had fallen, provided the necessary sense of scale and contrast which would make a picture work.

There are few things I know more enjoyable than photographing in a shallow stream – I think I may become a fly fisherman if I ever grow up – and the time spent that afternoon was joyful, perhaps because the colours were so vivid, but also because I was doing something different. The sun did find cloud to hide behind for a while, which caused some anxiety, but it shone long enough for me to make my exposures and explore a couple of variations on the theme.

I returned to Falling Foss twice more last autumn. The light was different each time, as it always is, and by my third visit the shedding of leaves meant that many of the trees now looked decidedly bleak and wintry. Yet, in spite of the overcast sky, I still found a photo to do, using the rocks, leaves and stream, a few hundred metres above the waterfall.

Falling Foss will probably not inspire you with the awesome power of nature. For me it was much more intimate than that, allowing me to question my own attitude to picture-taking, and what I thought could constitute a photographic subject. Challenging our own assumptions, thinking laterally, exploiting the conditions however unpromising they may at first appear to be – all of this is part of the photographer's journey. And you don't need to travel to Yorkshire to discover that! ❖

Above The falls are a challenge to photograph in their entirety, as they are surrounded by extremely dense tree growth. There are a few gaps to be found, however! This is the 'standard' view of Falling Foss, framed by trees from the valley side. Here, overcast conditions produce soft, controlled contrast, and luminous colour. A warming filter removed the ambient blue cast. A long exposure was inevitable given the need to stop down for depth of field in such subdued lighting, and when using a slow film like Velvia
Ebony 45SW with 90mm SW Nikkor, Velvia, four seconds at f/22½, 81D warmup filter

Planning

How to get there Falling Foss is about six miles south of Whitby. The waterfall itself is deep in a valley which runs north off Pike Hill in the North York Moors. Sleights is the nearest village and, if you approach from the west, you are likely to drive through the splendidly named hamlet of Ugglebarnby. A detailed map is essential for finding Falling Foss.

Where to stay Whitby is one of England's most photogenic towns, and is well served by hotels and guesthouses. There are also camping and caravanning sites to the west, and the east of the town and further south at Robin Hoods Bay. The coast here is photographically outstanding as well.

What to take Wellington boots! If you happen to have the super-long fishing variety, so much the better. As ever, a tripod is essential. Don't be afraid to set it up in the river. Light balancing filters will be necessary for colour transparency users, especially if it is overcast.

What to shoot While the waterfall itself is the obvious subject, there are numerous 'miniature' landscape possibilities. A varied population of broad leaf trees provides graphic and colour potential, and the stream itself with its currents and rocks gives scope for reflected light and long exposure experimentation.

Best time of day This will be a surprise, but probably midday. Being in a north facing valley means that light is at a premium and almost any light is good light.

Best time of year Autumn for colour, winter for ice and frost, spring for fresh green leaves and wild flowers. Forget about summer.

Nearest pub The nearest pubs are in Sneaton, Sleights and Ruswarp. Too bad there isn't a Jugglers Arms in Ugglebarnby...

Ordnance Survey map Landranger 94; Touring Map and Guide sheet 2; Outdoor Leisure 27

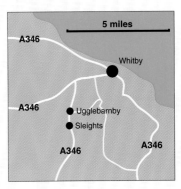

 Each winter, **Guy Edwardes** pulls on his wellies and heads for the Somerset Levels, a huge area of land which is submerged for several months each year

SOMERSET LEVELS

BETWEEN THE Quantock, Brendon and Blackdown Hills, seven rivers drain into 64,000 hectares of low-lying wet meadows and marshland as they make their way, slowly, towards Bridgewater Bay in the Bristol Channel. This flat expanse of Somerset, bisected by 5,000 miles of largely manmade drainage ditches, or rhynes, is a unique and internationally important area for a wealth of interesting, and in some cases rare, flora and fauna.

Many areas of the levels and moors are well below the high tide mark and this, coupled with the heavy autumn rains, results in annual floods that cover a huge acreage of land when the rivers Axe, Brue, Carey, Isle, Tone, Parrett and Yeo breach their banks. These areas often remain underwater until the following spring, providing an ideal habitat for

Above West Sedgemoor, where this photograph was taken, is a Site of Special Scientific Interest, part of which is owned by the RSPB. It is also one of the best locations for photography. While shooting this scene, a small cloud briefly moved across the sun, so I was quick to take the opportunity of making a few exposures without the problems of flare. A two-stop ND graduated filter was positioned over the sky and the brightest part of the water to help balance the exposure, while still recording the gate as a silhouette
Canon EOS 5 with 28mm lens, Velvia, 1/15sec at f/16, two-stop ND grad, tripod

many species of wintering waterfowl, for which the area is well known. The scenes created by this flooding cannot be found with the same regularity anywhere else in the country.

Facts about the Somerset Levels

The Somerset Levels and Moors form the largest area of natural floodplain and lowland wet grassland in England, and are of international importance for their rich wetland habitats. Thousands of years ago this area of Somerset was a vast tidal inlet – part of the Severn Estuary – into which many rivers drained from the surrounding hills. Gradually the formation of sand dunes and an accumulation of marine

sediments at the mouth of the inlet closed it off from the open sea. The area became a huge, reed-filled swamp beneath which, over a long period, peat formed, turning the area into a low lying fen. Much later, man's creation of a maze of drainage ditches and river embankments resulted in the transformation to the rich marshy grassland present in this area of southwest England today.

Above King's Sedgemoor Drain is an artificially straightened section of the River Cary. On a previous visit I calculated the sun would rise above this stretch of the river in early spring, when viewed from the bridge on the A361. I included a lot of sky in frame, showing its reflection in the water, with the two areas bisected by the dark trees and distant hills
Canon EOS 5 with 400mm lens, Velvia, 1/60sec at f/22, tripod

Above Burrow Mump is like a smaller version of Glastonbury Tor. The short, steep climb to the top of the hill provides panoramic views over the levels, and is one of the best spots to photograph the mist-covered meadows at dawn. This view over Earlake Moor towards Glastonbury was taken at 5am one morning in May
Canon EOS 5 with 70-200mm lens, Velvia, 1/15sec at f/16, tripod

The surrounding hills are easily accessible and provide far-reaching views across the levels, the wooded slopes contrasting with the cattle-grazed meadows below. Lines of pollarded willows are a characteristic feature of the landscape; in the calm conditions of dawn and dusk their bulbous crowns and stout trunks reflect perfectly into the surrounding floodwater. Such expanses of damp ground result in the frequent formation of mist as the night air cools, providing evocative landscape scenes when the swirling layers hang above the floodwater.

The day I took the main picture shown opposite started as a dull, drizzly and rather windy mid-December morning. After a while, the cloud layer gradually started to break up over my home in Dorset, revealing patches of blue through which shafts of sharp winter sunlight were sent stabbing across the landscape. Following a week of heavy rain I knew prospects would be good for an afternoon of photography in the Somerset Levels. I wasn't disappointed. After a short drive I arrived under a clear blue sky at the village of Curry Rivel, on a ridge just above the flat expanse of West Sedgemoor.

Rather than work from the roadside, I decided to wade out onto the moor, so I followed a broken fence line, which I knew from previous visits bordered a long, wide track that was now under nearly a foot of water. As the breeze began to drop and the sun sank towards the horizon, I found myself surrounded by a vast, tranquil lake that was by now starting to take on the colourful hues of the late afternoon sky. After tackling the problem of how to get my camera gear out of a large photo backpack with nowhere to put it down, I was able to start shooting.

Just before the sun slipped below the distant hills I came across an isolated field gate. As it was not connected to a fence I wondered what purpose it served, other than a welcome foreground element. While moving around to find the best position to shoot from, my question was answered when my left boot filled with freezing ditch water. The gate was obviously positioned on a causeway over a rhyne that was hidden beneath the murky floodwater!

I quickly fitted a wideangle lens, onto which I attached a two stop neutral density grad to reduce the contrast within the scene. The shallow water was calm enough to provide a partially reflected silhouette of the gate in the foreground.

By the time the colour had drained from the sky and the light levels had dropped too far to continue shooting, half a dozen exposed rolls of Velvia were the result of another productive afternoon's work on the Somerset Levels. ❖

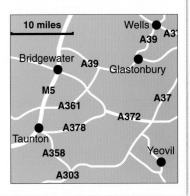

LOCKWOOD RESERVOIR

Better known to early rising fishermen, Lockwood reservoir near Guisborough also has a magical element for landscapes, says **Mike Kipling**

ONE OF THE GOOD THINGS about winter is you don't have to rise at an ungodly hour to shoot the sun rising. Also, for me, the soft warmer dawn and dusk light of November to February produces far more attractive results. A favourite location of mine where a good winter sunrise picture is almost guaranteed is at Lockwood Reservoir, a few miles east of Guisborough on the northern edge of the North Yorkshire Moors.

I am drawn to this location at least a couple of times every winter, usually waiting until the first snowfall or a crisp frost. Over the past few years snowfall in this area

has been conspicuous by its absence, but often there is a light dusting and some meaningful frost in November, even if the rest of winter is unseasonably mild. Frosty nights mean still air and a glass-like surface to expanses of enclosed water – a great asset for against-the-light photography. However, as soon as the rising sun heats the cold air, the resulting air flow produces ripples on the surface of the water and the effect is quickly lost.

I shot the above picture in mid-November last year at about 7.30am. About 45 minutes earlier, when I arrived, there was just a hint of colour in the eastern

Facts about Lockwood Reservoir

The reservoir is owned and managed by Northumbrian Water Ltd, who encourage responsible access. Interpretative information showing the paths and do's and don'ts is posted in the car park. The main users are fishermen, hence the rowing boats, but generally they have not arrived by dawn.

The open moor has unrestricted access but where the land is enclosed it is best to stay on the marked footpaths or ask. The access into the reservoir is off an undulating piece of fast road. Although there have been recent improvements, be sure to take special care when turning.

Above Another occasion when the fisher folk got there before me. Because there was movement I had to increase the shutter speed to 1/60sec at f/5.6. I used an 81C warming filter with a Cokin 1 grey grad to give a more emphasised result

Above Initially, I was going to shoot Freeborough Hill into the sun through the veil of bare birch branches, but then the cows arrived to check me out! *Bronica ETRSi with 50 mm lens, Fuji Provia 100, 1/30 sec at f/16, Cokin grey grad 1 and 81A warmup filters*

sky as I set up my camera. As the dawn approached and the sky took on pre-dawn hues I started taking pictures, but the rising sun was not yet lighting the underside of the clouds. I knew the light was likely to improve as dawn progressed. With sunrises and sunsets the light is constantly and subtly changing, so rather than miss the optimum I always start taking pictures early. And as it can be hard to visualise how film will react to long exposures, it's better to have shots in the bag than risk missing the moment. By the time I felt that this sunrise was at its best I had shot a whole roll of Velvia. About five minutes after this was taken, the sun lifted over the moor, the clouds burnt away and a gentle breeze rippled the water. The magic had gone.

I took the shot on a Bronica ETRSi with a 40mm lens, using a 0.3 ND grad over the sky area and an 81B to further warm the image. I used a light grad to tone down the brightness of the sky but at the same time ensuring the sky was just lighter than the water. Exposure was one second at f/16. It was important to retain detail in the frost on the jetty and the rowing boats so I bracketed to ensure I had a shot without blocked up shadows or too much light in the sky.

Above I took this shot from the Castleton road a few hundred yards above the reservoir on the open moorland. Freeborough Hill is in the far distance. The wet snow had frozen onto the tufts of heather and I wanted to catch this as a foreground *Bronica ETRSi with 45-90mm zoom at 45mm, Fuji Velvia, 1/5sec at f/22, polarising and 81B filters*

Almost every time I have visited this location I have come away with a successful result. On one occasion, however, when conditions were superb, I was beaten to the location by that other group of hobbyists mad enough to be out before dawn on a freezing morning – fishermen! They had flashlights, took out the boats and disturbed the water. I had to abandon the shoot. ❖

Planning

Location The reservoir is found alongside the A171 about six miles east of Guisborough.

How to get there To be there for sunrise you will have to go by car, although the Middlesbrough to Whitby bus service passes the reservoir. Four miles after leaving Guisborough on the A171 a steep rise takes you onto the moors at Birk Brow. Approximately a mile further on the right is the access to the reservoir, almost opposite the junction with Lingdale Road. Follow the access road for 200m to the car park.

What to shoot After shooting the sunrise, walk around the reservoir on the footpaths provided. If you are lucky enough to have a good frost or snowfall, the jetty and boats provide many picture-taking opportunities. Close by is the strange cone shaped mound called Freeborough Hill, which rises out of the plain to a height of about 400ft. There is much speculation about the hill's origins. Its name is evidently Saxon and is said to derived from Friga or Frea the northern goddess of love. Access is from Dimmingdale Road opposite the road to Moorsholm. Afterwards backtrack to Guisborough and visit the dramatic priory ruins, at their best bathed in warm winter sunlight.

What to take On freezing mornings warm clothing, stout footwear and gloves are essential. A tripod and cable release are mandatory for the long exposures necessary before dawn. If your camera is battery dependent take spares and keep them warm as batteries can quickly fail in cold conditions.

Nearest pub The Jolly Sailors, half a mile east of Freeborough Hill on the A171 (01287 660270)

Other times of year This area on the edge of the Yorkshire Moors is well worth visiting in late August when the heather is in full bloom and the hills are a blaze with a rich purple colour.

Ordnance Survey map Outdoor Leisure Map 26

Essential reading *The North York Moors Landscape Heritage* by D A Spratt and R J E. Harris, £9.95, ISBN 0-907480-58-6,

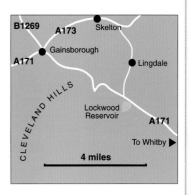

 The simple charm of Suffolk comes to life in the area around Southwold. The graphic shapes and colours are what lure **Gary Hacon** there regularly

SOUTHWOLD

SOUTHWOLD HOLDS many diverse areas of interest for the photographer, so with each visit it is worth deciding beforehand which element to concentrate on. The town is a bustling centre for local people and visitors alike, with an array of quaint shops, and it is rich in architecture with many well-maintained buildings. The lighthouse, standing high above its neighbours, is painted brilliant white, and nestles among pretty cottages on the clifftop. Moving south from the lighthouse, one comes across the coastguard lookout and a row of old cannon pointing out to sea, still posing a defence from times past.

Down on the promenade you are met with the sight of dozens of smart beach huts, all different colours and named individually by their owners. At sunrise there is nothing between these huts and the morning light. Viewed from the beach they stand side by side with the

Above This small fishing boat is typical of the type that are still used inshore off Southwold, as much for pleasure as profit, I suspect. The river is called The Blyth, which runs back to an estuary and the village of Blythburgh. The shot was taken early one August evening, facing south with the warm sunlight coming in from the right. The mooring rope runs in on the diagonal to lead the eye to the boat, with its reflection captured in the water
Nikon F90X with 24-120mm lens, Sensia 100, polarising filter

cliffs rising up behind and the rooftops of the town above breaking the skyline.

Walking along the shingle beach and sand dunes to the south of the town brings you to the mouth of the river Blyth. This is the source of many photographic opportunities. From the car park, an unsealed road heads inland for approximately half a mile. To the right of this road are numerous old black painted fishing huts

Facts about Southwold

This is a pretty Suffolk seaside town with enough charm and interest to satisfy almost anyone. With its lighthouse, beach huts, and river dotted with watercraft, this area provides a wealth of interest for the photographer. Largely unspoiled by modernisation, Southwold has managed to retain its character and provides a glimpse of life as it once was. The town has a pier, which is currently being re-built. Away from the seafront, there is a market place, which has small markets on Mondays and Thursdays, as well as an interesting town hall, museum and the UK's only amber museum. Expect to see plenty of bird life in the area, too.

Above These are just three of the brightly coloured beach huts that sit on the lower promenade of Southwold's seafront. The colours, shadows and repetitive patterns always make them an appealing subject. A polarising filter was used to make the most of the contrast between huts and sky
Nikon F90X with 24-120mm lens, Sensia 100

Right Sunset looking west along the river Blyth, near the footbridge to Walberswick. Taken on a summer's evening, the grasses were alive with mosquitoes, which were very hungry! Metering from the grass around me controlled the exposure. I find this method most reliable in almost every case
Nikon F90X with 24-120mm lens, Sensia 100

from which the local fishermen sell fresh fish. To the left is the river, which has several wooden landing stages, some on piles, some floating. These landing stages provide mooring for numerous boats, both local and visiting. Their type, colour and condition provides an endless supply of photographic images. Several of these craft are sitting at the water's edge rotting away, showing off their wonderful texture and construction with rusting metal and peeling paint in abundance. To capture the boats at their best, early mornings and late afternoons are most favourable.

At the end of the dirt road there is a pub, and the road cuts right across a sluice, over Reydon Marshes and back to town. Beyond the pub, a small footbridge crosses the river, giving access to the village of Walberswick. From the footbridge, the view inland leads to a disused windmill, minus its sails, and beyond are Reydon Marshes. The sun sets along this section of the river, giving good reflections of the evening skies. Those interested in birds will also have much to see. On our last visit, as we left the area we watched a marsh harrier wheeling above the reedbeds.

The diversity of the area is satisfaction guaranteed, with enough interest to keep the family happy too! ❖

Below This beach hut stood out because of its wonderful colour. It was so striking against the blue sky. As a graphic image it really appealed to me
Nikon F90X with 24-120mm lens, Sensia 100

THE MANOR HUT

Planning

Location Southwold is on the east coast of England, in the county of Suffolk.

How to get there Take the A12 between Ipswich and Lowestoft. At Blythburgh take the A1095 towards Southwold. Parking is readily available and often free.

What to shoot Architecture in the town, beach huts on the prom, sand and stone patterns on the beach, boats on the river and sunsets/ sunrises over the marshes.

What to take Prepare for the English weather; a tripod is a must; insect repellant and good footwear.

Accommodation and refreshment Both the town and river areas have ample selections for refreshment and, being a seaside location, there is no shortage of accommodation.

Ordnance Survey map Landranger 156
Local tourist information 01502 724729/722366

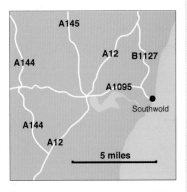

RIVER WEY

Surrey is not entirely a suburban extension of London. **Derek Croucher** says the River Wey has provided him with many inspirational landscapes

WE ALL LOVE to head for the most dramatic areas of Britain in search of something special to capture on film, and we can't really complain at the variety of landscapes on offer within a few hundred miles. But there is another way to take equally good shots without the need for long distance travel or the costs involved. Explore your home ground.

Now, I don't have the luxury of living in, say, the Lake District, or near the Yorkshire Moors – but that doesn't mean that I can't find plenty of material within a day's travel of my front door. And I've also heard all the jokes about my home county of Surrey – like the one saying that if Kent is the garden of England, then Surrey must be the patio. Despite this, there are plenty of subjects on offer, and this shot was taken along the River Wey just a mile from my home in the village of Send.

We all live within a short distance of some stretch of water or other, and places that are photographically uninspiring most of the time can be transformed by the right weather pattern at this time of year. Undoubtedly my favourite conditions are calm, crisp autumn or winter mornings with mist or fog, so I'll keep an eye on the forecasts and whenever things are looking promising, set the alarm and pop down to the river to see how it looks. But with sunrise being so late at the moment, and with such a short trip up the road (and being able to nip back for a hot breakfast to warm up), this doesn't seem like hard work at all. It may not be Glencoe or Derwent Water, but when shooting locally, you have the luxury of being able to choose your moment so conditions are at their best.

There are a number of good viewpoints in this area, but I often end up at this spot, where a small bridge gives a good view along what is actually one of the canal sections of the Wey Navigation. Locks and sections of canal were built along the River Wey in the 17th and 18th Centuries to allow horse drawn barges to carry goods between Godalming and the Thames. Nowadays it is owned by the National Trust and is busy with pleasure craft and dog walkers. Any spell of prolonged rainfall in this area will cause many of the fields to become flooded.

Left This is the view in the opposite direction from the same bridge, with Triggs Lock in the distance. I feel this is one of those shots where nothing is particularly striking, but the various elements come together to create a pleasing scene worth taking.
Mamiya RZ67, 110mm lens, Velvia, 1/8sec at f/16

Below left On this morning I had been to the river early, but the fog was far too thick for any photography so I returned home. Then at about 11 o'clock the sun began to show through, so I grabbed the camera and returned in time for a series of shots looking into the light.
Mamiya RZ67, 50mm lens, Velvia 1/30sec at f/11, 81A warm up, ND graduate

Some say that the straight sided, raised banks of the canal do not make such a good composition, but I have always liked the symmetrical feel, in particular the grouping of the trees on the banks. This shot was taken nine years ago, and was one of my first on large format, having just acquired an old 5x4in MPP. I used a 90mm wide-angle lens with neutral density graduate to even up the exposure difference between the sky and the land.

The moody conditions only lasted a while, and soon the frost melted, so I was off back home for a nice hot cup of tea and breakfast. That's the life for me. ❖

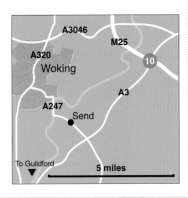

Planning

Location This section of the River Wey lies between Woking and Guildford in Surrey.

How to get there Best approach is via the A3. From the north use the Ripley exit, or from the south look for the Send/Woking sign. There is limited parking by Send Church with a footpath leading to the river. Avoid the church later on Sunday mornings – instead park at Sutton Green village on the other side of the river.

What to shoot There is plenty of variety in the area – locks, boats, bridges, reflections and swans all make great subjects. Try spending some time exploring to find the locations you like best, then return early morning when the forecast is for calm, clear conditions.

What to take Wideangle lens for general scenics, telephoto for compressing the lines of trees along the riverbank. Since you are likely to be shooting into the sun, a ND graduate will probably be needed to reduce the contrast range. Wellington boots are vital in the fields in winter, though in places even these may not be high enough to stay dry.

Nearest pub Try the Bulls Head in nearby West Clandon. Good pint and great food (01483 222444).

Other times of year Summer would be good for boats and the abundant insect life along the banks.

Ordnance Survey map Explorer 145, Ref 019543 for Send Church.

Essential reading *100 Walks in Surrey* by Clive Scott. The Crowood Press, ISBN 1 8522 3806 2.

HARDKNOTT PASS

Not only do early mornings give you the best light in the Lake District, but you'll also avoid the inevitable traffic jams. **Steve Day** always sets his alarm clock to go off at an ungodly hour

HARDKNOTT PASS derives its name from the feeling in your stomach as you negotiate the terrors of the twisting, turning mountain road leading to it. Well, it would do if I was writing its history.

It certainly is an interesting road. The views are wonderful, but in many places it's only wide enough for one car, and the summer season sees streams of cars shuffling backwards and forwards as they try to edge round each other.

Get up early on a late September/early October morning and you have the place to yourself. So I found as I tumbled blearily out of my camper, about an hour before dawn, despite Michael Fish's depressing forecast of a warm front, bringing long periods of rain and low cloud the night before. Always get up early, regardless of the forecast – when I'm buried I'd like the words, 'You never know...' on the headstone.

It's important photographically to be up this early. Any half-decent landscape photographer knows that the first and last couple of hours of the day are the best, but for some reason many assume that the day starts at dawn. Well, it doesn't, because you don't need direct sunlight to make a picture.

Don't feel you have to be at the top of a pass for the best view. This shot was taken halfway between Hardknott and Wrynose Passes, a couple of hundred yards from the road. It looks east, over Wrynose Bottom towards Little Langdale. Autumn mist fills the distant valleys north of Windermere, Little Langdale Tarn is a bright splash a little nearer, the bright sky highlights the tiny River Duddon and the reflected warmth of the rising sun lights the foreground grass and bracken.

I spent a happy 10 minutes shooting various vertical and horizontal compositions, using different lenses, before the forecast rain and cloud came rolling in.

There are many other good pictures to be had in the immediate area. On the western side of Hardknott Pass, on the way to Eskdale, are the remains of Hardknott Castle – a Roman fort. Alternatively, head down the road east from Hardknott. Explore Wrynose Bottom then continue downhill and take a short detour right to Duddon Vale where the River Duddon flows through a very pretty valley. Return to your original road, continuing towards Little Langdale. Just beyond Fell Foot Farm turn left onto the Blea Tarn road. Stop and look back to the farm.

In the space of these few miles you'll find a wealth of subjects. When you've done them all, turn round and go back – by then the sun's moved and everything looks different. And remember – 'you never know...' ❖

Opposite page I managed just 10 minutes of photography that morning – this picture alone was worth it. The picture is deceptive. It is glowing with colour yet there is no direct sunlight at all. The only light on the land is that reflected from the sky. To the naked eye the sky was overpowering, leaving the ground dark and lacking in detail. Fitting a strong neutral-density graduate solved that problem and brought everything into balance. A wideangle was used to give a broad view and to enable inclusion of the foreground rocks to add depth to the shot
Canon EOS 600 with 20-35mm lens, Velvia, 2 seconds at t f/16, neutral density grad

Left There are several portrait and landscape alternatives to the main picture – including this view. I used a variety of lenses to make different compositions, all from the same viewpoint
Canon EOS 600 with 20-35mm lens, Velvia, 2 secs at f/16, ND grad

Left The Roman Fort, with Border End hill behind. A reasonable shot, but it would have been so much better late in the afternoon. Ah well, you can't shoot everything at the right time!
Canon EOS 600 with 20-35mm lens, Velvia, 1/15sec at f/11, polariser

Planning

Location Southwest area of Lake District National Park

How to get there By road, A593 west from Ambleside then minor road west one mile beyond Skelwyn Bridge through Little Langdale. Alternatively, from just south of Ravenglass on the coastal A595 take the minor road east through Boot, along Eskdale and up to the pass. For detailed travel information see the website www.travelcumbria.co.uk/ or contact the Lake District National Park Authority (01539 724555).

What to shoot The place is a dream. Stunning landscapes abound, and the ever-changing weather gives variety to the views. Don't get hooked on the lakes themselves – there's so much to see in the surrounding hills. Go to a likely spot, get out and explore.

What to take Good walking shoes, waterproofs, warm clothing (regardless of weather forecast, which you have, of course, checked beforehand), OS map, a compass if you're going away from the road, a tripod and a range of lenses in a backpack.

Nearest pub To the west, at Boot in Eskdale, is The Burnmoor (01946 723224). To the east is the Three Shires in Little Langdale (01539 437215). Both have bedrooms.

Best time of year Autumn is best, and relatively peaceful. Winter frosts and snows make for stunning pics, but beware of closed high passes. Avoid summer – it's is heaving, the traffic jams are awful and you're deafened by choruses of 'ooohs' and 'aaahs'.

OS map Landranger 90 or Outdoor Leisure 6; map ref NY 230 015

Essential reading Too many to list. See www.cumbria-the-lake-district.co.uk/ for a list of publications.

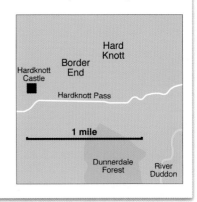

GRIMSPOUND

Ducking storms and sliding in sheep muck may not be everyone's idea of fun, but when he heads down to Dartmoor, **Lee Frost** wouldn't want it any other way

ASKED TO chart their careers, the majority of landscape photographers could probably cite a particular region where their love-affair with the land was first confirmed. For me, that place is Dartmoor. The latter half of my teenage years was spent living on the south Devon coast, and as my interest in photography began to take off, I discovered what until then had been nothing more than an empty brown patch on maps of the south west.

This had as much to do with curiosity as anything else. I could see its barren fringes from my bedroom window and often wondered what surprises lay hidden among its wooded valleys, desolate moorland and mysterious tors. Then I reached the grand old age of 16, scraped enough money together to buy an aging 50cc motorbike, and set about discovering the land, armed with an Olympus OM1N and a couple of secondhand lenses.

Facts about Grimspound

Lying in a fold of hills between Hamel Down and Hookney Tor, Grimspound is one of Dartmoor's best-known Bronze-Age settlements. Dating from around 1,000BC, it contains the remains of 24 small huts enclosed by a boundary wall some three metres thick. There are no references to its name before the end of the 18th century so its origins are unclear, though 'pound' clearly relates to the fact that Grimspound was an enclosed settlement while use

of the name 'Grim' in other place names is always in reference to the devil, suggesting the Saxons associated the settlement with diabolic forces. The setting of Grimspound, which would have been hard to defend against attack, and its proximity to a stream running through the north side of the enclosure, indicates it was home to pastoralists eager to protect their livestock from the wild beasts that once roamed Dartmoor.

This photograph, of the Bronze-Age settlement of Grimspound, was taken more recently, during the making of my book on the region. It was mid-afternoon and I had spent much of that dismal autumnal day sitting in the car, sheltering from frequent bursts of heavy rain and taking very few pictures. But strong winds were pushing boiling clouds across the sky at a rate of knots, and experience had taught me that anything could happen, so I persevered.

Once the rain began to abate, I headed briskly up the paved pathway to the village and within seconds of arriving at the walled enclosure, bright sunlight exploded through the stormy sky, illuminating the land around me and creating a scene of high drama. Instinctively, I set up the tripod and grabbed my camera – a Pentax 67 already fitted with a 55mm wideangle lens and 0.6 neutral density graduate filter.

Then came the moment every photographer dreads. Frantically rummaging for the tripod head's quick release plate, I suddenly realised why I couldn't find it. It was still screwed to the bottom of my panoramic camera, which I'd left sitting in the boot of the car, and I foolishly hadn't packed a spare (something I now do religiously). For a few brief seconds the sound of expletives sent sheep rushing in all directions, before I decided to take positive action. What followed would have made the British Olympic team proud as I slid, leapt and bounced my way back down to the car in record time, feet hardly touching the ground, grabbed the item in question then made the return journey, hoping and praying my efforts wouldn't be in vain.

Switching to autopilot, the next few minutes disappeared in a blur: fix camera to tripod, compose shot, set focus using depth-of-field scale to ensure front-to-back sharpness. Align ND grad, attach cable release, make sure film is advanced. Take spot reading from sunlit grassy foreground, set exposure – 1/8sec at f/16 – activate mirror lock, allow camera to settle for a few seconds, trip shutter. Advance film, check meter reading, mirror lock, wait, trip shutter. Repeat.

In all I managed to expose half a roll of 120 film (five frames) before all traces of sunlight were angrily snatched away by a thick band of cloud. And then, as quickly as it began, it was over, leaving me a sweating, steaming wreck, standing before a scene of sublime beauty in this harsh, unforgiving land and trying to imagine what life must have been like 3,000 years ago for the simple Bronze-Age folk of Grimspound. ❖

Above Located some three miles south of Manaton, Hound Tor is definitely worth a visit while you're in the area. Its jumble of enormous granite boulders offers lots of photographic potential and successful shots can be taken at either end of the day. I prefer early evening, when low, raking light reveals the coarse texture of the granite. This view looks south southeast towards the familiar sight of Haytor Rocks
Pentax 67 with 45mm wideangle lens, Velvia, one second at f/16, polariser and 81B warm-up filters

Above If grey, overcast weather puts paid to shooting sweeping views, concentrate instead on smaller details, which are revealed at their best by the soft, low-contrast light of a dull day
Pentax 67 with 105mm standard lens, Velvia, 1/15sec at f/11

Planning

Location Grimspound can be found approx three miles west (as the crow flies) of the village of Manaton, within the Dartmoor National Park, Devon.
How to get there From Moretonhampstead take the B3212 towards Postbridge and Two Bridges. After approx seven miles, turn left down a minor road to Challacombe and after two miles, where the road crosses a small stream at Firth Bridge, park then walk the paved pathway up to Grimspound.
Where to stay Plenty of B&Bs and hotels in Moretonhampstead. The market town of Chagford, a few miles further north, is also a good bet.
Nearest pub The Warren House Inn (01822 880208), two miles west of Grimspound, on the B3212 Moretonhampstead-Postbridge road.
What to shoot The best shots are to be had at closer range, where remains of the stone huts can be used as foreground interest. Other locations worth checking out – Hound Tor, Bowerman's Nose and the village of Widecombe-in-the-Moor.
Best time of day Dawn and dusk are ideal times for ancient, mysterious places like Grimspound, though any time of day can work. I personally favour dramatic, stormy weather.

Best time of year Autumn and winter tends to yield more changeable weather and dramatic light.
What to take The walk to Grimspound is short but can be boggy and slippery, so a good pair of walking boots is essential. It can also get rather cold and windy, so a fleece and wind/ waterproof jacket is advised. Wideangle lenses are the order of the day to capture the huts in their harsh surroundings, plus a sturdy tripod.
Ordnance Survey map Outdoor Leisure sheet 28
Essential Reading *Dartmoor* by Lee Frost and Ian Robinson, Colin Baxter Photography, ISBN: 1 8410 7039 4, £9. For general info on Dartmoor and its history, Crossing's *Guide to Dartmoor* is the definitive publication – now available only from Forest Publishing, £24, tel 01626 821631.

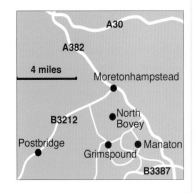

PEWSEY DOWNS

Even **Steve Day**, advocate of the early rise and off-the-beaten-track photograph, from time to time succumbs to the temptation of the easily accessible scene

ONE OF THE MANY delights of Wiltshire is that it is awash with views. Pewsey Downs National Nature Reserve (NNR) is only eight miles away from Martinsell Hill (see page 72), and is part of the same range of downland.

About two thirds of the county is chalk. It is the least-populated of the southern counties, and as most of that population is concentrated in the lower valleys the hilltops give views unsullied by modern civilisation. Nearly all of the hills have ancient trackways running along the ridges, so access is easy.

Knapp Hill, and the adjacent Walker's Hill, are both part of Pewsey Downs National Nature Reserve and are managed by English Nature. Like most such sites in Wiltshire they are littered with Iron-Age terraces and hillforts, but there are a couple of extras – the Alton Barnes White Horse (one of seven in Wiltshire) and The Wansdyke – an ancient defensive ditch, thought to have been built in Saxon times.

There's often a price to pay for good views in the form of a long hike, and there's something to be said for having to make an effort, but Knapp Hill is made for idle photographers. A small country road runs over the ridge, and there is a car park about 100 yards from this view.

I hasten to add that I did explore a little to get the shot shown above, which looks along the line of hills towards the east. It's a scene I'd tried to capture in the summer, which was the first time I saw it. I say 'tried' because I couldn't do it justice – long, sweeping views like this are often difficult to get right. Shooting in the first or last hours of the day is the only way to give three-dimensionality, especially in the summer, but from this viewpoint the sun's direction was wrong at that time of the year. I concluded that January would be best, with the sun rising to the right of the picture. All it needed to complete the scene was a good coating of frost, to lend some sparkle.

The right conditions duly arrived, and I was there at

Facts about Pewsey Downs

Knapp Hill is part of the English Nature National Nature Reserve (NNR) that encompasses a large part of Pewsey Downs, and is a classic example of traditionally-managed chalk grassland, with a wealth of flora, and insect fauna. Apart from its nature interest the area abounds in pre-historic hillforts, the ancient Wansdyke defensive bank and ditch (which subsequently became a track) and medieval cultivation terraces. For more information contact English Nature for a leaflet, e-mail enquiries@english-nature.org.uk, tel 01733 455000 or see their website www.english-nature.org.uk.

Above This one of the seven White Horses in Wiltshire, viewed from the bottom of Walker's Hill. The light covering of snow reflects the white chalk of the horse, while the furrows in the field lead the eye towards the undulating hills in the distance. The low sunlight creates large areas of darker shadow, which serves to reveal the dips and troughs in the land
Canon EOS 50E with 75-300mm IS lens, Velvia, 1/8sec at f/16, polariser

Above Keep your eyes open. I felt this stack of straw bales on the top of Milk Hill, lit by the fast-fading evening sun, was a worthy contender for the Turner prize
Canon EOS 50E with 20-35mm lens, Velvia, one second at f/16, polariser

dawn, to find a persistent veil of cloud (the one that seems to follow me around), giving weak light, so I waited impatiently for over an hour before it cleared. And only just in time, too – another half hour and the shadows on the hillsides would have filled in, and those beautiful, flowing shapes would have changed into flat cardboard cutouts. A combination of sharp winter light and the frost lends an almost metallic quality to the picture.

A 20-35mm wideangle lens ensured I could include some foreground, to give depth. I used a polariser – the uneven blue of the sky, characteristic of a polariser on a wideangle, gives this away. No matter, I don't think it spoils the picture. Finally, a weak warm-up was fitted because I felt the scene was too blue, and I don't like 'cold' pictures. It's all a matter of taste, though. An aperture of f/22 ensured that everything was in focus from front to back, and a tripod, cable release and mirror lock-up coped with the long exposure of one second (a half-stop extra exposure was given as the bright frost was fooling the meter).

Composition was difficult – with a wideangle, moving just a couple of feet either way can dramatically affect a picture. I settled on this because I felt the lines of the terracing bottom right pulled the eye naturally towards the hills, where it follows and explores the ridge, finally resting on the shadowed slopes. Any temptation to wander out of the picture to the right is stopped by the dark zigzag of lines at the foot of the hills which naturally return you to the start point, and off we go again.

That's the theory, anyway! ❖

Above Whee – snow in Wiltshire! This could almost be the Lakes, or the Scottish hills. Low evening light gave detail on the ground. Note the happy people sledging down Knapp Hill, in the background – snow brings out the kiddie in us all
Canon EOS 50E with 28-135mm lens, Velvia, 1/4sec at f/11, polariser

Planning

Location Wiltshire, about five miles southwest of Marlborough.

How to get there From Marlborough head west on the A4 for two miles. At Fyfield take the turning left to Lockeridge. Continue through the village heading southwest for three miles to the car park.

What to shoot Knapp Hill, Walker's Hill (with Adam's Graves – a hillfort), Milk Hill and Tan Hill (the highest point in Wilts) are all part of the Pewsey Downs NNR, and within short walking distance. The ancient Wansdyke runs behind the hill and there is a fine White Horse. The whole area is superb in summer for flowers and insects. It has another attraction – crop circles (though the farmer may not agree with the word 'attraction'). The sweeping fields to the south of the hills are a favourite spot for the tricksters, and each summer there is a row of tents pitched high on the hill, with gullible fools sitting outside eagerly awaiting the 'aliens'.

What to take Good walking shoes, waterproofs, a tripod, a range of lenses and something to drink.

Nearest pub The Barge Inn at Honeystreet (01672 851705), about one mile due south of Knapp Hill, just past Alton Barnes – excellent food and beer, and on the banks of the Kennet & Avon canal, though full of crop-circle spotters in summer (see the pub's website http://cropcircle.dsvr.co.uk/anasazi/barge99.html).

Times to visit Spring and summer for nature and fine landscapes from the hills, autumn and winter for landscape shots of the hills themselves.

Ordnance Survey map Explorer 157 (Marlborough & Savernake Forest). OS Refs: Park at SU 116 637. Knapp Hill is due east of the car park. The picture was shot about 100 yards from the car park, at 115 635, just over the fence by the road.

Essential reading *Exploring Historic Wiltshire (Vol 1)*, by Ken Watts, Ex Libris Press, ISBN 0 9485 7885 8, *The Vale of Pewsey*, by John Chandler, Ex Libris Press, ISBN 1 9033 4107 8.

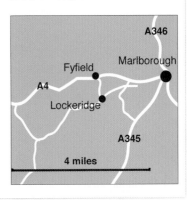

MALVERN HILLS

When the valleys of Hereford and Worcestershire are covered in mist **Steve Gosling** heads for the inspiration that can be drawn from the Malvern Hills

THE JAGGED OUTLINE of the Malvern Hills rises from the flat plain of the River Severn in Worcestershire and their contrast with the surrounding countryside makes them instantly recognisable for some distance away. The hills offer excellent ridge walking, with beautiful views east and west over rural England and into Wales.

I lived in Worcester for 10 years and grew to love these hills and, although I moved from the area several years ago, I return regularly with my family to walk and take photographs. I have therefore seen them at all times of day and year but consider early morning in the autumn to be my favourite for atmospheric photography. The variety of weather conditions that prevail at this time of year can result in dramatically different photographs from one day to the next.

It was on a cold and misty autumn morning that I dragged myself out of bed at about 5.30am and looked

Above Worcestershire Beacon, the highest point in the Malvern Hills, rises above an early morning autumn mist
Canon EOS 1N, 35-135mm USM zoom, Kodak Elite EC100, 1/5sec at f/22, 81B & grey graduated filters, Slik tripod

out of the window to be greeted by a thick grey mist concealing all but the closest details. Joy of joys! I knew that these weather conditions would be ideal for the photograph I had planned. Frequently, when the valley is cloaked in mist the tops of the hills are clear.

I had chosen my viewpoint carefully: I wanted to capture the highest point of the Malvern Hills, the Worcestershire Beacon (1394 ft) rising out of the mist. I therefore had to seek high ground. To get a clear view and to be able to look down on the mist in the valley below, I chose to shoot looking north from the Herefordshire Beacon, (also known as 'British Camp Hill'

Facts about the Malvern Hills

The rocks of the Malvern Hills are so old they were formed before life existed on earth. Some of the rocks date from before 200 million years ago. For over 100 years they have been looked after by the Malvern Hills Conservators (tel. 01684 892002). This independent body attempt to balance the protection and preservation of the hills against their

value as a site for a variety of leisure pursuits, which today includes walking, horse riding, mountain biking and hang-gliding. One of the attractions of the Malvern Hills is their accessibility. There are numerous car parks (a small charge is levied by the Conservators – see *Planning*) and the ridge can be reached by a multitude of routes of varying difficulty.

– height 1109ft). This viewpoint has the added advantage of being a short climb from the car park.

The scene before me was magical and justified the early rise. The sun was shining brightly on those parts of the landscape emerging from the mist, which was rolling backwards and forwards across the valley, like the tropical sea that would have surrounded the ridge of these hills 500 million years ago. The landscape below me was constantly changing as the mist revealed and concealed at one and the same time. Occasionally the mist would lap at my feet - I knew I would have to work quickly if I was to capture the view on film.

I framed the shot to accentuate the mist in the foreground and to emphasise the isolated Worcestershire Beacon rising out of it in the distance. To retain detail in the sky I fitted a light grey graduated filter to cover the top of the frame. I also experimented with both 81B and 80B filters to respectively 'warm' and 'cool' the image – while both versions work, it is this warmer version that I prefer. ❖

Below I arrived on the hills at 7am and the mist was so thick that I couldn't see further than 20 yards. I waited and my perseverance paid off – two hours later the mist began to clear
Canon EOS-1N with 20-35mm USM lens, 81B and grey grad filters, Ektachrome Elite 100, 1/16sec at f/22, tripod

Planning

Location Great Malvern (the largest of the communities around the hills) is situated on the A449 and is approximately 12 miles from Worcester and 8 miles from Ledbury

How to get there Access by car is easy (the M5 and the M50 are not too far away) and there is plenty of car parking at various locations around the Hills (charge of £1.50 per day). Public transport access is good - the area is served well by local buses and there are rail stations at Great Malvern, Malvern Link and Colwall.

Where to stay There are numerous hotels, B&Bs and pubs offering accommodation in the area - contact the Malvern Tourist Information Office for more details (tel. 01684 892289) What to shoot: The area offers a great variety of landscape opportunities, the rolling green countryside of Herefordshire contrasts with the flatter Worcestershire scenery. The Malvern Priory Church in Great Malvern or Little Malvern Priory, (near British Camp Hill) offer potential to those interested in architectural photography. Further afield are the cathedral cities of Worcester, Gloucester & Hereford or picturesque villages with black and white timbered cottages such as Elmley Castle, Weobley, Pembridge and Eardisland, as well as many historic houses and gardens (again Malvern TIO can provide further details).

What to take A wide range of lenses (from 28 to 300mm will cover most eventualities), walking boots, additional clothing (windproof & waterproof) to enable you to 'layer'. At early morning or late in the day, it can be chilly on the top of the hills, even in summer. Always take a sturdy but preferably lightweight tripod and a torch if you plan to walk to your chosen viewpoint before sunrise or after sunset.

Nearest pub There are several pubs in Great Malvern. Alternatively there is The Malvern Hills Hotel (tel. 01684 540237) situated on the A449/B4232 below the Herefordshire Beacon, or the Brewers Arms (tel. 01684 568147) located off the B4232 in West Malvern.

Other times of year Spring offers similar lighting conditions to autumn. The hills can be easily approached during winter for dramatic scenery, especially after a dusting of snow. Ordnance Survey Map: Landranger 150, grid reference 775459

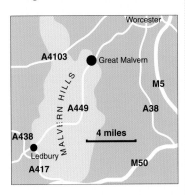

VIEWS FROM ROBINSON

Sometimes a climb is the only way to do justice to the sheer expanse of the Lake District. But, as **Derek Croucher** explains, you must be prepared

THE GOLDEN RULE for the colour landscape photographer has to be to concentrate efforts on shooting during the first rays of morning sunlight and then again as the sun heads towards the western horizon. This way of working comes into its own in coastal areas, using the morning sun on the east coast and utilising the evening light in the west. A problem arises, however, when shooting in areas such as the Lake District, where the hills have the uncanny knack of casting rather large shadows just where you don't want them. By the time the sun is above the mountains it has lost all its vital, warm quality. This is what prompted me to climb to the tops in order to catch the early rays of light as they appeared.

The first job, though, was some research. After scouring the maps I decided my viewpoint would be the peak of Robinson above Buttermere, shooting to the northeast towards Skiddaw and Blencathra with the autumn sun rising to my right. I also wanted to walk the route in good daylight beforehand so I could be sure of finding my way in the darkness before sunrise. To this end, I set off on a research walk starting in the village of Buttermere, carefully noting any landmarks I passed. After one mile, however, the Lake District proved its unpredictability when heavy rain forced me to turn back.

The next day I tried again, but only got half a mile this time when the wind, increasing with altitude, took my legs from under me before I knew what was happening. Just five minutes previously I had been walking along the top of a sheer drop, so the warning was heeded and I beat a second retreat. Back in the comfort of my bed and

Facts about Robinson

Robinson is one of the more modest Lake District peaks, reaching 737m (2,418 feet). Most of the area is under the protection of the National Trust, which has a reputation for keeping pathways in good, safe condition. In any case, the walk to the top from Buttermere is fairly straightforward, perhaps encountering a little bogginess in the dip between High Snockrigg and the peak, and a slightly rocky path over the last section. Views to the north and east are superb, taking in well-known peaks including Skiddaw, Blencathra, Causey Pike and Cat Bells, as well as the Newlands Valley, Derwent Water and Keswick.

While parking is not a problem at 5am, bear in mind that if you arrive later in the day this area becomes very busy during peak holiday times.

breakfast I was able to catch the weather forecast – fine and sunny with winds still strong but decreasing. The next day would have to be the one; the first hint of daylight helping me to find my way over the section I had not been able to research fully. My next decision concerned equipment. I wanted a fairly narrow format for this type of landscape, so I packed my Linhof Technikardan with a 6x9cm film back, along with a selection of lenses and a lightweight tripod.

was still pretty strong since the clouds show some blurring due to movement.

A couple of hours after dawn, the cloud became more and more dense, so I decided to make my way back down to civilisation. A fell runner stopped for a brief chat, and seemed surprised to see me coming down the hill at such an early hour. The only person who wouldn't have expressed such surprise would have been another photographer! ❖

The lonely lakes

It creates a real sense of loneliness, parking the car at 5am in the darkness, to set off up a track that would normally be busy with hikers. The walk, which was only in the dark for the first half hour or so, proved to be fairly easy, and I was greeted by blue skies with some cloud to add interest and provide a patchwork of light.

A couple of different compositions presented themselves immediately and the main shot was taken with a 65mm lens fitted with a polariser, using Velvia exposed for 1/2sec at f/22. You can see the wind

Below I used a 90mm lens to pick out this detail showing the peak of Causey Pike with Skiddaw in cloud
Linhof Technikardan with 6x9cm film back, Velvia, 1/2sec at f/22, polariser

Planning

Location Robinson lies to the northeast of Buttermere. My walk began in the village, though there are various routes to the top.

How to get there From Keswick take the B5289 through Borrowdale. From Cockermouth take the B5292 then the B5289. To approach via the Newlands Valley, turn off the A66 west of Keswick through the village of Braithwaite. There is limited roadside parking in the valley, or continue on to Buttermere.

What to shoot Views will all be distant, so choose a day with good clarity. Please don't shoot at midday under plain blue skies – you will be disappointed when you see the results.

What to take Waterproof walking boots, extra clothing, whistle, torch, compass, map, food and drink. Mountains can be very dangerous. Ask yourself whether you could find your way down if visibility dropped to 10 metres. Use a good quality photographic backpack – a shoulder

bag is very bad for the back.

Nearest pub There is a good pub in Buttermere, which gets very busy at peak times.

Other times of year Autumn or winter mists hanging in the valley make great pictures. Springtime, while the greens are still vivid and fresh.

Ordnance Survey map Outdoor Leisure 4, The English Lakes Northwest area; map ref 203168.

Essential reading *On Foot in the Lake District, Northern and Western Fells: Vol. 1*, by Terry Marsh, £9.99, David and Charles, ISBN 0-7153-0943-9

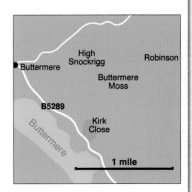

 There's still a dusting of snow to be found at this time of year, and it can add an extra dimension to your landscapes, as **Michael Szarelis** explains

THE PEAK DISTRICT National Park was our first national park, and next year it celebrates its 50th birthday. The road network into the park is very good, which it has to be, as one in three of us lives within an hour's drive of its boundary, and each year the park has more than 22 million day visitors, making it the second busiest national park in the world.

But even with all these people, you can still find solitude if you wish, and take some cracking shots as well. The main photograph of Mam Tor shown here was taken early one Sunday morning in February, and was planned the previous year in late spring when poor weather had ruined the day's photography.

Because the park has such a wide range of landscapes in such a small area, the possibilities for planning and taking shots are endless. Having planned the shot I wanted of Mam Tor at sunrise in the winter months, it was a matter of waiting for the right weather conditions and that little bit of snow that can transform those landscape shots.

One Sunday morning, having got up well before dawn and loaded the car with my gear, I drove to the Peak District. As I reached the boundaries of the park, where I could see over several of the hills, I saw that dragging myself out of bed at that cold, inhospitable hour had paid dividends. There was a dusting of snow sitting atop several of them.

From the car park at the foot of Mam Tor, it was a short walk up the summit to my location. Soon the tripod was set up and I was viewing the scene with the viewfinder of my Fuji panoramic camera. I chose the 105mm lens and fitted that to the camera body. This would allow me to get foreground interest as well as the distant hills in the shot. I focused the camera and set the polarising filter using the focusing screen.

Below On a trip to Mondal Head near Bakewell, I found myself down in the valley by the River Wye. I shot the scene using a 180mm and 105mm lens. The former, for me, produced the best picture
Fuji 617 with 180mm lens, Velvia rated at ISO 32, 1/2sec at f/22, 81B warm-up and polarising filters

MAM TOR

On the 105mm lens is a centre filter designed for the 6x17cm camera. This distributes light evenly from corner to corner for a well-balanced image. Because I was using a handheld meter, I allowed one stop for this filter and then allowed for the use of polariser and 81A warm-up filter. I also used a 0.6 ND grad on the sky.

Having obtained a meter reading, I then bracketed the exposure to make sure I had the shot I wanted. With only four images to a 120 roll film, you can sure use some film when bracketing!

After this shot I moved positions around the summit, as there were many more potential images to take looking down and across the valley below. I spent the rest of the morning walking along the ridge from Mam Tor to Lose Hill and back, taking pictures all the way. ❖

Below This was shot at Tansley Dale near Litton, in the late morning. One of the most characteristic features of the White Peak (as this area is known) is the network of limestone walling. As soon as I saw the landscape covered in snow with the walls bisecting it, I knew I had to have this shot. The wind was blowing the heavy snow clouds towards me, so I had to work fast. Two frames later the light was lost as heavy snow blew into the shot
Fuji 617 with 180mm lens, Velvia rated at ISO 32, 81B warm-up and polarising filters

Planning

Location Mam Tor is a few minutes drive from the village of Castleton. It can be seen from the village, but you get a better view if you climb up to the Peveril Castle.
How to get there Take the A625 through Castleton and head up Winnats Pass. Turn right along the B6061 and then rejoin the A625 at the base of Mam Tor. There is parking here and then it's just a short walk along the path.
What to shoot From the summit of Mam Tor you get some atmospheric sunrise and sunset pictures. You can shoot up the Hope Valley, over towards Castleton with Peveril Castle perched above the town, or shoot over towards Edale and Kinder Scout. From the car park you could walk up Rushup Edge to Lords Seat and catch the sunlight on Mam Tor as the sun sets to the west of the peaks.
What to take Warm clothing, boots, gloves, a hat, tripod, cable release, a range of lenses and a spare battery. I carry my gear in a Lowepro Mini Trekker. I always take a notepad and compass as well, so I can make notes about where sunrise and sunset will be at other times of the year.
Where to stay Castleton is a good base and offers a full range of accommodation. For details of hotels,

B&Bs and self-catering cottages in the area, call 0114 262 0777. There is a youth hostel in Castleton, call 01433 620235.
Nearest pub There are several pubs in Castleton, try the Castle Inn (01433 620578), it has good food and accommodation.
Other times of year You can shoot all year round in the peaks, although some areas offer more potential than others.
Ordnance Survey maps OS Outdoor Leisure 1 (Dark Peak) and 24 (White Peak). For the Mam Tor area use the OS Dark Peak map, grid ref 128835.
Essential reading Too many to mention, as there are a lot of good local travel guides. Contact Castleton Tourist Information on 01433 620679, or Edale on 01433 670207. For more information on the Peak District visit www.peakdistrict.org

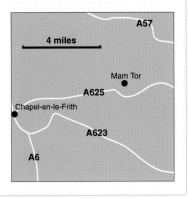

Facts about Mam Tor

Mam Tor is looked after by the National Trust, and to reach it from the village of Castleton you must drive up through the spectacular limestone gorge of Winnats Pass, and park at its base. It has also been called the 'Shivering Mountain', because of the unstable nature of the layers that make it, which easily crumble to cause landslips. At some time in the past, one such landslip left the sheer, exposed face shown in the photograph. On the 1,695ft summit of the tor are the earthwork remains of an Iron Age hillfort. Covering 16 acres, it stands on the site of a Bronze Age settlement dating back to 1,000BC – or earlier! It is the largest hillfort in the Peak District. Mam Tor dominates the head of the Hope Valley, and you get spectacular views from its summit.

SWALEDALE

Looking for the classic picture of the much photographed Yorkshire Dales? **David Tarn** always makes a beeline for Swaledale for his pictures

SWALEDALE and Arkengarthdale are the northernmost dales of the Yorkshire Dales National Park. If you were asked to supply a photograph of a typical Yorkshire Dales scene, chances are it will be of Swaledale. Field barns, dry stone walls and rolling green hills dotted with sheep – this is Swaledale.

Staying nearby is easy, you have a choice of towns and villages starting with Richmond at the eastern end of the dale, progressing through Reeth, a large market town sometimes referred to as the capital of Swaledale. Further

along the valley you pass through Grinton, Healaugh, Feetham, Low Row, Gunnerside, Muker, Thwaite and Keld. All can offer you accommodation of one sort or another, though Keld is bereft of a pub!

To find Swaledale, leave the A1 at Scotch Corner and take the A6108 to Richmond. Richmond is a large hilltop market town with a cobbled town square and an impressive castle overlooking the river Swale. Continue out of Richmond on the A6108 towards Leyburn, then take a right turn towards Reeth on the B6270 which

continues all the way to the far end of Swaledale. A few minor roads take the higher routes through the dale, and these are worth exploring to find other good viewpoints. But the best way to explore much of the dale is on foot.

Because the Yorkshire Dales are under pressure from so many visitors, the Park authority is keen to encourage the use of public transport. However, it is a sad fact that the hours photographers keep, and the need to move on whenever the light and conditions take you, necessitates the use of a car. Walk as much as you can once you are in the area you want to photograph. This way, you will always find more viewpoints and remember to stay on footpaths through the flower meadows. If we all stay on the footpaths we won't destroy what we have come to see and record. We will also avoid any unpleasant encounters with the farmers, whose efforts over the years are largely responsible for the way the dales now look.

Below The dominant colour of the landscape during summer is green, so the wild flower meadow makes an interesting subject. A polarising filter has saturated the colours and the deep blue sky contrasts well with the buttercups in the field. This view is from the road between Richmond and Gunnerside *Pentax 67 with 55mm wideangle lens, Velvia, Gitzo tripod and polarising filter, half a second at f/22*

Far left This picture was taken further along the valley just outside the village of Muker. I don't use filters for this sort of effect very often, but this picture benefits from a soft focus filter, and a sunset used as a warm up. The overall effect makes the photograph more impressionistic *Mamiya RB67 with 180mm lens, Velvia, soft focus and sunset filters, 1/30sec at f/16*

Left Within every scene there are always details. For this picture I wanted to concentrate on the flowers and just leave an impression of the barn and walls. A shallow depth of field also meant I could use a faster shutter speed and not worry about any movement which the breeze might cause *Pentax 67 with 55mm wideangle lens, Velvia, Gitzo tripod and polarising filter 1/60sec at f/4*

Having said that, much of the wonderful scenery in Swaledale can in fact be captured from the roadside. This wonderful scene (opposite page) is taken from a lay-by just outside the village of Gunnerside. The row of three barns running diagonally across the valley floor never fails to attract photographers. With the composition being so well made already, I always feel you need to be extra careful over light and other elements in the scene to make the picture stand out. The wild flowers add a dash of welcome colour, and this was an especially bright day last June, with fresh, clear air.

This picture was taken using a Pentax 67 and 135mm lens on a Gitzo tripod, and with a polarising filter. I use Fuji Velvia almost exclusively these days. Exposure was half a second at f/22. ❖

Planning

Where to stay Swaledale is full of good pubs, hotels, guesthouses, youth hostels and self-catering cottages. I can recommend the food at the Kearton Country Hotel at Thwaite. It's named after the Kearton brothers who were the first natural history film-makers in these parts and used imitation rocks and cattle to get closer to their subjects.

What to shoot In Swaledale there are a number of good waterfalls to find, especially near the village of Keld. Wain Wath Force can be seen from the roadside just beyond the village of Keld. If you are prepared for a little walking, Kisdon gorge and the waterfall are well worth a visit, especially after rain.

What to take The obvious: waterproof walking boots, rucksack (for your flask and sandwiches as well as camera gear), polarising filter and a sturdy tripod.

Other times of year The Yorkshire Dales can be good at any time of the year. In winter when it snows, the walls and barns make great patterns in an otherwise white landscape. Spring and autumn bring their own colours and both warrant a visit.

Ordnance Survey map Outdoor Leisure 30

Essential reading All the James Herriot vet books. They have nothing to do with photographing the dales, but they vividly record the life of a bygone era.

Website www.yorkshirenet.co.uk, or alternatively call Richmond tourist information on 01748 850252.

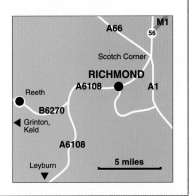

 It's difficult to get off the beaten track in southern England – and it will be even more difficult after **Steve Day** reveals his favourite spot for photography

I HAVE RESERVATIONS about revealing one of my favourite Wiltshire views. For me it's a special place. Other spots in the county have equally as good views, or interesting prehistoric earthworks, or varied flora, but Martinsell Hill has them all. One of the principal joys is that it's tucked away in the middle of nowhere with only narrow country lanes leading to it, and so is not on the tourist trail. At dawn I have always had the place to myself. Later in the day there are a few people about, but by then I've gone.

The Hill lies at the eastern end of Pewsey Downs which are, in turn, the southern flanks of the Marlborough Downs. Downland has a unique beauty – its curving, flowing, chalk is almost wave-like – and it cries out to be photographed. Martinsell is a classic case

Above Snow is a rarity in Wiltshire, but the previous night's weather forecast had promised a light covering. I was there the next day at dawn, and it was worth it. There had been a fine dusting of snow, like icing sugar. The sky was an intense blue, with a beautiful crescent moon adorning it and the light was a dream – sharp and clear, with a strong warmth that needed no filtering.

This view is but a few yards from where I'd parked my camper van that morning, and I love the way the eye is pulled into the picture by the curve of the downland. This is just one frame of the two rolls that I shot, all within a few yards of this viewpoint

Canon EOS 50E with 20-35mm wideangle zoom lens, Velvia, one second at f/16, polariser, tripod, mirror lock-up

Facts about Martinsell Hill

Martinsell Hill is one of the finest examples of chalk downland in the UK. Most of it is under Countryside Stewardship, so is freely open to walkers. For landscape photographers the views are superb. For nature lovers it has a wealth of wildflowers, some interesting trees and a thriving insect population. History buffs won't be disappointed either – there are two Iron-age hillforts (one at each end) and some ancient flint-diggings. Roman remains have been found there, and its medieval history shows in the form of the strip lynchets (cultivation terraces) that lie below the western end of the hill. It has long had significance for locals, and until 1860 was the regular site of Palm Sunday celebrations. It's a prominent feature in the countryside, and its name derives from Saxon terms that refer to rounded hills that served as landmarks.

MARTINSELL HILL

in that it contains examples of just about everything that such land has to offer.

This area makes a fine walk, and is best approached from the east, where the steep escarpment provides initial drama. This is best shot at dawn, simply because, being so steep, it's hopeless in the evening – it loses the sun around 3pm, even at the height of summer. Despite many attempts, I've yet to manage a satisfactory shot later in the day. Now there's a challenge for some photographer out there!

A little further on are stately beech clumps, so characteristic of Wiltshire's downland. I spend hours exploring the graphic, graceful shapes of these trees – they are studies in shape and form. They're followed by the remains of ancient flint-diggings, a fascinating area of pits and mounds that can easily use up a roll of film. Next come the eastern defensive banks of an Iron Age hillfort, high above the steep escarpment, lined with beautiful, gnarled, stunted, weather-beaten beeches that defy the strong easterly winds that often blow here. Stop, and look back. The long, sweeping lines of the steep escarpment lead the eye to the start of the walk. Just don't do as I did and leave your bright white camper-van in full view!

Shortly you reach the top of the hill, crowned by a solitary Scots pine that's seen better days – strong winds have hastened the death of this exposed tree. The view south over the tranquil Vale of Pewsey is superb. This valley has escaped modern life in that it has no significant roads whatsoever. True, there is a

Below One of the beautiful, weather-beaten beeches that line the steep bank of the hillfort. These are the sort of trees I imagined populated the landscapes of Tolkien
Canon EOS 50E with 28-135mm lens, Velvia, four seconds at f/11, tripod, mirror lock-up

concession to the current world with the main west railway running through it, but this is a minimal interruption in a scene that is quintessentially rural. Across the Vale lie the gentle slopes of the northern edge of Salisbury Plain, and in clear weather the distant spire of Salisbury Cathedral can be seen; a needle-like point piercing the horizon.

Near the western end, where the land slopes down to the village of Oare, there are stunning views over a horseshoe-shaped combe. Rainscombe House nestles snugly here, surrounded on three sides by the sheltering slopes of beech-clad downland. There are yet more prehistoric earthworks to explore too, in the form of the Giant's Grave, standing defiantly on the sharply-jutting western promontory, and below lie the contour-like lines of strip lynchets.

Finally, walk down to the village of Oare, pausing to look back at a more gentle view than the eastern end, but equally photogenic. Then go to the pub, savour the memories of your walk, and work out how to get back to your starting point! ❖

Above Rainscombe House is what I'd buy if I won the lottery. It's a pity I don't do it... It's tucked away in the horseshoe combe formed by Huish, Oare and Martinsell Hills. The beeches on the slopes are at their best in the autumn, but the combe makes a lovely subject at any time of the year
Canon EOS 50E with 100-300mm lens, Velvia, 1/15sec at f/8, polariser

Planning

Location Wiltshire, about 2.5 miles south of Marlborough.
How to get there From Marlborough (on the A4), take the A345 south for two miles. At the signpost left for Clench Common take the minor road for half a mile. Just as you emerge from a small stand of beech trees (called Starlings Roost) there is the car park on your right, marked 'P' on the OS map.
What to shoot There is something for everyone. Views, prehistoric hillforts and defences, trees, flowers, insects. This is a place where your biggest problem will be running out of film.
What to take Good walking shoes, waterproofs, a tripod, a range of lenses and something to drink.
Nearest pub The White Hart in Oare (01672 562273) – excellent, especially the food.
Times to visit Anytime of the year really, depending upon your interest.

Scenically, the eastern end is best at dawn, whereas the western end is best late in the day
Ordnance Survey map Explorer 157 (Marlborough & Savernake Forest); Refs: start at SU 183645, walking to Oare at 158631.
Essential reading *Exploring Historic Wiltshire (Vol 1)*, by Ken Watts, Ex Libris Press, ISBN 0 9485 7885 8; *The Vale of Pewsey*, by John Chandler, Ex Libris Press, ISBN 1 9033 4107 8.

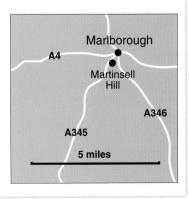

 Winter is a favourite time for **Bill Hall,** who likes nothing better than to venture into the Peak District when there are few people about

WHEN YOU MOVE to a new area, there's nothing like meeting someone with local knowledge to help you settle in – and, in my case, to help your photography. So it was with much gratefulness to Mick, my next door neighbour, that these pictures came about. A keen walker, he is a mine of information on the Peak District – an area I was keen to discover after moving to Derby from northeast England. It was also around this time that I became interested in photography, so I joined the Rolls-Royce Photographic Society – where I worked at the time – and, 18 years on, I'm still a member.

At the club, I was inspired by some of the lectures on landscapes by the likes of Ken Bryan, now resident on Skye, who produced some wonderful work. Early

Above The starkness of the bare tree attracted me to this scene, with the two trees in the background providing balance and a sense of scale. In retrospect, an ND grad across the grass would have balanced the exposure more effectively

attempts at emulating the pros were met with the usual problems that beset beginners; trying to make do with cheap film and poor equipment, as well as the usual being in the right place but at the wrong time – usually too late in the morning or too early in the evening. I soon learned that my best pictures were taken in autumn, winter or early spring, say November to March. This still holds true today, and I usually don't bother taking landscapes at all in summer. In fact, a change of job meant that I was to do a

EDALE

Facts about Edale

Edale Village, in the Vale of Edale, is really a string of five ancient farming communities, or booths, isolated between the Rushup Edge/Mam Tor ridge to the south, and the imposing massif of Kinder Scout – at 2,088ft, the highest point in the Peak – to the north. This is the start of the Pennines, 'the backbone of England', and the official starting point of the Pennine Way, Britain's longest pathway at 256 miles. The route takes you up either Grindsbrook, or via Upper Booth to Jacobs Ladder, named after a

packhorse leader or 'jagger'. Nearby, are the famous caves in Castleton, the grit-stone edges of the east moors, a Mecca for climbers, and the dams of Ladybower, Derwent, and Howden, where the dambusters did their practising. Nearest towns are Hathersage and Buxton, while Sheffield is the nearest city. The moors around Edale are open land owned by the National Trust, made public after the famous mass trespass protest in 1932. Fieldhead Information Centre, 01433 670207, is open daily.

lot of work abroad, and for the next 15 years or so I concentrated mainly on travel pictures.

It was only a couple of years ago that, while round at Mick's one Boxing Day, he told me he was leading a walking party from work the next day. It was to be to the top of Kinder Scout, the purpose of which was to work off some of the Christmas excesses, and to look for some of the 57 aircraft wrecks up there, including a Wellington bomber, a Boeing Superfortress and a German V1. Usually these aeroplanes had been trapped between a low cloud base and rapidly rising ground, although some were casualties limping home, others were lost or running out of fuel, and they ended up ploughing into the peat troughs on the desolate isolation of Kinder and Bleaklow. I decided to tag along with my camera gear, but parted company with the others in the Main Street at Edale, by the Nag's Head pub, the official starting point for the Pennine Way.

Spying a composition

Mick and his group went straight up Grindsbrook Clough, but I opted for the alternative route up Crowden Gully to the west side, skirting Broadlea Bank. Here on the flanks on the way back down, I

Above This is overlooking one of my favourite locations, Overstones Farm, below Stanage Edge. The first snows of the year had fallen, and although it was tricky driving on untreated roads, one advantage of the conditions was that there were no other cars out. Normally there is a line parked along the road below Overstones, which can be a terrible distraction, as can the road itself, which divides the view into two halves in a horizontal shot. This is why I chose this vertical viewpoint. To round off the picture, the kind farmer had conveniently lit a fire, and the smoke coming out of the farmhouse chimney just sets it off for me
Nikon 801S with 70-300mm Nikkor lens, Sensia 100, 1/125sec at f/11, Uniloc tripod

noticed two gnarled old hawthorns that I, and I suspect many others, would normally pass by without seeing their photographic possibilities. I first saw the composition as a black and white, and took a few shots on FP4 on one of my Nikon 801S bodies. After this, I decided to give colour a go, too, shooting a few frames on Sensia 100, using my other camera body. Both the black and white and colour versions were shot with a 20mm Nikkor. The grasses in the corner were a nice lead in and, to keep it all sharp, I stopped down to f/11 and focussed one third of the way into the picture. To steady the camera I rested it on my backpack, as a Uniloc tripod's legs get in the frame when using a 20mm close to the ground. Bracketing from +2/3 to -2/3 stop, the non-compensated version turned out to be the best shot of the day, and although the +2/3 version shows up the distant Edale Valley much better, the grasses are too light. With hindsight, I could have used a grey grad filter diagonally across the bottom corner to darken them a touch. These filters can be used to bring down the contrast of more than just skies – a tip I picked up from OP's regular contributor, Joe Cornish.

Above This is a double exposure technique. One is sharp, stopped down to a small aperture and one is out of focus, taken wide open. The image size changes with the defocus, so use a zoom lens on a tripod to re-size the shot. Both are over-exposed. Sandwich the two together and you will be amazed at the effect on the colour, and glow about the image *Nikon FE2 with 35-70mm, Ektachrome 100, 1sec at f/16, and 1/30sec at f/4*

Planning

Location and how to get there The Village of Edale (grid ref SK123857) lies at the end of a minor un-numbered road looping off the A625 between Mam Tor and Hope (frequently closed in snow, the easiest access is from the Hope end). It can also be reached by rail as the station lies on the picturesque Stockport/Sheffield line. Parking is restricted in the narrow single lane of the village, but there is a large public car park next to the station.
What to shoot Wild moorland, grit stone edges, the spectacular Kinder downfall in wet seasons, tumbling streams and stone barns. Wildlife includes grouse and mountain hare.
What to take Usual wide to mid-tele lenses, best carried in a backpack. Clothing should be warm and

waterproof, and good boots are the first essential.
Nearest pub The Nag's Head (01433 670291)
Ordnance Survey map Outdoor Leisure 1, Peak District, Dark Peak Area, grid ref for main picture SK113857.
Essential reading *The Peak National Park* by Roland Smith, £8.99, David & Charles, ISBN 1 8986 3001 0.

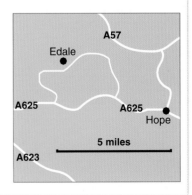

WESTONBIRT ARBORETUM

Westonbirt Arboretum welcomes photographers and their tripods, says **David Cantrille**, and late October is the best time to go there for the autumn colours

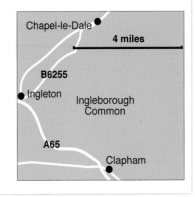

Above During the winter a setting sun over the Irish Sea spotlights Ingleborough in glorious shades of purple and combines with spectacular cloud effects
Fuji GX617 with 90mm lens, Velvia, 6 secs at f/32, centre spot ND filter, Tiffen warm tone polariser

Above Situated at the top of Fell Lane, on White Scars, this is one of the most photographed trees in Yorkshire. I managed to take this shot after a rare sprinkling of snow, coupled with strong, winter light. Panoramic photographs tend to work most effectively when they have three areas of interest, and here Ingleborough, the tree and the snow-covered path entering from the bottom left hand corner demonstrate this perfectly
Fuji GX617 with 90mm Fujinon lens, Velvia, 1 sec at f/32, centre spot ND filter, Tiffen warm tone polariser, Gitzo tripod

after. I was fortunate that the conditions were wind-free, an important factor as I was using a shutter speed of half a second with my selected aperture of f/22. A spotmeter reading taken from the mid-tone shadows on the limestone gave me the exposure, but I still played safe by underexposing by half a stop on the next frame. I was pleased to see, when they returned from the processors, that both exposures were acceptable.

By waiting a few minutes for the rays of the lowering winter sun to hit the top of the main tree, I managed to capture the warm, fiery glow on its branches, enhancing their shape against the sky, and making them almost appear like flames. The clear, blue sky really brings the shape of the trees into sharp relief.

As I shoot for a number of stock libraries as well as my own, I always try to extract as many variations from a subject as possible. The three trees work well both in landscape and portrait formats, and subtle changes in composition can be achieved by the use of slightly varying wideangle lenses.

I can visualise the trees looking their best after a heavy snowfall, but with our recent mild winters this is becoming increasingly difficult to capture. One final point. Always wear strong boots and be very careful where you walk. This type of landscape can be very dangerous, so tread with care. ❖

Planning

Location Ingleborough lies in northwest Yorkshire, and covers a roughly triangular area, with Ingleton to the west, Clapham to the east and Chapel-le-Dale to the north. To reach the three trees in the main photograph, take the minor road to Beasley Farm (which is the half way point on the famous Waterfall Walk). Follow the path marked Scar End for half a mile, then take the steep track up the fell side on the right. After a couple of steep bends you will see the trees on the left.

How to get there A65 to Ingleton from Leeds/Bradford; B6255 from the east; M6/A65 from north and south. There is a regular bus service to Ingleton and a rail service to Settle, which is 15 miles to the southeast.

What to shoot Limestone pavements, isolated trees, waterfalls, fell lanes, geological erratics or limestone boulders left stranded on minute rock pedestals, all make for a wide variety of subject. Soft, overcast light works best for the waterfalls, and strong hard light for the other subjects. Ingleborough's most photogenic side faces west, therefore afternoon light is preferable, especially in autumn and winter.

What to take Strong walking boots and layered waterproof clothing – this area is very exposed if the weather closes in. Tripod and cable release are essential, as are polarising and neutral density graduated filters, along with a range of lenses.

Nearest pub There are plenty of good pubs in Ingleton, together with the Hill Inn at Chapel-le-Dale (01524 241256) and the New Inn at Clapham.

Nearest accommodation Numerous guesthouses in Ingleton.

Other times of year Rare wildflowers and ferns on Southerscales Nature Reserve above Chapel-le-Dale in early summer. Sparkling glens and waterfalls, especially in spring and autumn.

Ordnance Survey map Landranger 98
Essential reading *Walks in Limestone Country*, by A Wainright

 Visiting familiar locations to work quickly in fading light is one of **Steve Gosling**'s specialities, as he has to fit his picture taking around a fulltime job

STUDLEY DEER PARK

AS A PART time photographer who, like so many of us, fits photography around home and work commitments, I have to make the most of any available opportunities to venture out with my camera and tripod. Frequently this means heading at short notice, when the light looks promising, to a location I know from previous visits.

It was on such an occasion that this photograph above was taken. I was driving home from the office one summer evening and found myself distracted by

the quality of light. Forcing myself to concentrate on getting home safely, I resolved to collect my equipment and capture what was left of the dramatic light.

I knew from many frustrating hours spent chasing the light (you know the sort of thing – jump in the car, drive around in circles looking for a suitable shot, return home with only a bad temper to show for your efforts), that I would have to visit a well known and previously researched location. From my earlier visits I knew that Studley Royal Deer Park would present

Facts about Studley

There have been deer in Studley Park for 400 years. Today it is home to more than 500 red, fallow and Manchurian Sika deer. As well as the deer, there is a large lake, treelined avenues, walks around the River Skell valley and the 19th century St Mary's Church. The National Trust now owns the whole estate, which also includes Studley Royal Water Garden and Fountains Abbey, and the Trust's usual restrictions on commercial photography apply. However, there are no restrictions on amateur photographers in the park or on other parts of the estate.

Common sense should be used – the deer are wild animals and must be respected as such. In June the female

deer, having given birth to their young, are prone to disturbance, and there is danger they might abandon their offspring. In the autumn rutting season the males are at their most photogenic, but also their most aggressive.

The deer park is open during daylight hours. The opening times of the water garden and Fountains Abbey vary – it is always best to check with the Estate Office (01765 608888) when planning a trip. There is also an admission charge to the water garden and abbey (although it is free to NT and English Heritage members). Again the estate office can provide further details of current charges and any discounts for large groups.

Opposite page
Although I was pleased with the original, I thought it could be improved with additional manipulation. I therefore re-copied the shot onto Kodak Ektachrome 100 film, using a Jessops zoom slide copier (which had the benefit of increasing contrast) and added an 81C filter to further enhance the warm feel of the original

many quickly accessible photographic opportunities.

The sun was sinking fast and time was working against me. Fortunately there is a large car park situated in the heart of the park – I leapt out of the car and headed for high ground, reasoning that I would get more photographic time out of the valley in which the lake and the tiny River Skell sit.

By this time the light was stunning – low, raking rays picking out texture and highlighting every blade of grass. As I climbed upwards I saw the bank of trees and thought they would look good lit from the front – right, but wrong! They looked great, but the front lighting lacked the atmosphere and mood of the backlit shot. I returned to the lower viewpoint and sought an angle that emphasised the dramatic light. I wanted to capture its quality, produce a shot that had a strong design element (the diagonal band of light) and at the same time avoid flare.

Having found the right angle, I fitted a telephoto lens

Above This is the photograph as it returned from the processors, before I re-copied it
Olympus OM4Ti with Tamron 70-210mm lens and 81B filter, Agfachrome 100, 1/125sec at f/11

to 'pull in' the trees and the foreground, as well as emphasising the graphic elements within the frame. An 81B filter was added to assist mother nature in warming the scene. Finally, I took a spotmeter reading from the lit areas of grass. Over the years I have found a spotmeter invaluable for situations like this, where there are dramatic differences between highlights and shadows, and the light is changing rapidly. ❖

Below Although it is possible to photograph the deer at any time of year, I have captured more atmospheric shots in the winter months. Because the deer are accustomed to the park's many visitors they are relatively easy to photograph with a moderate telephoto lens
Olympus OM4Ti with Tamron 70-210mm lens, Scotchchrome 1000, 1/500sec at f/11

Planning

Location Ten miles north of Harrogate, three to four miles west of Ripon (off B6265 to Pateley Bridge; follow the signs to Studley Roger).
How to get there Access by public transport is difficult, so it's advisable to go by car – not least because you can then time your arrival and departure to suit your photography. There is ample car parking which is free to NT and English Heritage members/£2 non members.
Where to stay There are numerous hotels in the Ripon and Harrogate areas – contact the local Tourist Information Offices for details (Harrogate: 01423 537300, Ripon: 01765 604625).
What to shoot Avenues of trees, single trees, close-up shots of foliage and tree bark detail, the deer, geese and water birds (such as great crested grebes, tufted duck, whooper and mute swans) and St Mary's Church. There is also great potential for candid shots of people feeding the geese and birds at the lakeside.
What to take Walking boots are useful, but not essential at this time of year; take bread to feed the ducks and geese if you want to entice them closer to your camera.

Nearest pub There are several pubs in nearby Ripon – I would particularly recommend The Water Rat, Bondgate Green (01765 602251). Alternatively, for non-alcoholic refreshment, there is a lakeside tearoom at Studley Royal, near to the car park, which is open daily from April to September.
Other times of year Autumn is a particularly good time to visit as the variety of trees (including beech, horse chestnut and lime) provides a rich tapestry of colour. In winter – other than the deer – photographic potential includes frosty scenes (general shots of the parkland, frost on trees and fallen leaves) and a greater variety of visiting geese and water birds on the lake.
Ordnance Survey map Landranger 99

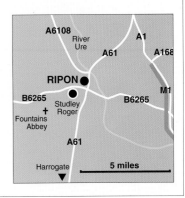

GOLITHA FALLS

 When you know a location, and have an idea for a picture in your head, don't let it blind you to other photographic opportunities, says **Ross Hoddinott**

THERE ARE SO MANY beautiful spots hidden in the rugged Cornish countryside that it is difficult to prefer one to any other. But Golitha Falls is one place I always return to. Golitha is found on Bodmin Moor, a short drive from Jamaica Inn, made famous by author Daphne du Maurier and smugglers of years past. You can also discover the legend which surrounds the Hurlers, a Bronze Age stone circle west of nearby Minions.

Golitha has a wealth of natural history, too. Otters frequent the river, although count yourself very lucky to see one! Woodpeckers, nuthatches and treecreepers are among the birds you can see and hear, but they rarely come close enough to photograph. In autumn many species of fungi grow here and can make great pictures.

Do not visit expecting an impressive waterfall. Instead, it's a gentle river winding through an attractive oak and beech woodland. The falls are a beautiful stretch of river where the water flows over many giant Cornish granite boulders, and it was this I intended to photograph one day last October.

We had just had several days of rainfall – something you get quite used to living in Cornwall! I knew the falls would be impressive. But as I walked through the woodland I found it was the freshly fallen beech leaves which caught my eye. All the warm, rich colours of autumn could be found covering the woodland floor. The roots of the trees, which had harvested the leaves, were still visible and creating beautiful natural patterns.

Just off the path I found some very prominent roots which I decided were ideal for the picture I now had in mind. I wanted to emphasise the colour and pattern by allowing the woodland floor to dominate the frame. I attached a 28mm wideangle to my Nikon F90x camera and attached an 81C warm up filter to further saturate the leaves' colours. I had deliberately chosen an overcast day for my visit, as this kind of light reproduce detail far better on film than harsh, contrasty light. This did mean I needed a tripod, as the shutter speed was slow due to the weather and the small aperture of f/22 I had selected to maximise depth of field. I always believe in using a tripod when the opportunity allows. Not only does it give stability, but it also makes you think much more about your picture's composition. I

bracketed the exposure and then also experimented – less successfully – with a lower viewpoint.

The reserve is managed by English Nature and, in recent years, has become popular with tourists and walkers. But in autumn visitors are few. Like many beautiful areas, Golitha is a well-photographed location. So when I visit such a place I am always very conscious of trying to produce a different angle or viewpoint. I find less satisfaction from reproducing what other photographers have taken before. Always discipline yourself to find an original view, because that is surely what makes our profession/hobby so enjoyable – if a little frustrating! The pure pleasure of producing a unique image, which others might also enjoy, always proves a great motivation. ❖

Left The falls at Golitha are beautiful but well photographed. Try to choose a different angle. With this picture the impressive granite rocks covered in leaves make an interesting foreground and lead your eye through the frame. Then a slow shutter speed has blurred the water. A well used technique, but still very effective
Nikon F90x with Sigma 28mm lens, Sensia 100, two seconds at f/22, 81B warm up filter, Manfrotto tripod

Below left Golitha falls is home to many species of bird, but few venture close enough to photograph well. Robins, though, are always curious and in winter a few crumbs can entice them to briefly pose for you!
Nikon F90x with Sigma 400mm lens, Sensia 100, 1/125sec at f/8

Planning

Location Southern tip of Bodmin Moor on the river Fowey. Nearest villages are St Neot and St Cleer.

How to get there Take the A30 from Launceston and turn off left at Jamaica Inn (signposted). Follow a minor road for around six miles. Park in the large car park adjacent to woodland. Can also be reached from A38 west of Liskeard.

What to shoot Great landscapes and close ups of beech and oak trees in autumnal colours. Also photograph the falls using long shutter speeds. Look for fungi, lichen and moss.

What to take Always take walking boots, as it can be soft under foot in places. A tripod is a must and warm up filters will help saturate colours. A pocket reflector is always useful when doing macro work. And a few bars of chocolate in case you get hungry!

Nearest pub It could only be the famed Jamaica Inn (01566 86250)

Other times of year In the spring the fresh new growth is very attractive, and woodland flowers can also be seen and photographed.

Ordnance Survey map Landranger 201; grid ref SX 227 690.

Essential reading West Country Wildlife by Kelvin Boot and Elaine Franks. Covers local wildlife and lists the nature reserves of the area, and what you can expect to see at each.

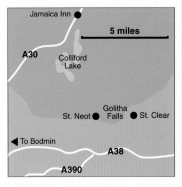

CLUMBER PARK

Clumber Park near Nottingham offers rich pickings for the landscape photographer in the warm low light of autumn, says **B. Baskar**

CLUMBER PARK is a popular location and in the summer can become crowded with visitors, making any attempt at serious landscape photography difficult. I have found that a visit later in the year offers the best photographic opportunities when the number of tourists has diminished and the low autumn light picks out the natural features of the landscape.

The main entrance to the park leads into Lime Tree Avenue, a double row of lime trees stretching over two miles, I first saw Lime Tree Avenue on a dull day in December. The trees were bare and the leaves on the ground had lost their colour and were beginning to decay. Although the scene presented a strong architectural shape, the lack of colour and the flat lighting did not inspire me to photography on that occasion, but I made a mental note to pay a visit in the autumn.

Good landscape photography is nothing without good lighting and a spectacular view can be made to look mundane if the quality of the light does not do the scene

Above Looking down Lime Tree Avenue, taken around 10am in early November. The strong side lighting has backlit the leaves perfectly and the telephoto lens has compressed the perspective *Canon EOS 5 with 75-300mm lens, Velvia 1/45sec at f/22, polarising filter and 85c warming filter*

justice. As the end of October approached, I was hoping that the unpredictable British weather would favour me. My prayers were answered! I arrived at the park around 9am, to make most of the crisp morning light, to find that the scene had undergone a magical transformation in the glorious morning sunshine. The fallen leaves had formed a rich carpet on the ground, and yet there was enough foliage left on the trees to close the view of the sky almost completely. The space between the rows of the Lime trees was transformed into a magnificent 'botanical tunnel', which was gloriously lit by the low autumn sun. This was what I wanted to capture in film.

Metering was not a major problem as the scene was lit

Facts about Clumber Park

Clumber Park is located between historic towns of Worksop and Mansfield in Nottinghamshire. Originally the seat of the Dukes of Newcastle, Clumber Park was purchased by the National Trust in 1946. The park covers over 3000 acres and contains a man-made lake, a walled kitchen garden and glass houses which date from the 19th century. There is also a small chapel which is a fine example of gothic architecture.

Left This is the arch at the entrance of the Lime Tree Avenue. This is not a view that is particularly impressive during the middle of the day, but it appears as a magnificent silhouette against the setting sun. The arch is located at a much higher level than the rest of the park and, as a result, one gets an uninterrupted view of the sky through it
Canon EOS 5 with 75-300mm lens, 4sec at f/8, Velvia, polarising filter.

uniformly and I let my Canon's evaluative metering decide the exposure. I composed the picture with the wideangle end of the 28-80mm zoom lens. That emphasised the foreground well but the rest of the trees seemed to disappear in the distance and I was not entirely satisfied with what I was seeing. So I went to the other extreme, changed to the 300mm end of the 75-300mm lens. The compressed perspective did the trick and the view was, quite simply, amazing!

I tried both landscape and portrait framing of the scene but found the landscape format to be more visually satisfying. It remained sunny well into the evening and I managed to get some wonderful sunset shots as well. It was a very rewarding day. ❖

Above This is a close-up view of the lime tree branches with their beautiful autumn leaves. I liked the blue background of the sky and used a polarising filter to enhance it.
Canon EOS 5 with 28-80mm lens, Kodak Elitechrome Extra,1/45sec at f/8, polarising filter and 81C warming filter

Planning

Location In Nottinghamshire between the towns of Worksop and Mansfield
How to get there Take A1 to Worksop and Newark-on-Trent. As you approach Worksop, take A614 to Ollerton and Nottingham. After a few hundred yards you will see Clumber Park on the right.
Time of Day Last week in October and first week in November is the best time. Timing is crucial, as the leaves will be gone almost overnight after this period. On a sunny day get there by 10am. The hour before sunset is good too.
What to shoot Lime Tree Avenue of course! The lake and the chapel also offer good potentials. On a dull cloudy day, trees covered with autumnal leaves, the fallen leaves and tree barks are all there to be photographed.
What to take Tripod, both wideangle and telephoto zoom lenses, macro lens. Warm clothing including pair of gloves with finger holes. A flask of hot tea can be rejuvenating!
Nearest pub Plenty of pubs in nearby Worksop. Clumber Park Hotel with a bar and restaurant (01623 835333) is a few minutes drive down the A614. There is a cafeteria and restaurant in the park.
Opening times The Park is open daily during daylight hours throughout the year.
Useful web site www.mansfieldpages.co.uk/clumber.htm

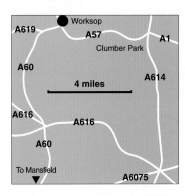

 The millstones in the Peak District National Park take on a dramatic quality in snow, says **Mark Hamblin**. In these conditions Stanage Edge is his favourite destination

STANAGE EDGE

IMAGINE THE SCENE. A thick blanket of virgin snow cloaks the landscape while above the sun beats down from an azure blue sky. Everything has been transformed by this transient white covering as the countryside takes on a magical appearance. These conditions are a landscape photographer's dream, but unfortunately nowadays it seems to be more of a dream than a reality.

When I first moved to Sheffield, in the mid-eighties, I was amazed at the amount of snow that fell each winter. Back then it was more of nuisance than anything else and I remember having to dig my way out of the back door on several occasions. Those days seem to be gone for the time being as the climate has changed, bringing milder winter weather.

It still does snow, of course, but not as often and it usually turns to slush within a couple of days. When it happens as I drop everything and head out into the Peak District. With limited hours in which to work during the winter and with access only via the main roads, I tend to stick to places that are easy to reach.

One popular location for landscape photography at any time of year is Stanage Edge in the northern Peak District. Here the grit stone of the Edge meets heather moorland and offers some spectacular views across the Pennines. However, my favourite view includes the old millstones that litter the ground beneath the Edge.

Until a couple of years ago I had never photographed the millstones in the snow. I came close one November following a sprinkling of the precious white stuff and was pleased with my results. However, later in the winter there was a major fall of snow that was exactly what I had been waiting for and I couldn't wait to make a return visit. The problem was that so much snow had fallen that many of the roads in and out of the Peak District were impassable. The next day was dull with further flurries of snow, but the following day was clear and sunny and by now I was chomping at the bit.

I decided to chance the road conditions and headed off. The road out of Sheffield was fine but on reaching the Peak District boundary I ran into snow. Oh, for a

4WD. I was still a few miles from Stanage Edge but, taking it very slowly, I crawled onwards. I knew the picture was waiting to be taken and I just had to get there. Eventually, I made it only to find a trail of footsteps leading up to the millstones. Someone had beaten me to it!

I trudged the short distance from the car and began to assess the situation. There were footsteps all around, but by carefully selecting my viewpoint I was able to hide most of them behind the millstones. I take most of my landscape pictures using a Pentax 67, but because it is unwieldy I use my 35mm camera to check out the various viewpoints. Once I had settled on the view I wanted (in the most awkward spot, as usual), I set up the tripod for the Pentax.

The snow-covered millstones were to be the main focal point of the picture but I wanted to include the background landscape that extended into the heart of the Dark Peak. I therefore chose to use the 55mm lens, the widest lens I have for the Pentax (equivalent to 28mm on a 35mm system). I have never trusted the meter in my Pentax and so I used my EOS1N to take a meter reading from a mid-blue section of the clear sky. This gave me a reading of f/22 at 1/15sec for Velvia, which I set manually on the camera. Before making the exposure I locked up the mirror to avoid camera shake and took several frames, bracketing 1/2 stop in both directions. The original exposure, however, proved to be correct. ❖

Right Prior to taking the main picture I made a visit to the millstones after a light dusting of snow in November. I chose to include a section of Stanage Edge in order to provide a link between the millstones and the rock from which they were formed
Pentax 6x7 with 55mm lens, Velvia, 1/8sec at f22

Planning

Location The Millstones lie beneath Stanage Edge, near Hathersage in the Peak District.

How to get there Leave the M1 at junction 29 and take the A617 into Chesterfield. From here take the A619 to Baslow, continue onto the A623 and turn right in Calver at crossroads onto the B6001. After about two miles turn left (B6001) to Hathersage. On reaching T-junction turn right through village and then left on to a minor road that takes you past the church and up onto the moors. Follow this road for about $1^1/2$ miles and park on the verge where the road reaches the top of the climb. From here there is a marked footpath that takes you directly under Stanage Edge. The millstones can be found about 300m along this footpath at OS 250830.

Where to stay The Peak District is full of B&Bs. Hathersage makes an excellent base to explore Stanage Edge and the rest of the Dark Peak.

What to shoot A wideangle lens will allow you to include both the millstones and Stanage Edge. Try various angles that include different portions of the background. Be careful not to include the cement works in the far distance.

What to take It is an easy walk but you will require stout boots or possibly wellingtons if there is deep snow. Typical warm winter clothing.

A tripod that will extend to 5-6 feet. A wide-angle of at least 28mm (for 35mm), a wide-angle zoom would be useful.

Time of day Plan to arrive early in the morning for the best lighting. Later in the morning side-lighting emphasises form and texture. The millstones can be photographed in the afternoon but the composition and background is not so good.

Other places of interest The whole of the northern part of the Peak District is fantastic for landscapes. Stanage Edge catches the last of the sunshine in the afternoon when photographed from below. There are impressive views in all directions from the Edge itself. Include the rocks as foreground interest. Stormy skies over the valleys below look great.

Ordnance Survey map Landranger 110 or Outdoor Leisure 1 (highly recommended to help find the exact location).

Recommended reading The Peak District, The Official National Park Guide (Pevensey Guides) ISBN 1-898630-10-0, £8.99

Tourist Information Centre Bakewell (01629) 813227

Right It's hard to find a viewpoint at Avebury that shows the stones in their setting. October or November is just right, however, because the sun rises over Fyfield and Overton Downs behind the stones of the South Circle. Standing on the top of the high outer bank to the southwest gives a fine view. The picture was shot with a telephoto to compress the stones and exaggerate their importance. A weak neutral-density grad was used to balance the brightness of the sky
Canon EOS 50E with 100-300mm lens, Velvia, several seconds at f/16, Manfrotto tripod

AVEBURY

Beyond Stonehenge you'll find a far more inspiring and varied prehistoric site – photographically speaking. **Steve Day** weaves his way through these ancient standing stones

AVEBURY'S STONE CIRCLE is rather like a younger sibling forever living in big brother's shadow. Stonehenge's overpowering lure ensures that Avebury is an afterthought. Excellent! At Stonehenge the heaving hordes process in circles, shuffling like prisoners in an exercise yard, yet a few miles north those in the know can wander unfettered through Avebury's ancient stones in relative peace.

Of course, in these tourism-obsessed times, even Avebury is fairly busy in summer; but go there between October and April and you'll have the place to yourself. This time of the year is also the most photogenic, with the promise of early morning mists enhancing the magic and mystery of these ancient stones.

Avebury was begun about two hundred years after Stonehenge, in 2,600 BC, but only came to the attention of the outside world in the mid 17th century. It is far larger than Stonehenge, with a huge outer ditch, the Great Circle of stones inside this and two smaller circles in the centre. Unfortunately, in the 18th century, many of the sarsen stones became buried or were broken up and used for building. However, subsequent excavations and restorations have ensured the site remains a remarkable testament to the imagination and engineering skills of its original builders. Equally unfortunately, the main Devizes-Swindon road runs right through the middle of the site. If ever there was a case for Millennium funding this is it – re-routing the road around the henge would be a tremendous improvement.

Nevertheless, dawn on an October morning is a wonderful experience. The curve of stones of the South Circle, seen from the high bank of the ditch to the south, lead the eye to the rising sun, its intensity muted by morning mist over Fyfield Down. This is symbolic, for Fyfield and Overton Downs are the source of the stones that were so laboriously hauled here. It's well worth walking the two miles to see the thousands of 'grey wethers' that still litter this landscape.

Don't forget the evenings, either. Most tourists leave fairly early on, and near sunset only a few die-hards are left to blot this primitive landscape. And you don't have to become obsessed with the grand view – shots of the individual stones will be at their best when lit by the golden, glancing light.

And there's more. Avebury village lies within the stones and there are many fine buildings to be photographed, not forgetting St James' church (dating from Saxon times), the 16th century Avebury Manor and the adjacent 17th century Great Barn that houses the fascinating Wiltshire Rural Life museum.

As if this isn't enough, the stones lie at the centre of a wealth of prehistoric remains. Radiating from the circle are West Kennet avenues of stones and the few remains of the Beckhampton avenue. Nearby is The Sanctuary, and the West Kennet Long Barrow – one of the few where you can explore the interior – and minor round barrows dot the landscape.

To cap it all, visible for miles around is the massive mound of Silbury Hill – a huge, man-made earthwork whose purpose still defies. It also defies photography – finding the right view that presents this mound at its best is a real photographic challenge. ❖

Left Silbury Hill, and the death of so many photographers' hopes. The River Kennet had flooded, leaving the mound floating like an iced cake. Cold, but worth it
Canon EOS 50E with 20-35mm lens, Velvia, two seconds at f/11, polariser, wet feet from leaking wellies

Left In golden morning light, somewhere there will be a stone that's beautifully side-lit. I included the other stone to emphasise the size of the one in the foreground, and exaggerated the effect by shooting about a foot off the ground
Bronica ETRSi with PE45-90 zoom, Velvia, 1/2sec at f/16, polariser and warm-up

Planning

Location In the middle of Wiltshire, about 6 miles west of Marlborough
How to get there The A4 runs just to the south. At the Beckhampton roundabout take the A4361 north and park in the NT car park. From the north take the A4361 south from Devizes and park in the village car park, by the Red Lion.
What to shoot A combination of overall views, the ditch and bank, the beautiful beech trees on the bank, individual stones, Avebury Manor and Barn, the church and village, the Avenues, Fyfield and Overton Downs nature reserves, The Sanctuary, West Kennet Long Barrow and Silbury Hill should ensure excellent profits for Fuji.
What to take Good walking shoes (the ditch banks are steep), waterproofs, a tripod and a range of lenses.
Nearest pub The Red Lion, smack in the middle of the stone circle.
Times of year October to April is relatively quiet, though any time of the year is good for photography provided you're prepared to get up before dawn or stay until sunset. During the

summer months, the sun comes up and goes down like a rocket and you've only got half an hour or so at sunrise/set before the light becomes flat and uninteresting.
Ordnance Survey map Explorer 157
Essential reading See English Heritage's site at www.engh.gov.uk/archcom/projects/summarys/html98_9/2257aveb.htm, or try www.henge.demon.co.uk/wiltshire/avebury.html; *Footprints through Avebury*, by Michael Pitts, Stones Print; *The Prehistoric Temples of Stonehenge & Avebury*, Pitkin, ISBN 0-85372-710-4; *Prehistoric Avebury*, by Aubury Burl, Yale University Press, ISBN 0-300-03622-1

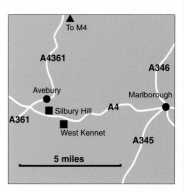

Wet weather is not often associated with nature photography, but rain can enhance the atmosphere of a forest in autumn, as **Colin Varndell** explains

NEW FOREST

THE NEW FOREST in Hampshire falls within a rough triangle between the towns of Salisbury, Bournemouth and Southampton. It is the largest tract of lowland forest in Britain, covering an area of 145 square miles. The landscape comprises three main habitats: lowland heath, conifer plantations and mature broad leaved woodland. Together with valley bogs, agricultural land and amenity areas these habitats support a greater range of flora and fauna than any other single location in Britain.

The forest is peppered throughout with photogenic oak and beech woods, but my own favourite areas for photography are the Bolderwood and Rheinfield Ornamental Drives which run north and south of the A35 between Lyndhurst and Christchurch. The Rheinfield Ornamental Drive is principally an arboretum with impressive North American redwoods

Right Even in the remarkably beautiful location of the New Forest finding good compositions which fit the rectangular format is not easy. Simplicity is the key, but searching for it takes a lot of legwork. Once I have found a scene that suits my choice of composition I tend to return and photograph it in all seasons. These three beech trees stand at the edge of the forest road along the Bolderwood Ornamental Drive, and were crying out to be photographed. An 81C warm up filter was added here to intensify the autumn colours
Nikon FE2 with 24mm lens, 1/30sec at f/11, 81C warm-up filter

Above It was raining steadily when I found this group of beeches at Brock Hill. The foreground at the base of the tree gives a sound foundation, and I excluded the sky as bright highlights coming through the canopy would distract from the main subject
Nikon FE2 with 70-200mm lens at 100mm, Velvia, one sec at f/11

lining the forest road. Bolderwood is made up of ancient beech woods interspersed with plantations of both conifer and hardwoods.

This was once managed woodland and the beeches were pollarded to encourage growth of straight branches

for use by the Royal Navy. Sadly many of these magnificent trees were lost in the storms of the 1980s, but the few that remain offer a wealth of photographic potential.

The beech woods are at their most colourful from late October to mid November when the deciduous leaves change from summer green to vibrant yellow. This golden stage lasts for only a few days before the colours fade to deep rust prior to leaf fall.

Capturing the atmosphere of woodland in autumn can be one of the most rewarding challenges in nature's annual cycle. At this time of year I particularly like to photograph woodland scenes in wet weather. When rain coincides with that brief stage of autumn gold the effect can be sheer magic. Thick rain cloud acts as a massive diffuser, eliminating shadow. Raindrops saturate the foliage, enriching the warm, autumn colours and the wet trunks darken to contrast with the bright leaf colour. ❖

Below The ancient trees and abundance of dead wood are perfect hunting grounds for fungi pictures. I think the most photogenic is the fly agaric which thrives on the dead roots of silver birch. The silver birch is a naturally predominant species of the forest so these speckled crimson toadstools are often plentiful in autumn. The white specks on the cap are the shrivelled remains of a veil which protects the fruiting body as it pushes up through the earth
Nikon FE2 with 100mm macro lens, Kodachrome 64, 1/30sec at f/11

Planning

Location The New Forest is in Hampshire between Bournemouth and Southampton. The main A31 trunk road cuts across the middle of the forest.
How to get there From London take the M3 and join the M27 westbound. At the end of the motorway leave the Cadnam roundabout and take the A337 to Lyndhurst. A car is essential for moving between locations within the forest but overnight parking or camping is not permitted in the forest car parks. There are official camp sites in the forest that are open between April and September. There are public toilets at both ornamental drives and also near the Bolderwood Deer Sanctuary.
Where to stay The Cloud Hotel, Brockenhurst (01590 622165) Knightwood Lodge Hotel, Lyndhurst (02380 282502). The New Forset Tourist Information Centre can provide up to date accommodation lists (01590 689000).
What to shoot In autumn, beech trees, deer, fungi and forest ponies. I also like the spring when the beech trees burst into life with fresh, lime-green foliage.
What to take The main problem when shooting in rain is keeping the equipment dry. When using waterproof covers changing lenses or film can be tricky, so in wet conditions I prefer to use a large golfing umbrella, preferably with an assistant to hold it! Working from a shoulder bag I can stand at the tripod with the bag open and everything is protected by the umbrella. The beech woods are often extremely boggy in places so it is advisable to wear Wellington boots.
Ordnance Survey map Outdoor Leisure series 22
Essential reading *Explore the New Forest*, published by HMSO, ISBN 011 710021 8

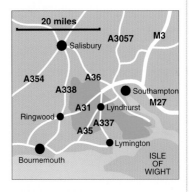

MONTROSE

The tidal lagoon at Montrose Basin is an important fishing ground for migratory waders. **Niall Benvie** focuses on the grey herons that feed there in June

THE SCOTTISH WILDLIFE TRUST'S centre overlooking Montrose Basin is an ideal place from which to survey the 2000 acre tidal lagoon. The Basin is noted for its migratory geese, ducks and waders, but it is also used by many other birds throughout the year.

In June, it is quite common to see up to 50 herons, both adults and youngsters, fishing on the Basin, or trying their luck in the muddy creeks which feed into it. This is not Florida, however, and an open approach simply drives the birds away. A more covert method is definitely called for.

I am often surprised by how readily some otherwise very shy birds accept a hide. Grey herons are a case in point. Indeed, I've been able to float in my amphibious hide to within 12 or 15 yards of some individuals without them figuring out a photographer was on board. And it

was this hide I chose when I decided to stake out a nearby pond used by a group of recently fledged youngsters. The hide has the advantage of providing a low perspective and the facility to support the camera and lens on a beanbag. On the downside, the user needs to wear chest waders and be prepared for a few hours of kneeling. I therefore decided to set up my hide in an especially muddy area – mainly to save my ageing and aching knees.

Early bird

From watching the activity on the pond over a few days, I learned that the young birds arrived there a little before first light and realised that I would need to be in position while it was still dark. That meant being in the hide – which had been left out from the previous

Facts about Montrose Basin

Montrose Basin is a local nature reserve and as such is governed by certain bylaws. If you want to use a hide, apply in the first instance to: **The Ranger, Scottish Wildlife Trust, Montrose Basin Wildlife Centre, Rossie Braes, Montrose, Angus DD10 9TJ (01674 676336)**. The shoreline can be accessed at several points, the best being from the pier at Old Montrose and the mains of Dun Car park. The

ranger can advise on those areas to avoid when birds are nesting. Although a permit is required to photograph herons at the nest, there are no legal restrictions at a pond or estuary. The mortality rate amongst first year herons is about 70%, the principal cause being starvation, so minimise disturbance, especially when young birds are still practising their fishing skills.

afternoon – before 4am! I was much encouraged when herons began to arrive within 10 minutes of me entering the hide. But as the sky lightened, I realised that I would have a frustrating hour or so before direct light reached the pond. During this time I watched as the birds stalked, paused, then lunged viciously at imaginary fish, honing their technique, but going hungry in the meantime.

A heavy dew had come in with the dawn so when, at around 5am, light began to kiss the edge of the pond, the fringing reeds sparkled and drooped. One of the herons had shown its tolerance of the hide by pecking at it but my attention was focused on another grey heron hunting at the other side of the pond, just 20 yards away. It was moving slowly, looking, pausing and probing in the shallows.

When it turned to the sun, I took a spot reading from the heron's back and wings; I wanted that to be the mid-tone value in the picture. It was in this subtle morning light that I appreciated the light-gathering powers of my Nikkor 300mm f/2.8 telephoto lens. The metered exposure was only 1/30sec with the aperture wide open at f/2.8, on Fujichrome Sensia 100. With the lens supported on a beanbag, I had no concerns about camera shake. Thankfully, it wasn't too cold either. It was then simply a matter of waiting for that moment of harmony between the light, the pose of the bird and the shapes of the reeds. ❖

Bottom The car park at the Montrose Basin Wildlife Centre has been planted with various species of wildflower, including the dramatic Viper's bugloss. The plant's height means that it is rarely still in this open location, but the wind is less likely to be a problem in the early morning or late evening. An overhead viewpoint with a very wideangle lens gave the impression of the flower spikes rocketing towards the camera.
Nikon F4s with 20mm lens, Velvia, SB25 flashgun set to -1.7ev, 1/8sec at f/5.6; tripod

Left The nearby beach at Usan offers all sorts of close-up possibilities, including these blunt periwinkle shells. I shot these as soon as the sun had dropped below the horizon (to avoid disruptive shadows), under a bright sky. An 81A warm up compensated for the slight blue cast that can be expected in these lighting conditions.
Nikon F4s with 90mm lens, Velvia, 81A filter, 1/2sec at f/11; tripod

Planning

Location Montrose Basin is a tidal lagoon on the Scotland's east coast, lying between Aberdeen and Dundee.
How to get there For the wildlife centre, follow the A92 Montrose-Arbroath Road out of town; the centre is about one mile out of town. Montrose is on the east coast mainline for rail travellers and the Basin and its surroundings are easily accessible by bike. For the Old Montrose pier, leave the A92 to join the A934 for Forfar and turn right at Maryton Kirk. After about a mile, a track to the right, just after a bridge over the creek, leads to a small car park.
Where to stay There is plenty of good B&B and hotel accommodation in Montrose. Especially recommended are the Limes Guest House (01674 677236) and the Links Hotel (01674 671000).
What to shoot The Basin is home to a large flock of mute swans, some of which are quite accessible. There is a typical saltmarsh flora on the west side of the Basin and nearby, the big sandy beaches at Montrose, Lunan Bay and St Cyrus NNR provide good scenic opportunities.
Other times of year Up to 40,000 pink footed geese visit in October; eider ducks and wading birds can be photographed through the winter.
What to take If you want to shoot scenics from the railway bridge, a tripod is likely to get in the way of other bridge users. There is a wide metal parapet to rest a beanbag on instead. Even in summer a fleece jacket is normally called for early and late; it is often five or six degrees cooler in Montrose, compared with Brechin, just nine miles inland
Nearest Pub Sharky's (01674 677 375) and Roo's Leap (01674 671 230).
Ordnance Survey map Landranger 54
Essential reading Leaflets and information about the Basin are available from the SWT Wildlife Centre. road and turn left at the junction then take the low road and take the next right at the slip road.

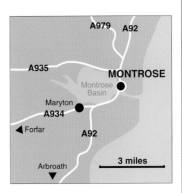

Dornoch is one of those areas in Scotland where the beach meets the golf course. However, as **Steve Austin** explains, there is more to it than that

DORNOCH

THIS ATTRACTIVE part of Sutherland is found on the east coast of Scotland. In particular, there is an area of grassland near the beach which is worth exploring for the numerous grasses, wild flowers, birds, butterflies and – probably most impressive of all – the Six Spot Burnett moth.

These moths are most active in bright conditions and they fly everywhere, feeding on the flowers and looking for a mate. The easiest ones to start photographing, then, are a mating pair, as these can stay motionless and locked together for hours and are easily approached. The best conditions are calm and bright, with thin cloud cover. The lack of wind allows a small aperture to give the necessary depth of field, while the diffused light from the thin cloud gives a less contrasty picture.

If it is breezy, you can shield your subject with pieces of semi-opaque plastic sheet cut to about 18x12in – DIY stores sell this sheeting. In very sunny conditions, contrast is always a problem, with burnt out highlights and deep shadows. To combat this, the same sheeting can be used to shield your subject from the direct sun. This will soften the light, taking about half to one stop off the light level, resulting in a noticeable decrease in the contrast and more detail in the shadows.

A further improvement can be made by placing a white reflector (white card will do) under the subject to bounce some light into the shaded parts. If you are thinking that by now you won't have any spare hands with which to take your picture, try modifying your cable release so you can hold it between your teeth,

Facts about Dornoch

Although there are some interesting flowers to photograph in the area described here, such as wild thyme, biting stonecrop and various orchids, a much greater diversity can be seen close by at the Dornoch Common Grasslands, which is surrounded by dunes and saltmarsh. This grassland, between the dunes and the golf practice area, is a type of grassland rich in flowering plants which has become rare throughout much of Britain; in fact, part of it is now a Site of

Special Scientific Interest. This low-lying wet ground, which was once saltmarsh flooded by tidal seawater, is particularly rich in species such as yellow rattle, ragged robin, grass of parnassus, northern marsh orchid, frog orchid, common twyblade mouse-ear hawkweed, sea rocket and meadowsweet. There are no restrictions on movement, or photography, but of course do not pick the flowers, keep off the golfing green areas and watch out for golf balls!

Far left The seed heads look great against the sky, so use a low viewpoint. Carefully clear a small foreground area, using a polarising filter to darken the sky. Experiment with exposure time, to introduce movement *Canon T90 with 20mm lens, 1/8sec at f/11, Velvia, tripod*

Left A pair of skylarks were taking food to a nest, so I went back early next morning with a post. While the birds were away foraging I stuck it in the ground nearby. As I waited in the car, they used it straight away. I moved the car nearer each time they were away, until I was close enough for some pictures. Signs of distress, such as the birds hesitating to go to the nest, means you are too close and should back off
Canon T90 with 400mm, 1/350sec at f/5.6, Provia, bean bag

triggering it with a small bite action! This also has the advantage of producing a surprisingly fast response time – especially useful when waiting for that 1/2sec lull in the wind in which to take your shot.

However, because my moths were still moving slightly with the wind and I was using f/22 (in order to get the antennae sharp), I decided to use two flashes mounted either side of the camera. If only one flash is used, it creates the same problem with contrast as would bright sunlight.

Usually, when using two flashes, each would have a slightly different output, or you could fit a plastic diffuser, or even tie a single layer of a white handkerchief over one head, to give light of slightly differing intensity on either side. However, since this composition was so symmetrical, I decided to light them evenly. Using my Ricoh XR-X with a Sigma 50mm macro lens and two Ricoh Speedlite 300P flash units, the exposure was f/22 with an automatic TTL exposure.

Once you are happy with your technique on a static subject, try following some of the flying moths and photograph them when they land to feed on the

flowers. As this requires hand-holding, you will need to use flash here to freeze any movement, but make sure the background is close to your subject or it will appear very dark and unnatural. ❖

The grassland area leads down towards the beach car park, while the bank up to the golf course is on the left.

Planning

Location Grassland near the beach (NH 804894). From The Square in Dornoch go along Church Street and continue until you pass the caravan site on your right and the last building on your left. Between here and the beach car park (at the end of the road) is a modest area of grassland which rises up to the golf course; on the left, while on the right you will see several places where you can park on the grass. Dornoch Common Grass Land: (NH 802885) is about 10 minutes walk south, through the golf practice area, towards the landing strip: you can also park here, at the large building and you will find some information lecterns about the area.

How to get there Follow the A9 north and after going over the Dornoch Firth Bridge, take the A949 for Dornoch. The nearest railway station is Tain, and buses run from Inverness to Dornoch every hour, via Tain.

What to shoot Wild flowers and grasses, Burnett moths and butterflies, birds such as skylarks, pipits, yellowhammers and linnets, beach life such as kids playing and kite flying.

What to take Macro, wideangle,

standard and tele lenses, plastic sheets as described and a flash set-up for the moths. Clothing should be everything from warm clothing and waterproofs to swimwear, plus a stout pair of shoes.

Nearest pub Dornoch Inn, The Square, Dornoch.

Other times of year Many birds are there all year round, as well as wintering wildfowl, waders and seaducks (Oct to Mar), Dornoch cathedral (all year), Loch Fleet NNR – five miles north (all year).

Ordnance Survey Map Landranger 21
Essential reading A flower identification guide, such as Wild Flowers, published by Collins.

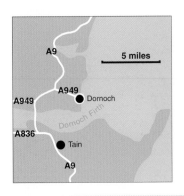

 Buttercups are not obvious subjects but, says **Colin Varndell**, there are exciting possibilities for pictures of these flowers and the wildlife they attract

KINGCOMBE

THE SMALL HAMLET of Lower Kingcombe nestles comfortably in the Hooke valley, just north of Toller Porcorum in west Dorset. This ancient farmland comprises a labyrinth of small meadows, marshy ground, and gloriously overgrown copses and hedgerow thickets. The fields have never been treated with chemicals or subjected to modern farming methods. The result is a varied habitat, abundantly rich in wild plants and teeming with birds, mammals and invertebrates.

Kingcombe Meadows nature reserve is managed by the Dorset Wildlife Trust as a working organic livestock farm and covers an area of 400 acres. On lower ground, the wet meadows remain undrained to provide perfect conditions for a profusion of wild flowers. Species of note include ragged robin, knapweed, frog orchid,

heath spotted orchid, lady's mantle, corky-fruited dropwort, and bog pimpernel. But it is the lowly buttercup which energises this corner of Dorset with a magnificent explosion of vivid yellow in early summer.

Rabbits are plentiful at Kingcombe, especially on higher ground, where the fields are sufficiently dry for burrowing. I had come up with the idea of shooting rabbits in buttercups for the BBC *Living Britain* television series, and was subsequently commissioned to shoot stills for the accompanying book.

Erecting a hide

I first sought permission from the Dorset Wildlife Trust to erect a hide to photograph wild animals during the buttercup season. My only restriction was to keep to the

Facts about Kingcombe

Footpaths cross the reserve in various places and are clearly marked. It is important to stick carefully to these paths partly because their sympathetic layout causes minimum disturbance to wildlife, and also because the mosaic of bogs throughout the reserve are extremely hazardous. It is not possible to erect a hide at Kingcombe without permission from the Dorset Wildlife Trust and, more importantly, the reserve warden (I had cultivated friendships

with both in order that our relationship had mutual benefits). Plenty of other subjects at Kingcombe can be photographed without special permission. When low evening sunlight stabs across the yellow fields in June, bands of golden light are interspersed with long hedgerow shadows and the effect on the buttercups can be sumptuous.

Contact your nearest county wildlife trust to ask about possibilities for hide work on your local nature reserves.

Opposite page Shiny yellow buttercups will reflect a lot of light and can confuse the camera's meter, so I took a TTL reading from the adjacent hedgeline, which was bathed in full sunlight. I chose Kodachrome 200 as the extra speed would compensate for the one stop lost through using a converter. With the lens set at maximum aperture the effective exposure was f/5.6 at 1/250sec
Nikon F301 with Nikkor 500mm f/4 IFED lens and Nikkor 1.4 teleconverter, Kodachrome 200, f/5.6 and 1/250sec

field edges to avoid damaging the hay crop. This suited me, because rabbits are naturally shy creatures and it was necessary for me to be concealed within a hedge. For a hide I used camouflage netting (the same material used by the army) draped over four lightweight poles. Two main considerations were wind direction and lighting. I really wanted side lighting to give texture to the animals' fur, so I chose a south facing hedgebank in which to set up my hide. Wind direction is crucial and is most often from the west in this part of Dorset, which would be quite favourable in this position.

Several hours after settling in my hide, rabbits began to emerge from the hedgebank to feed on the succulent flowers. Young rabbits of the current annual vintage were much bolder than the mature adults, due no doubt to their lack of experience and youthful hunger.

The main problem I encountered while shooting wildlife at Kingcombe was human disturbance. The reserve is open to the public all year, and humans have the uncanny knack of turning up just at that crucial moment, blissfully unaware of ruining the shot I had waited hours for! ❖

Below Sometimes it can be an advantage to own a noisy old manual Nikon. When this roe buck entered the meadow, I took one shot on my FM2 and the deer was alarmed by the sound of the MD12 motordrive. He moved closer and stood looking intently at me. I made another noisy exposure and he advanced again. This continued until he was close enough for a portrait, the tilt of his head emphasising his curious attitude
Nikon FM2 with Nikkor 500mm IFED lens; Provia 100, f/4 and 1/250sec

Far left This scene of yellow, green and blue was taken prior to one of my rabbit vigils. A polariser emphasised the cloud formation and deepened the blue sky. I mostly use f/11 for landscapes because my lenses seem to produce the finest detail at this setting
Nikon FE2 with Nikkor 24mm lens and polarising filter, Velvia, f/11 and 1/60sec

Left These backlit buttercups were shot from my hide as I waited for rabbits to appear in the evening sunlight. I was struck by the way the buds and hairy stems were rimlit by the low sunlight. I focused upon the best composition I could find and allowed everything else to blur into diffusion
Nikon F301 with Nikkor 500mm IFED lens, Provia 100, f/4 and 1/500sec

Planning

Location Kingcombe Meadows nature reserve is one mile west of the village of Toller Porcorum, near Dorchester in West Dorset.

How to get there Public transport in West Dorset is limited mainly to the towns. There are bus services from Bridport and Dorchester to Toller Porcorum, but these are infrequent and do not run every day. If travelling by car, take the A37 west from Dorchester towards Yeovil as far as Grimstone. After Grimstone turn left onto the A356 towards Crewkerne. One mile beyond Maiden Newton turn left onto a minor road signposted Toller Pocorum. In the village of Toller take the first right next to the Swan pub (now closed) which leads to Lower Kingcombe. There is a visitor centre in Kingcombe at Pound Cottage with toilet facilities and ample parking.

Where to stay The Marquis of Lorne Inn (01308 485236/www.marquis-of-lorne.co.uk) at Nettlecombe, and the Three Horseshoes Inn (01308 485328) at Powerstock are both small country inns offering accommodation and excellent food.

What to shoot Photographing wildlife at Kingcombe is difficult without the use of a hide, but this is a most picturesque area with a wealth of wild flowers in summer. The hay meadows are at their best in June.

What to take Wellingtons or water-proof walking boots are essential, as the lower meadows and footpaths are always wet and often under water, even in mid summer.

Other times of year In early spring the ancient hedgerow banks are adorned with spring flora such as primrose, town hall clock, campion, yellow archangel and bluebell. From September through autumn and winter the valley is often submerged in morning mists which create ideal conditions for atmospheric pictures.

Ordnance Survey maps Landranger 194

Essential reading Leanet on Lower Kingcombe Meadows, available at Pound Cottage or from the Dorset Wildlife Trust (01305 264620).

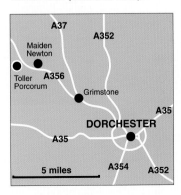

LEWESDON HILL

 October is the best time, says **David Cantrille**, for photographing fungi – the strange and beautiful shapes that litter the forest floor of Lewesdon Hill in Dorset

Facts about fungi

There are many thousands of species of fungi, only a few of which have popular names like fly agaric (the red spotted toadstool) or glistening inkcaps. The season for most species is autumn, before the first frosts. It is best to visit weekly to see what has appeared since your last foray. Particularly interesting or attractive species include amethyst deceiver (*Laccaria amethystea*), fly agaric (*Amanita muscaria*), stinkhorn (*Phallus impudicus*), shaggy inkcap (*Coprinus comatus*) and coral spine fungus (*Hericium coralloides*). While many fungi are harmless, a few are lethally poisonous if eaten. Ensure a specimen is identified by an expert before taking it home for breakfast. *Amanita phalloides* – the death cap – is the deadliest toadstool in the world. Good sites include the New Forest, Puddletown Forest near Dorchester, Forest of Dean, Ebernoe Common National Reserve (near Petworth, West Sussex), Horner Woods, Exmoor (near Porlock). Any woodland site should yield some species.

LEWESDON HILL is a wooded hilltop in beautiful rolling Dorset countryside, the summit of which is owned by the National Trust. There is quite a steep climb to the top but you are rewarded by wonderful views, and beech woods in which to wander and search for fungi.

Photographing fungi is fascinating – I look forward to its season every year. However, you may find you are following a budding mycologist round the wood and most of the best specimens have been carted away in a basket! I haven't seen this happen on Lewesdon, though.

The main characteristic of the porcelain fungus (*Oudemansiella mucida*) featured in the main picture is that at first the cap is domed. It then expands and flattens with age. The cap is whitish and semi-translucent with a slimy, glistening surface. Gills are widely spaced and white. It is edible but not recommended as it is glutinous and slimy – much better to take photographs of it!

Porcelain fungus grows almost exclusively on trunks and branches of beech trees. This photograph was taken from quite low down with the sun glancing over the outer cap, causing minute star bursts. I had to work quite fast for this effect, so I placed a foil reflector underneath the gills and took a few shots before the sun passed over. To take this underside, I used an angle finder attached to the viewfinder of my Canon EOS 1N, (so I wouldn't get a crick in my neck). I fitted a 100mm macro f/2.8 lens, and exposed for one second at f/22.

Angle finders are particularly useful for taking fungi as one often has to get very low down and look up underneath the specimen. It also helps to align the lens on an even plane with the fungus. The reflector I use is a simple piece of aluminium kitchen foil stuck onto cardboard and made to fit the front compartment of my

rucksack. Generally speaking, I try to avoid sun or flash on any fungi shots – though this was an exception.

For most fungi work a tripod such as a Benbo will enable the photographer to get down to ground level. A Benbo is more than capable of acting like a demented octopus, with legs going in all directions, but nothing compares with it for this kind of work. ❖

Below left Small clusters of gill fungus (Pholiota) are found on deciduous trees especially beech; sometimes on fallen trunks. This group was found on a rotting branch and as the sun shone on the caps I decided that the best view would be of the gills and stems. Again, the low angle was necessary, coupled with the anglefinder and warm-up filter. It is always worth remembering with this type of photography that if your equipment is fitted with a mirror lock-up device then it is wise to use it, particularly in conjunction with the self timer and remote cable release. All these help to prevent any vibration
Canon EOS 5, with 100 mm f/2.8 macro lens, Velvia, 1 sec at f/22, Benbo tripod, Cokin warm-up filter

Below Glistening inkcaps (Coprinus micaceus) are one of my favourite fungi. On the caps are mica-like particles, rather like sugar granules, which make it easier to focus accurately. Very common, they are often found in large clumps on rotting stumps of broad-leaved trees. Getting this picture was definitely a 'lying down in wet boggy ground' job – but I think it was worth it!
Canon EOS 1N with 100mm f/2.8 macro lens, Kodachrome 25, five seconds at f/22, Benbo tripod

Planning

Location Lewesdon Hill is situated in west Dorset, a few miles inland from the coastal town of Bridport

How to get there Take the B3162 from Bridport to Broadwindsor. Lewesdon Hill is found a couple of miles south of Broadwindsor. The wooded summit is owned by the National Trust. There is limited parking space for a few cars only at the bottom of the hill. The nearest railway station is Crewkerne (Paddington to Exeter line), about five miles from Lewesdon.

Where to stay There are B&Bs in Broadwindsor and Bridport, also hotels in and around Bridport.

What to take The compulsory tripod (one which will get very low down, preferably the bent bolt variety), angle finder, reflectors, filters, 100mm macro lens, remote release, flashgun, spare batteries, films, waterproof footwear, bin liners for kneeling or lying on, old Barbour jacket. Perhaps also a 200mm macro to shoot fungi (such as porcelain fungus) higher up on branches.

What to shoot Moss (eg star moss) and lichens, beech tree portraits.

Best time of day For fungi – any time of day is suitable as woodland is always quite overcast. October is probably the best month.

Nearest pubs The Anchor Inn at Salwayash (01308 488398) and the White Lion in Broadwindsor (01308 867070).

Ordnance Survey maps: Landrangers 192 and 193

Essential reading For magnificent photographs and informative text it would be hard to beat *Photographing Fungi in the Field* by George McCarthy, GMC Publications, ISBN 1 86108 236 3, £16.95. For reference, try: *Encyclopaedia of Fungi* by Michael Jordan, David & Charles, £25

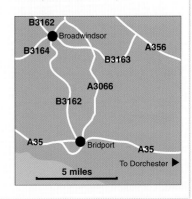

FIELDS OF blood-red poppies make a dramatic impact upon the landscape in mid summer, often appearing like magic where they have not been seen before. Similarly, return to a poppy field the following year and there will be no sign of them. The Romany lifestyle of this most photogenic annual wildflower is linked to its main habitat requirement – disturbed ground. Poppies tend to be most successful on chalky soils, occurring in arable fields, and on the verges and banks of new roads.

When a field near my home erupted in a sea of red flowers, the first shot that came to mind was one which included a deep blue sky, because primary colours usually work well together. Once I had achieved a composition which fitted this, I turned my attention to details of individual flowers and noticed how the hairy stems and buds were emphasised by backlighting. It was mid morning and the sun was high, so I decided to come back later in the day when the lower angle of the sun would produce a more dramatic result. Armed with some hazel sticks, I returned and, after inspecting nearly every plant in the field, identified a few suitable buds and marked each with a stick.

Diffusion and depth of field

In order to create a red blur into which the stems would blend, I pushed a nearby poppy flower directly in front of the lens. The result is that everything dissolves into total diffusion before it meets the frame edges.

Usually I like to achieve totally diffused backgrounds by using a telephoto set at its widest aperture, to limit the depth of field and make the main subject stand out. However, this technique would not work with these three poppy buds, because they were not all on the same plane of focus. To bring them into sharp focus it was necessary to stop down to f/11, which of course made the distracting background foliage sharper. To overcome this, I set up a board mounted, matt finished print of out of focus green foliage behind the poppy buds. Due to the low angle of the sun, the background was in shade, which increased the contrast further, enhancing the effect of backlighting on the

Nikon FE2 with Nikkor 105mm micro lens, Velvia, 1/30sec at f/11

POPPY FIELD

Here one season, gone the next, such is the frustrating habit of field poppies, gypsies of the plant kingdom. **Colin Varndell** tracks some down

Facts about poppies

Due to their nomadic habitat, poppies can occur just about anywhere, especially on chalk where the soil is disturbed. Learning to identify plants by foliage is a good way to predict an impending colour explosion. Check your own local arable fields in spring. Always seek permission for access, and if you are local, this might also lead to other photogenic subjects. As a matter of courtesy I always give landowners a print afterwards.

This area of West Dorset is very photogenic, with a succession of lush green rolling hills, interspersed with steep wooded valleys. There is always a wealth of wildflowers in summer, both in the country lanes and along the spectacular coastline.

Above Next to the set aside field was a barley crop, where I noticed the occasional poppy flower encroaching into the corn. I shot this with a 300mm lens set at full aperture in order to limit the depth of focus to the poppy head and the few ears which were close to it
Nikon FE2 with Nikkor 300mm IFED lens, Velvia, 1/500sec at f/2.8

buds. The lens was shaded from the direct rays of the evening sun to prevent flare from spoiling the effect. I knew the dark background might confuse my meter, so I calculated the exposure by reading off the foreground poppies, which were bathed in full sun. ❖

Below This view of the poppy field was taken with a wideangle lens to portray the impact of the red flowers on the landscape. A polariser removed the sheen from the flowers and foliage, and also enhanced the blue sky.
Nikon FE2 with Nikkor 24mm lens and polarising filter; Velvia; f/11 and 1/30sec

Left I returned to this field several times during the few days that the poppies were at their best. One morning was overcast but very still, so I set off armed with a small step ladder in order to shoot from above. A 24mm lens was used from a high angle, which makes the blooms explode to the corners. The bold spray of red poppies (bottom left) was placed on the rule of thirds position to provide a degree of anchorage to the picture
Nikon FE2 with Nikkor 24mm lens, Velvia, f/11 and 1/15sec

Above This image was created using a 500mm lens at full aperture to achieve maximum blurring. I was not totally happy with the result, as I had hoped to achieve just one poppy flower in a total diffusion of the mixed flowers' colours
Nikon F-301 with Nikkor 500mm IFED lens, Provia 100, 1/250sec at f/4

Planning

Location The location for these photographs was an arable field near to the village of Uploders in Dorset, adjacent to the A35.

How to get there The most scenic area of Dorset is centred around the small market town of Bridport. A car is essential. From Dorchester, take the A35 west to Bridport. From Yeovil take the A30 to Crewkerne and join the A3066 south to Bridport. From Exeter take the A35 east to Bridport.

Where to stay The Bull Hotel, East St, Bridport (01308 422878) has 20 rooms and a renowned restaurant. As this is predominantly a holiday area, there are plenty of good B&Bs in the town.

What to shoot Don't miss Eggardon Hill, three miles east of Bridport. This ancient iron age hill fort commands the most spectacular views in Wessex, and is good for landscape photography in all seasons, both morning and evening.

What to take The steep, hilly terrain necessitates a good pair of walking boots with ankle support.

Nearest pub The Royal Oak, Bridport (01308 422657) and The Loders Arms,

Eggardon Hill (01308 422431).

Other times of year The late summer harvest offers a feast of images, from fields of round bales to the corn stooks which grown for the thatching trade. In winter sunlight the coastline is at its best. But it is the leafy lanes of west Dorset when they explode in an uproar of spring flora which I find most appealing.

Ordnance Survey maps Landrangers 193 and 194

Essential reading: *A New View of Dorset* (Dorset Books 1996), ISBN 1 871164 30 3; *The Natural History of Dorset* (Dovecote Press 1997), ISBN 1 874336 40 7

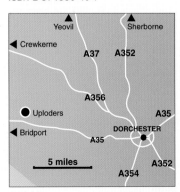

Looking every inch like a French chateau, the little known Dunrobin Castle in north east Scotland proved an inspiration for **David Tarn** one fog-bound August morning

DUNROBIN CASTLE

VERY RARELY do I work on commission, but a couple of years ago I had the delightful prospect of weeks of paid work through the summer taking photographs for a book of drives and walks in the countryside. Expense accounts, mileage, film and processing paid for – oh joy, oh heaven. Oh responsibility.

It is bad enough when you are funding the trip yourself and have travelled to some far flung corner of empire on the back of a questionable weather forecast, but when you are doing so at a client's expense you simply must come up with the goods. So it was with a sense of impending doom that I sat in the car drinking flask coffee, half listening to the radio, waiting for a blanket of thick sea fog to blow away so I could start the walk I was being paid to photograph.

It was more in desperation than hope that I noticed

this particular route took in the Dunrobin Castle, and I wondered if I might be able to take a photograph there rather than waste the whole day. I reasoned that even if the weather didn't lift I would at least gain some benefit from a look at the castle. When I first entered the grounds the castle was shrouded in fog, almost invisible even from the gardens. I had the hope, though, that the fog might shift. It was clearly blowing around. I must have wandered around for an hour or so before the fog began to give way and a clearer sight to the castle emerged. When it did, I realised the same fog that had been my enemy all morning was soon going to be my friend. Not simply by leaving, but by leaving slowly, and by endowing the castle, as it came into view, with a romantic quality more real than anything a soft focus filter could hope to create.

Using large format for perspective control

The best way of correcting converging verticals is to use a camera with movements for perspective control. You can buy perspective control lenses for most 35mm and medium format cameras, but in my view there is no better tool for photographing a building than a large format camera. These cameras offer full movements and a rising front with all the lenses they take. You need to be aware that the image projected towards the film is, in fact, a circle and that by

employing the movements you are taking your picture closer to the edge of that circle. Indeed, it is possible to go too far and lose the edge of the picture altogether. It is also possible to over-correct a picture so that the building still looks like it is going to fall over, but on top of the photographer rather than away from him. If the building is so tall that this is a problem the answer is to use only so much correction, and then tilt the camera the last few degrees to take in the top.

Far left I was able to reduce the area I was using for the picture by fitting a 6x9cm roll film back and raising the lens so that the castle was in the centre of the ground glass where the 6x9cm film would sit. The picture was taken as the sea fog began to disperse. Traces of it can still be seen on the left of the frame *Horseman 45HD with 90mm lens, 6x9 roll film back, Velvia, 1/15sec at f/22, tripod, no filters*

Left A 90mm wideangle lens on a 5x4in camera took in most of the castle before requiring any tilt or raising of the lens. The castle was well within the picture, if a little too close to the top *Horseman 45HD, 120mm lens, Velvia, 2sec at f/22, polarising filter, tripod*

For photographs of any tall building we have to contend with the problems of perspective distortion. Tilting the camera in order to include the top of the building in the frame causes this. Sometimes you can move far enough away from the building so that little or no tilting is needed. This was possible here from the garden with the fountain. I stood under a tree and, using a wideangle lens, was able to include the whole castle without tilting the camera. A spirit level that slips into the hot shoe is useful to tell you if the camera is perfectly level or not.

For this picture of Dunrobin Castle only a little correction was needed. There is sufficient distance between the castle and the viewer so that a wideangle lens takes in most of the castle before you tilt the camera or raise the lens. With a 90mm lens on a 5x4in camera the castle was well within the picture, if a little too close to the top. I was able then to reduce the area I was using for the picture by fitting a 6x9cm rollfilm back and raising the lens so that the castle was in the centre of the ground glass where the 6x9cm film would sit. The picture was taken as the sea fog began to disperse, although traces of it can still be seen, particularly on the left of the frame.

Eventually the fog cleared and I was granted a wonderful afternoon light for photography. I could probably have stayed in the grounds of Dunrobin Castle all afternoon, but I still had a walk to do for my client. Thank goodness the days are long in August.

Facts about Dunrobin

Dunrobin Castle is the ancestral home of the Duke of Sutherland. As we see it today the current building is a result of a remodelling undertaken by in 1845 by Sir Charles Barry. His job was to change the castle from a fort to a house in the Scottish baronial style, which is clearly influenced by the chateaux of the Loire Valley. Barry is best known for his design work on the Palace of Westminster. Two buildings less alike it is hard to imagine.

Planning

Location North east coast of Scotland above the Moray Firth and the Dornoch Firth, next to the village of Golspie.

How to get there From Inverness take the A9 coast road north through Tain, then cross the bridge over the Dornoch Firth and continue north to Golspie. The castle lies just beyond the village. Golspie has a train station.

Where to stay I stayed at the Ardmore Lodge Hotel (01862 821266) at Edderton by Tain and found it a friendly enough place. Check out tourist information for details of other places to stay.

What to shoot This is an underexplored corner of Scotland. Lacking the wild grandeur of the Highlands it is often ignored in favour of the more obvious delights close to hand. The nearby villages of Portmahomack and Rockfield and the Tarbat Ness lighthouse are all worth a look, as is the famous Glenmorangie distillery in Tain.

What to take Wideangle lenses are needed for pictures of the castle from its grounds. For the second picture in the formal gardens with the fountain it is possible to get far enough away from the castle so that you don't need rising front on your camera. A polarising filter can make the white castle stand out brilliantly from a blue sky.

Nearest pub The Dornoch Bridge, Tain
Ordnance Survey Map Landranger 17, Helmsdale and Golspie
Essential reading Dunrobin Castle, £2, Pilgrim Press, ISBN 1874670242

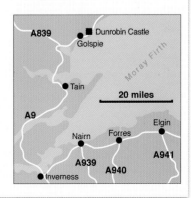

SALISBURY CATHEDRAL

Right The *Heaven's Gate* sculpture from last year's Salisbury Festival complements the cathedral spires as well as providing foreground interest in the close
Canon EOS 50E with 20-35mm zoom, polariser, Velvia, 1/8sec at f/16

To take a trip to Salisbury cathedral is to take a trip back in time, and, says **Steve Day**, there is no shortage of material for the photographer

Photography in the cathedral

The foundations were laid in 1220, and the elegant, tapering spire completed in the early 1300s. The spire was an afterthought, and the supporting columns have bowed, resulting in various bouts of strengthening over the years. The cathedral has a liberal view with regard to photography. Apart from the chapter house (which houses the Magna Carta) and during services, amateur photographers are welcome and both flash and tripods can be used. No fee is charged, but you can make an offering to the cathedral fund. It costs a fortune to keep the place up, and photographers have a duty to contribute. Pro photographers must contact the chapter office (01722 555100) for permission.

tall buildings, but the large close around the cathedral allows you to get far enough back without having to resort to tilt-and-shift lenses. However, the bare, sweep of grass means suitable foreground interest is lacking.

An ideal solution is provided by the annual Salisbury Festival where open-air activities centre around the close. 1999 saw the *Shape of the Century* sculpture exhibition, and the picture opposite arose from this. The purpose of the picture was to show the sculpture (*Heaven's Gate* by Tim Harrison, 1990) in its setting. There were a couple of problems. Best light was just after dawn, but the sun lit the north-facing side of the cathedral too much, overwhelming the sculpture. By waiting two hours, the sun was still relatively low, giving good, directional light, and the building was thrown into relief, making it more three-dimensional. The other problem was the scaffolding. Over the years I have become expert at hiding it behind various 'props'. Here it simply restricted my choice of view.

Fortuately, the scaffolding covering the magnificent west front has now been taken down, which means it can be photographed for the first time in 10 years. ❖

EVERYBODY KNOWS Salisbury cathedral, if only from Constable's paintings. Loads of tourists bang off a few snaps, then sally forth to Stonehenge and beyond. It's a pity, because the cathedral deserves more than that.

It lies in a valley but no matter which road you take to Salisbury, you will see the spire well before arrival. The cathedral's setting makes life relatively easy for the photographer. Converging verticals are a problem with

Far left In high summer, from the watermeadows to the south east of the city, the sun sets behind the cathedral. Choose your viewpoint carefully and you can catch the cathedral reflected in the waters of the River Avon
Canon EOS 50E with 28-105mm lens, Velvia, 1/2sec at f/11

Left These are the Cloisters, a beautiful covered walk to one side of the cathedral. Patience is the key here – it's simply a question of choosing your lighting and waiting for the tourists to go away
Canon EOS 50E with 20-35mm lens, Velvia, 1/30sec at f/16

Below left Despite this being *Outdoor Photography*, you'd be an idiot not to explore the interior of the cathedral. This is the choir, high altar and east end of the cathedral. It was shot from the far west end, the main reason being to avoid converging verticals. Taken on daylight film, with no filters, it has resulted in the tungsten lighting giving a warm overall colour and the fluorescent lighting above the east end recording a delicate green
Canon EOS 50E with 75-300mm lens, Velvia, 30sec at f/11

Planning

Location Salisbury, Wiltshire
How to get there By train, Salisbury is on the Waterloo-Exeter line, with connections to the north at either Bristol or Basingstoke. By road it's south of the M3/A303 out of London, though the best approach is along the A30 (better views and less traffic).
What to shoot Just about everything. For festival info call 01722 323883. The cathedral dominates the city, and there are so many views that, even after 10 years, I'm still finding new ones. Nearby is Old Sarum (site of the original cathedral and the remains of a castle) and Stonehenge. It's also surrounded by some of the finest, wildlife-rich downland in the country.
What to take Being a city, see the weather forecast.
Nearest pub You're spoilt for choice, but I like the Haunch of Venison in Minster Street and the New Inn (very old!) in New Street. If you're staying there's something for every pocket – contact the TIC (01722 334956). I

recommend The Old House on Wilton Road (01722 333433) or, more expensive, but in a lovely setting, The Old Mill at Harnham (01722 327517).
Other times of year Any time
Ordnance Survey map Explorer 130 (Salisbury & Stonehenge)
Essential Reading *The Salisbury City Guide*, Pitkin (ISBN 0-85372-925-5) and *Salisbury & Stonehenge*, Jarrold (ISBN 0-7117-1005-8), are good. There are too many books on the cathedral to list, but nothing directly aimed at photographers, which is why I'm currently working on such a book.

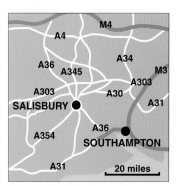

 One of the best ways to bring a much-photographed subject to life is to shoot it at the beginning or end of the day. **Steve Day** heads for the smoke

TOWER BRIDGE

YOU MAY THINK that London's Tower Bridge is a rather obvious subject that's been flogged to death but, as my mother used to say, there's more than one way to skin a cat (my mother was always 'saying' things, such as, 'Look before you leap', forgetting that, the day before, she'd said, 'He who hesitates is lost').

The main picture here took some planning. I wanted a pre-dawn shot, with Tower Bridge silhouetted against a colourful sky. The sun only rises in the right direction at the end of March, and again in early September. More important was the state of the tide – the reflections were a crucial part of the picture and so it needed to be just after high tide, when there is a short period of slack water.

Research done, I found myself pootling up the M3 at four in the morning, wondering if I was mad. By 5.30am I was in my chosen place on London Bridge, well-wrapped against the cold. Believe me, I'm no lover of cities, but early morning by the Thames was truly magical, especially on a morning like that. The masses of commuters that later stream across London Bridge were nowhere to be seen, and the city was still and silent.

Above This shot is from St Martin's Walk on the south bank. The lighting engineers do a grand job with the bridge, but I would have liked to be there 15 minutes earlier as the light in the sky is a little dark for my taste. Sadly, you can't be everywhere at once – so many pictures, so little time!
Bronica ETRSi with Zenzanon-PE 40-90 zoom lens, Velvia, tripod

Facts about Tower Bridge

Tower Bridge was completed in 1894, and is a lovely example of Victorian architecture. Its chief claim to fame is that it can be opened, to allow ships to enter the Pool of London. Back in the days when the docks were thriving this was a common occurrence, but these days this happens less often. The high-level walkway between the towers is now open to the public, as part of the 'Tower Bridge Experience', which includes a very interesting museum of the bridge.

Above The time, of day and year, matters. This picture was shot later in the year when the sun rises further north, and glances beautifully against the side of HMS Belfast – the open bridge with the sailing ship was a bonus
Bronica ETRSi with Zenzanon-PE 100-220mm zoom lens, Velvia, tripod

Sometimes everything falls into place. The tide was perfect, there was no wind to ruffle the water and the pre-dawn sky slowly coloured as sunrise neared. I had planned to wait a little longer but, as I peered through the viewfinder, I noticed a tug heading towards me (you can see it under the bridge in the picture) and I knew it would ruin the reflections.

I was none too happy about this as I had two shots in mind – a wideangle view that would be cropped to a panorama, and a closer portrait-format shot designed for the cover of a book I was working on. I had no time for both, and as I had the wideangle on the camera I went for the panorama. It was shot on a Bronica ETRSi, using a Zenzanon PE 45-90mm zoom, with no filters, using a tripod and mirror lock-up, on Velvia. Two shots in the bag, I frantically swapped to the 100-220mm zoom and took the close-up I was after, but by then, the mirror-like surface of the water was broken up, and by the time it settled the dawn colours had gone. Ah well…

Of course, there's more to Tower Bridge than a dawn shot. There are many opportunities for photography, throughout the day and into the night. Try shooting the same view, but at different times of the day, or year – it can be a singular lesson in how the changing qualities of light can transform a picture. Or stroll south from London Bridge, then head east on the south bank along St. Martin's Walk. HMS Belfast makes a good subject, followed by the classic view of Tower Bridge. Walk across the bridge itself – there's plenty of opportunity for striking, graphic shots of this fine, Victorian pile.

While on the bridge, look west along the Thames, especially at night – it's a stunning view, as is the sight of the Tower of London from the bridge, the old stone walls contrasting beautifully with the gleaming tower of the NatWest building behind, especially towards sunset. Then drop down from the bridge and head for St Katherine's Dock. This is a dramatically-redeveloped part of London and a good subject in

its own right, but beware, it's one of those places where 'jobsworths' will descend on you in droves at the first glimmer of a tripod or medium-format camera. Nevertheless, from the public walkway at the edge of the docks (where nobody can prevent you from taking photographs) there is a lovely view back towards Tower Bridge.

After this, head west along the north bank. From right in front of the Tower of London, on the public promenade (thus avoiding having to pay the extortionate entrance fee to the tower) there is a fine angle on the bridge. Having done the circuit, wait until evening and capture Tower Bridge in all its illuminated glory. ❖

Planning

Location Central London. Nearest tube for London Bridge is Monument, on the District & Circle line, as is Tower Hill, which is the nearest to Tower Bridge itself.
How to get there I refuse to tell you how to get to London!
Nearest pub Hundreds of them, especially the trendy, but pricey, places along the banks of the Thames
Times to visit March and September for sunrise shots similar to the main picture.
Essential information For tide times see www.tidetimes.co.uk/default.asp. There are precious few books on Tower Bridge, unless you're into serious engineering. For general info

see www.travelbritain.com/ london/tourism/thames/tower_bridge. html; www.theheritagetrail.co.uk/ industrial/tower/20bridge.htm; www.tourist-information-uk.com/tower-bridge-experience.htm; www.plus44.co.uk/london44/tour/ towerbridge.html

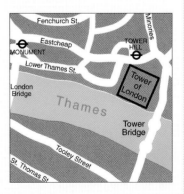

Colin Varndell explains how he was able to mix photography with a family holiday at one of Scotland's most photographed castles

EILEAN DONAN CASTLE

NATURE AND LANDSCAPE photography does not easily harmonise with the responsibilities of family life. The need to be out at unsociable hours to glimpse wildlife in the best lighting or weather conditions always seems to occur during important family occasions like my wife's birthday or a major school concert in which my children are playing.

My commitment as a father has meant that school holidays have provided the only unhindered opportunities for photographic assignments. But these days are also times for family fun and so, where possible, I have always attempted to blend these two fundamental requirements. Our annual holidays have therefore usually been taken in photogenic locations in order to combine a limited amount of landscape photography with family relaxation.

Although I had been to Scotland on previous photographic assignments I had not before spent time in the western highlands. Stock pictures of dramatic landscapes are always in demand in the publishing

Above The fast moving clouds hay have blocked out the sunset, but I turned then to my advantage with this long exposure which mixed the twilight with floodlight
Canon EOS 1N, 20-35mm USM, Slik tripod, Fuji Sensia 100, 20sec at f/11

world, and I knew the highlands offered abundant opportunities. It was with this in mind that last August, I took my family north to a rented cottage at Glenelg, near Glen Shiel.

Our aim was to enjoy family fun and do all the 'touristy' activities during the day, leaving a little time for landscape photography in either the early mornings or evenings.

We visited the famous Eilean Donan Castle one afternoon and I was amazed to observe the hundreds of tourists as they jumped from their coaches and immediately started taking photographs. This must be the most photographed castle in Britain if not the world, and it appealed to me very much as a subject. I did take

Facts about Eilean Donan Castle

The history of the castle dates from the 13th century when it was owned by the Mackenzie clan. It was destroyed by an English bombardment in 1719 during a Jacobite uprising. The castle on this site today is a total restoration which was

completed in 1932. It is open to the public during the summer from Easter until September. There is an extensive souvenir shop on the site which is also open to the public daily from I0am – 6pm.

Above Usually I shoot a couple of pictures of a subject at the first moment of contact. This approach serves two purposes. Firstly, I am anxious to get one 'in the bag', and secondly this record of how I first perceive the subject will hopefully be vastly different from the final shot. This was my first encounter with the castle on an August afternoon. *Nikkor 70-200 at 200mm. 1/60sec at f/11, Velvia*

a couple of straight record shots in pretty awful light that afternoon, and then spent some time driving around the loch to look at the building from various viewpoints.

In view of the fine, settled spell of weather at that time, and after some considerable persuasion, my family agreed to suffer a couple of sunsets at the castle. Actually it turned out to be me who suffered the ravages of highland midges at sunset while my wife and children went off to enjoy fish and chips in Kyle of Lochalsh. On neither evening was the castle floodlit on its most photogenic east side, and neither was the colour of the sky as spectacular as I had hoped when the sun sank into the loch.

After the second vigil I decided to cross the bridge and shoot the building from a viewpoint which would include mountains in the background.

I prefer shooting with prime lenses as I have always felt they have an edge over zooms when it comes to critical sharpness. But here on the edge of the loch my movements were restricted and the only way to obtain the composition I wanted was to use a zoom lens. By this time the castle was floodlit on its west side, and

Below Early one morning while my family were still fast asleep, I stole from the cottage on foot to Glenelg Bay. The tide was low in the loch and the lush green weed was exposed. I used a 24mm lens for this shot in order to include some weed in the foreground and still show the overall view of the loch, the distant landscape and the blue sky. The position of the sun was ideal for using a polarising filter to deepen the blue sky and remove unwanted reflections from the water surface. *Nikon FE2 with Nikkor 24mm wideangle and polariser, 1/15sec at f/11 on Fujichrome Velvia*

there was still light in the sky which I metered for. Although the sky was actually two stops darker than the floodlit castle I knew from experience that the floodlighting would require an additional stop which would in turn yield a slightly brighter sky and give a hint of detail on the distant mountains.

As in all extreme conditions when the opportunity allows, I bracketed in both half and full stops either side of my calculated exposure in order to ensure a result. As it turned out, my original exposure value proved to be the correct one.

The lens used was a Nikkor 70-200 zoom, actual focal length was 200mm. The exposure was 4sec at f/11 on Fujichrome Velvia.

Above It was late in the day when thick brooding clouds hung low over Loch Garry. Suddenly a shaft of sunlight stabbed into the loch and the water briefly sparkled against the dark mountains beyond. I metered directly from the water. *Nikkor 300mm, Velvia, 1/125sec at f/11*

Planning

Location Northwest highlands on A87 between Glen Shiel and Kyle of Lochalsh.

How to get there From Fort William take the A82 north to Invergarry and join A87 westbound. From Inverness take the A82 southbound to Invermoriston and join A887 westbound which eventually joins the A87. Please note, there is limited public transport but it is infrequent, and will not necessarily stop at photogenic sites. It is therefore essential to have your own independent transport

Where to stay Tourism is the main industry for this area of Scotland and therefore B&B's are abundant. Contact the local tourist centre at Kyle of Lochalsh for an up to date accommodation list. (Tel: 01599 534276).

What to shoot This area is so photogenic there seems to be a picture at every turn of the mountain roads. In addition to the wonderful landscape, the brochs at Glenelg are also of photographic interest. These circular stone structures are a type of small fortress unique to Scotland dating back to around 100BC.

What to take Be prepared for wet weather as this highland area attracts the highest level of rainfall in Britain. Waterproof clothing and footwear is essential, and take midge repellent and a hat For those tiny blood sucking insects which will descend upon you in swarms during the summer months.

Other times of year Photogenic all year, especially spring and autumn.

Ordnance survey map Landranger 33

Essential reading *The Which? Guide to Scotland*, ISBN 0340 55034. Packed with historical, geographical and other practical information like where to stay and places to eat.

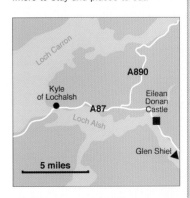

RIVER ALN

A gentle stroll down the banks of the River Aln takes in everything from castles to wildlife and landscapes. **Chris Weston** makes a day trip of it

THERE ARE several reasons why Northumbria is my favourite location for photography. There are its sandy beaches and rugged coastline, not to mention the abundance of wildlife, Roman ruins, historic castles and the rolling hills of the Cheviots. Not least, it is my home county and, being the most sparsely populated and least visited county in the UK, it is perfect for landscape photography. Alnwick itself is a small, bustling market town and a great centre from which to explore the rest of the county.

As you head north out of Alnwick over the Lion Bridge, a small gate leads to a footpath that follows the course of the River Aln past Alnwick Castle. On clear summer days the castle is perfectly reflected in the calm waters of the river. What struck me particularly about this scene was the fantastic warm glow of the light on

the castle walls and the stretch of early morning mist hovering ghostlike on the southern bank.

From the footpath there are numerous views of the castle from a variety of different angles and I considered various options before settling on this one. This position along the bank is one of very few that allows an uninterrupted view of the castle walls, and I felt it added to the overall presence of the imposing structure.

I also wanted to give the castle a sense of place, so I looked to include some foreground interest other than just the reflection in the water. The main problem was the reed bed directly in front of me that was both wide and dense. To include this would have created a barrier in the foreground of the picture. What I did like were the few tall grasses growing among the reeds. To

Facts about the River Aln

The River Aln winds its way peacefully from the area surrounding Alnham on the edge of the Cheviot Hills and the Northumberland National Park, cutting a swathe through rolling landscape to its end at the Aln Estuary in Alnmouth.

Along its course are numerous small towns and villages, most notably Alnwick where the castle sits majestically on its

banks. It is from here that you can follow the public footpath, starting from the Lion Bridge that eventually follows the course of the river to Alnmouth Bay.

There are no specific restrictions along this path though – as always in rural locations – it is important to abide by countryside etiquette.

Above Taken from a minor road connecting Alnmouth and the coastal village of Boulmer, showing the river glimmering in the golden light of sunset as it meanders past the village of Lesbury
Nikon F90X with 70-300mm zoom in 200mm range on Fuji Velvia, 1/30sec at f/22, 81B filter, Manfrotto tripod

Above On summer evenings the low tide at Alnmouth Bay leaves boats stranded. The warm light of sunset shimmering off the wet surface presents a kaleidoscope of vibrant colours
Nikon F90X with 24-120mm zoom in 24mm range on Fuji Velvia, 1/30sec at f/22, 81B filter, Manfrotto tripod

combat this problem I ended up with one tripod leg in the water and two bunches of reeds tied with string outside the image area. Not to mention, needless to say, two wet feet!

Creating depth

To create some depth within the composition I chose a 28mm wideangle lens with an 81B filter to enhance the warm tone. The sun was rising to my left out of view,

Taken from the north bank of the river, opposite Alnwick Castle looking east. This is the view that greets you as you begin the walk from Lion Bridge. Early morning is the best time of day, photographically speaking, to be here
Nikon F90X with 24-120mm zoom in 35mm range on Fuji Velvia, 1/15sec at f/22, 81B filter, Manfrotto tripod

but I used a lens hood nonetheless, to ensure no flare could spoil the image. Because the sky was slightly lighter in tone than the castle walls I metered from the grassy bank and then from the sky using the camera's spotmeter. This gave me a variance of around half a stop, so I added a 0.3 graduated neutral density filter to even out the tones. To ensure front to back sharpness I selected a small aperture – f/22 – which, using the given meter reading gave me a shutter speed of 1/30sec.

I was shooting with Fuji Velvia because I like its rich, saturated colours. Velvia, however, can be somewhat intolerant of high contrast so I often bracket shots when I am using it. However, given the low contrast in this scene, I was confident that the final image would record as I wanted it to, so on this occasion I decided not to bracket.

The result is an image rich in warm colour and atmosphere. The use of the wideangle lens has created some dynamism in the sky that adds life to an otherwise still scene. All in all, it was the perfect start to my journey following the River Aln to the sea. ❖

Planning

Location Alnwick – Alnmouth, Northumberland
How to get there By road take the A1 then the A1068. There is a mainline railway station in Alnwick and a regular bus service from surrounding towns.
What to shoot Alnwick Castle reflected in calm water; Alnwick castle from Lion Bridge; the meandering course of the river; Alnmouth Bay and harbour; Alnmouth beach; the Aln Estuary.
What to take As ever, a tripod and cable release are essential. Also take 81 series, ND grad and polarising filters; lenses from wideangle to medium telephoto with hoods; good walking shoes/boots; waterproof jacket/windcheater.
Nearest pub Alnwick and Alnmouth town centres.

Other times of year Coastal mist in winter; there are also spectacular autumn colours in nearby woods.
Ordnance Survey map Landranger 81
Essential reading Northumbria by Lee Frost, published by Constable, ISBN 0 09 477410 2, £20.00.
Useful websites www.northumberland.org.uk

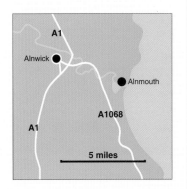

LEWES CASTLE

Ancient castles erected in the years following the Norman conquests are a feature of many towns in Sussex. *Outdoor Photography* editor **Keith Wilson** focuses on the 900-year-old ruin of Lewes Castle

I CONSIDER MYSELF very fortunate to work in an office located in one of the prettiest towns of England. Lewes is the county town of Sussex. It is steeped in history and home to some of the best preserved Tudor and Georgian architecture in southern England. Just a few miles inland from Newhaven and surrounded by the South Downs, Lewes is often bypassed by motorists speeding down the A23 to the fleshpots of Brighton or the A27 to visit granny in Eastbourne. Which is probably just as well, as Lewes doesn't get the same volume of traffic and tourists as the coastal towns. It has also largely escaped the ravages of the 60s town planners who had a dislike for anything charming and olde worlde, preferring to demolish such architectural delights in favour of concrete and glass eyesores.

Lewes high street is lined with wonderful buildings, some dating from the 14th century. It rises steeply up from the banks of the Ouse to an area known as Castle Gate, a cobbled path passing through the beautifully preserved barbican before winding up to the castle keep. In this part of Lewes, the castle is the dominant feature. It is perfectly positioned for photography as it occupies the highest point in the town centre. The Normans capitalised on this geographical advantage by building an earthen mound on top of which they constructed the

castle. As a result the castle is well lit by sunshine virtually all year round, but the best time of day to photograph it is the couple of hours before dusk when the castle keep is bathed in a warm light.

Because it is such a visible landmark in the town, it is possible to take pictures of the castle without having to pay £3.70 to enter the precinct, managed by the Sussex Archaeological Society. However, it is nearly impossible to frame the castle and mound from anywhere else without including the rooftops of surrounding buildings. This is no bad thing as the architecture spans many different periods with a diverse range of building and roof materials, including hanging earthenware tiles, glazed ceramics, slates and the proverbial bricks and mortar. These can be used as a foreground for your composition to complement the texture of the castle walls as well as to lead your eye into the frame, back through the ages, to the 11th century fortress. It also means a plentiful supply of midtones for metering, so I took a spot reading for my exposure setting.

For the main picture on this spread, I had to travel no further than the next room on the top floor of *Outdoor Photography*'s editorial offices in Lewes high street. I'm not lazy, just lucky, and as it is the view I see every day at work, it makes sense to share it with you. I set up the

Left: I always try to place a human figure in architectural shots, and the enveloping walls and arch of the barbican demands such a presence to show the scale of the subject. With a wideangle lens mounted on a tripod, I was able to stop down to gain maximum depth of field and then waited for someone to walk into the illuminated area beneath the arch
Canon EOS RT with 28mm f/2.8 lens, Velvia, tripod, 1/8sec at f/16

Below left: Trying to show the castle's barbican gate wholly within the frame demands a wideangle lens. Because of the grey sky I used the top of the arch above me to frame the top of the picture. At the bottom of the picture you can see the unmistakeable hanging tiles of a building in the high street
Canon EOS RT with 28mm f/2.8 USM lens, Velvia, tripod, 1/125sec at f/8

tripod and used an 85mm f/1.2 portrait lens mounted onto a Minolta Dynax 9 SLR, loaded with Kodak Ektachrome Elite 200. The 85mm focal length was ideal for framing the scene with the right amount of foreground detail offered by the roofs of a church and shops on the other side of the street, while including enough sky at the top to include the flagpole on the top of the castle. My elevated viewpoint allowed a glimpse of the mound between the rooftops and the base of the castle, vital to adding depth and perspective to the scene. The light was warm and golden, but I needed to give enough exposure to render enough detail and texture in the foreground rooftops as well as the castle walls. Finally, the rather innocuous flag needed to be in 'full sail' – the alternative of an otherwise limp looking piece of rag hanging forlornly from the pole would not have enhanced the picture. Fortunately the wind played its part right on cue. ❖

Planning

How to get there: From the M25, take the A22 turnoff to East Grinstead and continue on towards Uckfield. Just outside Uckfield, at the junction with the A26 turn right for Lewes and take this road into the town centre then follow the signposts to 'Lewes Castle', proceeding up the high street. A pay and display car park is situated at the foot of the castle wall in West Gate. Trains to Lewes leave London Victoria every half hour.

What to shoot: The homes of Virginia Woolf, Thomas Paine and Anne of Cleeves (the fourth wife of Henry VIII) are all within a few minutes walk of the castle. Down by the river Harvey's Brewery is worth a few frames.

What to take: Sensible shoes for the high street, boots for climbing the castle steps. A tripod is essential if you want to get absolute sharpness, plenty of slow slide film and a lens or lenses that will cover from wideangle (24 or 28mm) to short telephoto (135mm). If you don't have a cable or remote release, use your self-timer.

Other times of year: Guy Fawkes is a spectacular night in Lewes. The shop fronts of the high street are boarded up before the locals propel a succession of burning barrels down the hill.

Best pubs: Being the home of Harvey's ales, it's difficult to miss the local brew. The Elephant and Castle, Lewes Arms and the Royal Oak are OP's recommended haunts.

Ordnance Survey Map: Landranger 198, Brighton & Lewes

Essential reading: *10 Walks around Lewes*, £1, available from the local tourist centre.

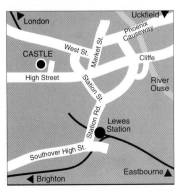

CORFE CASTLE

Steve Day's unhealthy obsession with studying Ordnance Survey maps paid off when he searched for a different view of the much-photographed Corfe Castle

CORFE CASTLE is an outstanding landmark in Dorset. The ravaged ruins, perched proudly on a high mound, have a romantic air that cries out to be captured in a photograph. And that's the trouble – it's been photographed to death. Take a look at the postcards in any of the twee village gift shops and you'll see it's been covered from just about every angle, in every light.

Now there's a challenge...

I can spend hours reading an Ordnance Survey map (a sad man). Poring over a large-scale one of Corfe, looking for a unique viewpoint, it struck me that the castle is strategically sited at a gap between two long, high, chalk ridges. All the shots I'd seen of the castle had been taken from fairly close, thus emphasising the height of the castle mound and the way it dominates the grey stone village below. Perhaps there was a way of showing its former crucial rôle of defending this narrow gap?

Corfe is about an hour from where I live so, one dull, dank, dismal day, I drove down to do a little research. From the map the view from the north looked promising

Above When photographing buildings or landmarks, we have a tendency to home in on the subject in order to emphasise it. Sometimes the reverse approach works. The aim here was to show the castle's strategic position defending the gap in the chalk ridge. Unlike painters, photographers have to work with what they see before them (though digital photography is changing this). It's often dangerous to have too clear a plan for a picture – real life doesn't always come up with what we envisage. In this case all the elements combined to provide just the shot I wanted. Without the morning mist the picture wouldn't have worked – the foreground layer gives the picture a sense of depth, and the silvery mist behind the castle makes it stand out against the normally dark background
Canon EOS 50E with 75-300mm lens 1/4sec at f/16, Velvia, grey grad to bring the sky down, polariser to cut through haze

but turned out to be a disappointment, with various features of the landscape in inconvenient places.

I decided that the view from the south looking back up

Facts about Corfe Castle

Corfe Castle was started in Norman times and slowly added to over the succeeding 250 years. Like so many such buildings it suffered during the Civil War, and was largely demolished by Cromwell's forces. That so much remains is surely a testament to the strength of the building. Now owned by the National Trust, it is open for visiting throughout the year.

Left Make the most of it when conditions are right. Shortly after taking the main picture I returned to the village and climbed the hill to the north of the castle. By now the sun had risen a little and the early morning light was streaming across the field below, turning the mist gold
Canon EOS 50E with 28-105mm lens, Velvia, 1/15sec at f/11, polariser

the village high street wasn't on – it's the most commonly-shot one, and was too close to the castle for what I had in mind. However, from the end of the main street the land drops away towards Corfe Common, and I headed there, hoping for a broader aspect. Not bad, but still not what I had envisaged.

After the common the landscape sweeps uphill towards another chalk ridge and so I headed for Kingston. There, a couple of hundred yards east of the village near Kingston Barn, was just the view I was looking for. At least, I thought it was, for the grey pall that hung in the valley all but obliterated the castle. My only worry was that both the flanking hills and the castle would be lost against the dark green background of the fields to the north.

Several weeks later, the last forecast of the night promised cloudless skies, a light northwesterly wind (wonderful clear light guaranteed) and early morning mist I hoped would delineate the hills and castle. I got up at 3.15am. Just for once, the forecast was spot-on. Too spot-on. The whole valley was completely foggy.

I climbed East Hill, in the hopes of capturing the castle floating ethereally in a sea of white, but to no avail, so returned to my planned viewpoint and waited. Patience paid off, and shortly after sunrise the fog began drifting away and there was the shot I had in mind. The castle stood out clearly against a background

of silver, the valley lay under a pale blanket and, glory be, with a small shift of viewpoint I could include some cows to give foreground interest and depth.

Sometimes getting up at silly times pays off, and planned viewpoints provide the shots envisaged. I even had time to return to East Hill and shoot more conventional views of the castle with layers of mist turned golden by the early morning sun. A good morning's work. ❖

Below left This is one of the more frequently-shot views of the castle. It was taken from the flanks of a hill north of the castle late in the evening
Canon ESO 50E with 28-105mm lens, Velvia, 1/8sec at f/8, polariser and warm-up filters

Planning

How to get there By road, half way along the A351 between Wareham and Swanage. By train to either Wareham or Swanage stations, then Wilts & Dorset buses 142, 143 or 144. There is also a steam railway service operating from Swanage. Call Swanage Railway on 01929 425800; e-mail: general@swanrail.freeserve.co.uk or see their website: www.swanrail.demon.co.uk/ for timetable.

What to shoot Don't let the fact that there are so many existing pictures put you off – you can always do better! There are many views, depending upon the time of day. Climb the surrounding hills for good overall shots, or close-ups with telephotos. Emphasise the castle's domination of the village by shooting along the high street with a telephoto. Go into the castle itself for different aspects of the ruins (NT property – tripods forbidden).

What to take Good walking shoes, OS map, a range of lenses.

Nearest pub There are several in the village within a hundred yards of the castle, and innumerable cafes and restaurants. The village also abounds in B&Bs.

Other times of year Any time

Ordnance Survey map Landranger 195 or Outdoor Leisure 15; OS refs: Corfe Castle – SY 959 823; viewpoint – SY 960 795.

Essential Reading The Story of Corfe Castle, Emmeline Hardy, £4.95, ISBN 0 946 159 505.

Website www.resort-guide.co.uk/ purbeck/corfe/index.html

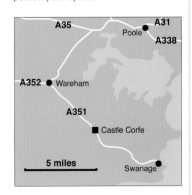

 You have to work hard to find a different view of Fountains Abbey, says **Steve Gosling**, but floodlights from late August to October make it worth the effort

FOUNTAINS ABBEY is owned by the National Trust and is visited by around 290,000 people every year. Not surprisingly, there are thousands of photographs taken of Fountains Abbey so coming up with something unusual requires time and effort. As a regular visitor to the abbey I think I have explored most of the usual angles and have photographed the abbey at different times of the day and at all times of year. But I am always aware of the danger of replicating the photographs taken by the many photographers who have been there before me. In reality, there are probably no 'new' viewpoints of Fountains Abbey – it is the quality of light that makes one photograph stand out from the others.

Above The fast moving clouds hay have blocked out the sunset, but I turned then to my advantage with this long exposure which mixed the twilight with floodlight
Canon EOS 1N, 20-35mm USM, Slik tripod, Fuji Sensia 100, 20sec at f/11

Every year the National Trust gives a helping hand to those photographers seeking something different from the standard tourist shot. Between August and October, the abbey remains open until 10pm (Fridays and Saturdays only), during which time it is dramatically floodlit. This provides a new Pandora's Box of photographic opportunities. If you will excuse the pun –

Facts about Fountains Abbey

Fountains Abbey was built in the 12th century and a hundred years later it was one of the richest Cistercian monasteries in the country. The abbey was surrendered to the crown in 1539, as part of Henry VIII's dissolution of the monasteries and over subsequent years it fell into disrepair. It was acquired by William Aislabie in 1768, who incorporated the grounds into the ornamental gardens of Studley Royal.

Today, the site, including Studley Deer Park (see *page 80*), is owned by the National Trust, which means the Trust's restrictions on commercial photography apply. However there

are there are no restrictions on amateur photographers.

The Abbey and Studley Royal Water Garden are open all year round but the estate is closed for a few selected days in the year – it is advisable to check specific open dates and times with the Estate Office (01765 608888) prior to making a visit.

There is an admission charge to the abbey and water garden – National Trust and English Heritage members free – again the Estate Office can provide details of current charges and discounts for large groups.

FOUNTAINS ABBEY

Left For floodlit shots like this, it is important to shoot before the sky goes black. This makes for more interesting images and a better definition between the sky and unlit areas of the building *Canon EOS 1N, 20-35mm USM, Sensia 100, 20sec at f/13, Slik tripod*

With favourable weather conditions I hoped to capture the clouds tinged with pink as the sun slipped below the horizon. After a lengthy wait it became apparent that the sunset was not going to materialise.

Fortunately every cloud has a silver lining, as the saying goes, and it was true in this case. Grey clouds that were obscuring my sunset were scudding across the sky – driven by the wind. By moving closer to the abbey with my 20-35mm zoom set to 20mm, I could capture the floodlit building against this dramatic sky.

Tilting the camera up made the walls of the abbey converge in the frame. This added to the drama by emphasising the sky. Setting a slow shutter speed to record the movement of the clouds, I bracketed widely around the indicated meter reading. I was aware of the danger of the floodlit highlights burning out due to overexposure but I wasn't going to waste this opportunity by being overly economical with film. ❖

Far left The arches, repeated in the main structure and the windows, make for good pattern photographs. Getting low, with a wideangle lens emphasises the size and impressive nature of the abbey *Canon EOS 1N, 20-35mm USM, Sensia 100, 10sec at f/16, Slik tripod*

the abbey can be seen in a whole new light. The atmosphere is incredible when this majestic building is lit and the night air is filled with Gregorian chant.

It was on one of these floodlit evenings that the main picture here was taken. It is the dramatic sky that makes this shot special for me. I had planned my visit knowing that the abbey would be floodlit. The weather forecast was for cloud cover but breaking, to give spells of sunshine, so I thought there was a chance of a good sunset. I arrived late in the afternoon intending to take a photo of the sun sinking behind the abbey tower. I set up the camera on the tripod and waited for the right conditions. My intention was to shoot as the sun was setting, positioned 50 to 100 metres away from the abbey with a 28 or 35mm lens.

Below The vaulted ceiling of the cloisters is very impressive. It can be seen at its best when floodlit - as in this shot. I framed to concentrate on the repetitive patterns of the arches *Canon EOS 100, 35-135mm USM, Sensia 100, 3sec at f/8, Slik tripod*

Planning

Location 10 miles north of Harrogate, four miles west of Ripon (off B6265 to Pateley Bridge; follow the signs to Fountains Abbey).

How to get there Access by public transport is not easy. It is best to go by car – there is ample free car parking at the visitor centre.

Where to stay There are numerous hotels in the Ripon and Harrogate areas – contact the local tourist information offices for more details (Harrogate 01423 537300; Ripon 01765 604625)

What to shoot Details of the abbey ruins: the vaulted ceiling in the cloisters, the arches in the nave aisle; the abbey in its rural valley setting surrounded by trees and the nearby River Skell. Studley Royal Water Garden has a wealth of photogrnic subjects with its formal lakes and architectural features.

What to take A wideangle lens for shooting the whole building as well as dramatic perspectives; a telephoto for picking out details. A tripod is essential for shots of the building when floodlit - it is well worth the extra effort involved in carrying it. A small torch is useful for when you're setting up, checking camera settings etc. A lens hood or piece of card to shield the lens from unwanted 'spillage' from the floodlights.

Nearest Pub There are several pubs in nearby Ripon – I would particularly recommend The Water Rat, Bondgate Green (01765 602251). Alternatively, there are licensed restaurant & cafe facilities at the visitor centre.

Other times of year Autumn is a good time to capture the abbey, when the leaves on the surrounding trees start to turn colour. It can also look splendid in the winter if we get a good snowfall (a rare event these days). The other advantage of autumn and winter is that there are fewer visitors around to wander into your shots.

Ordnance Survey Map OS Landranger series map no. 99; Grid Reference 276685

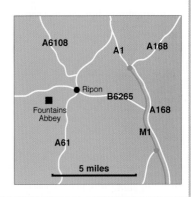

 With its imposing castle and empty, windswept beach, Bamburgh is a landscape photographer's paradise. **Lee Frost** returns to an all-time favourite location

BAMBURGH CASTLE

I'LL NEVER FORGET the first time I visited Bamburgh. Casually driving across country from the A1, I was suddenly shocked to my senses by the unexpected vision of a magnificent castle rising from the early morning mist. Even miles distant it appeared larger than life, but as the village neared it grew ever-bigger and, on arrival, I stood open-mouthed, gazing at one of the most amazing sights I had ever seen.

On closer inspection I soon realised that Bamburgh boasted not just a castle – though alone that would be enough for the photographer in me – but a huge, windswept beach over which the castle looks and breathtaking views out to the Farne Islands and up the coast to Lindisfarne.

Then there was the light. Northumberland has a quality of light that makes photography pure joy no matter what time of day or season of the year it is, and after five years and more than a dozen visits, my enthusiasm for Bamburgh is stronger than ever, if that's possible!

Facts about Bamburgh

In 547AD, the Anglo-Saxon King Ida invaded the Northumbrian coast and created a settlement where Bamburgh stands today. This became capital of the Kingdom of Bernicia and a place where the ancient kings of Northumbria were crowned. Bamburgh has had a castle to protect it since those times, perched high on an outcrop of the Whin Sill. First it was a wooden fortress, which the Vikings destroyed in 993AD, then in the 11th century the first stone castle was built by the Normans. Seemingly impregnable, Bamburgh became the first castle to be taken by artillery when, in 1464, Yorkists shattered its walls with canon fire. After lying in partial ruin for centuries it was rebuilt by the first Lord Armstrong between 1894 and 1903. The exterior you see today is pretty much how it would have looked in 1272. The name Bamburgh comes from Bebbanburgh – Bebba being the wife of King Ida's grandson, Ethelfrith.

Above Heading away from Bamburgh beach after sunset I turned for a final look and noticed this serene scene. Stopping my lens down to minimum aperture, I used a two second exposure to record motion in the waves and shot unfiltered
Nikon F90x with 28mm lens, Velvia, two seconds at f/22

Above This is one of my favourite shots of Bamburgh Castle, taken a few minutes before sunset on a stormy spring evening. Golden sunlight had broken through cloud to illuminate the castle, then as if by magic, a rainbow appeared
Pentax 67 with 55mm lens, Velvia, 1/2sec at f/16, 0.6 neutral density graduated filter and 81B warm-up

The main shot here on the left was taken around mid-afternoon during the spring of 1999, while I was in the area for a day. Arriving on the beach via The Winding, a narrow lane off Bamburgh's main street, I spent a while wandering up and down in search of a suitable viewpoint and, after 10 minutes or so, I found my spot, attracted by the wonderful colours and textures of a mollusc-encrusted rocky shelf and the reflections in a shallow pool beyond it that had been left by the receding tide.

For me, deciding where to shoot from is 75% of the battle over, because everything that comes after that is mere formality – rather like driving a car is once you've decided where to go.

I already had the composition in my mind, using a wideangle lens to emphasise the foreground and show the castle in its magnificent natural environment, so only fine-tuning was necessary once my Woodman 5x4in camera was set-up and fitted with a 90mm Nikkor lens (equivalent to 28mm in 35mm format).

While under the darkcloth, tweaking the composition, I applied axis tilt to the camera's front standard to increase depth-of-field and ensure front-to-back sharpness – one of the great benefits of using a large-format camera – before fitting polariser and 81B warm-up filters and rotating the polariser to achieve maximum effect. With light striking the scene from one side the polariser made a huge difference, deepening the sky to emphasise those cotton-wool clouds, removing glare from the surface of the water to reveal reflections on the sky more clearly, and boosting the colours and texture of the foreground. In fact, you're unlikely to get better conditions than that for letting a polariser do its job to full effect.

Even lighting made metering a doddle – I took a spot reading from the sunlit rock in the foreground using a Pentax digital handheld spotmeter, compared that to a second spot reading from the grassy slopes around the castle, and settled on one second at f/32 with Fuji Velvia. In all I exposed four sheets of film.

Since taking that photograph I have been back to Bamburgh on numerous occasions, but no matter how many times I return, I never fail to be inspired by its beauty.

The coastline of north Northumberland is a magical place, and with Bamburgh at its heart, to my mind it deserves the title 'Best-kept secret of the English landscape'. ❖

Planning

Location Bamburgh lies on the North Northumberland coast, approx 45 miles north of Newcastle-upon-Tyne and 10 miles south of Berwick-upon-Tweed.

How to get there Take the A1 north from Newcastle-upon-Tyne heading towards Berwick. Ten or so miles north of Alnwick, leave the A1 and follow the B1341 to Bamburgh.

Where to stay There are numerous B&Bs and hotels in Bamburgh. One of the best is the Victoria Hotel on Front Street (01668 214431).

Nearest pub Various to choose from on Front Street. I'd recommend the Victoria Hotel's bar where you can also buy excellent meals.

What to shoot The beach and dunes are the best places to shoot from, though you can also get a great shot of the castle towering over the village from Front Street (stand on the grass verge where the road forks). Go to the end of The Winding to capture sunset across Budle Bay with Holy Island twinkling on the horizon.

What to take Wideangle lenses are invaluable for emphasising foreground interest – a 24mm or 28mm will be ideal. Longer lenses are handy for homing in on the castle. Pack polariser, warm-up and neutral density graduate filters, a sturdy tripod and plenty of slow-speed colour film (ie Fuji Velvia!). Also, Bamburgh beach can be a windy place to hang around so wrap up and wear a hat!

Best time of day Sunrise, afternoon and early evening for shots of the castle and dusk for seascapes. Morning for shots of the village and castle from Front Street.

Best time of year Any season will reward you with great shots, though I prefer autumn, especially on a day of dramatic skies and sunny breaks.

Ordnance Survey map Touring Map and Guide 14, Landranger sheets 75 and 81

Essential reading *Northumbria*, by Lee Frost.

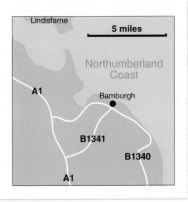

 Mow Cop stands on a rocky outcrop on the border between Cheshire and Staffordshire. **Peter Watson** finds this ancient folly an irresistible subject

MOW COP

DISTINCTIVE PICTURE taking is a result of being in the right place at the right time. Luck plays a part, but it is research, preparation and planning which increase the chances of success. I keep a list of locations I have previously visited and make notes about when would be the best time to return, including information about the most suitable time of year, time of day and the most

Above When photographing a building as a silhouette, take a meter reading of the sky (excluding the brightest part closest to the horizon). To maintain the twilight effect it will probably be necessary to then reduce exposure by approximately one stop. For safety I suggest you also bracket your exposures
5x4in Tachihara camera with 90mm Super Angulon wideangle lens, Velvia, one second at f/32

Facts about Mow Cop

Built in 1754 by local stonemasons John and Ralph Harding, Mow Cop was constructed to improve the view from Rode Hall, three miles away. It sits on a rocky outcrop on the exact boundary between Cheshire and Staffordshire. The Sneyd family from Keele owned the Staffordshire side and the Wilbrahams from Rode Hall, the Cheshire side.

Between 1807 and 1812 Mow Cop became the site of a number of large, open air evangelical meetings. One particular meeting, organised by Hugh Bourne and William

Clowes and attended by a crowd of several thousand, is generally considered to be the turning point which led to the expulsion of those known as 'The Ranters' from the orthodox (Wesleyan) Methodists.

Mow Cop is now owned by the National Trust. The usual restrictions on commercial photography therefore apply but the building and surrounding land is freely open to the public. Good vantage points are accessible from a number of positions and directions.

desirable lighting. This greatly reduces the chances of making a wasted journey and also improves the odds of photographing the subject at its best.

Having previously visited Mow Cop, which is perched on a hilltop in an imposing, elevated position, I had decided to photograph the ancient folly as a silhouette against a twilit sky. I very rarely record a subject as a complete silhouette, but my decision to do so on this occasion was influenced by the monument's interesting outline, its arches and windows and also its high westerly outlook, which would enable me to photograph the building against an evening sky at sunset.

The right conditions eventually materialised with the sun and moon in absolutely perfect positions. Arriving in good time (approximately two hours before sunset), and strolling around the hilltop, I realised that there was another photograph to be had, quite different but in its own way just as effective as the silhouette. The best position required an energetic scramble over rocky terrain, followed by a somewhat ambitious and quite precarious balancing act. As I carefully set up my camera, the evening sunlight gradually became more discriminating in its illumination of the landscape and as the light faded, the folly began to glow with an ever increasing intensity against the evening sky. As I watched, the grey stone of the building was bathed in a rich golden light which lasted for only a few seconds.

Picture taken, I then changed position and moved behind the monument to face west, ready to shoot the photograph I had originally planned. The magic continued. As well as a glowing horizon I was blessed with a crescent moon in a perfect position. If ever there was a 'right time, right place' this was surely it.

What often surprises people is the fact that both pictures were taken within 45 minutes of each other. Little wonder that most landscape photographers prefer early morning or late evening – it is because they know, from experience, that it is then when the power of light is at strongest. ❖

Planning

Location Four miles south of Congleton, Cheshire.

How to get there Leave Congleton via the A527. On the outskirts of the town, just past Mossley Hall Golf Club, turn right into a minor road. Continue for three miles then follow the signs to the Mow Cop car park.

What to take Mow Cop is easily accessible therefore no special equipment or clothing is necessary.

Other times of year Mow Cop can be photographed throughout the year. During the summer months you should arrive either early morning or late evening to (a) avoid people and (b) benefit from soft, directional lighting. Stormy weather would also be interesting because it would bring drama to an already dramatic setting.

Nearest Pub Alsager, an attractive village three miles west of Mow Cop, has a good selection of pubs, restaurants and hotels.

Other places of interest Three miles northwest of Mow Cop, Little Moreton Hall is possibly Britain's finest timber-framed moated manor house. A quite magnificent building, it photographs well and has an interesting knot garden. It is owned by the NT and is closed during the winter months, so check opening times before travelling.

Ordnance Survey map Landranger 118; grid ref 856 573

Essential reading Mow Cop appears in many local interest and travel guides.

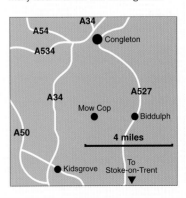

WHITE PEAK

There are still areas of Britain where you can find a profusion of meadow wildflowers. One of the best, says **Mark Hamblin**, is in Derbyshire's White Peak district

Useful tips

● When photographing at a new place, take time to walk around and search for good specimens and viewpoints before reaching for your camera.

● Don't be put off by dull, wet or windy conditions. Droplets of rain on foliage or the movement of tall plants swaying in the wind will add an extra dimension to your pictures.

● Invest in a tripod that will operate at ground level and use it to aid composition and support the camera.

● When working with long exposures in low light, lock up the mirror (if your camera has this facility) and use a remote shutter release to reduce the risk of camera shake.

● Consider the background to the main subject. For wideangle shots, include something of interest and stop down the lens for maximum depth of focus. To isolate a flower use a short telephoto set at a wide aperture. Check the effects of different apertures using the depth of field preview button.

● Use a reflector to bounce light into dark shadows. In bright sunshine, a diffuser will reduce harsh contrast.

● Choose a film that gives you pleasing colours. Fuji Velvia is great in overcast conditions, while Fuji Sensia is a good alternative in bright sunshine.

Conservation

Many of the flowers of the White Peak are found in fragile habitats that must be respected. Where flowers are growing en masse, photograph from the edge of the group to avoid trampling plants, and be very careful if lying down to photograph or when setting up your tripod to ensure you do not destroy other nearby flowers. If a flower or plant is in an awkward or unattractive situation, do not be tempted to 'garden' around the subject, but look elsewhere for a more suitable specimen.

A copy of the Code of Conduct for the Conservation and Enjoyment of Wild Plants can be obtained by sending an sae to The Botanical Society of the British Isles, The Natural History Museum, Cromwell Road, London, SW7 5BD.

A WILDFLOWER meadow in early summer, vibrant with colour and full of newborn birds and animals forms an idyllic picture. Chocolate box scenes depict swathes of buttercups and poppies swaying in a gentle breeze, while skylarks sing from high in an azure blue sky. Despite the many changes in agriculture over the past few decades, there still remains a wonderful diversity of flowers and plants within the British Isles, many of which are quite easily accessible to photographers throughout the country.

Within easy reach of some of the most populated areas of Britain lies the White Peak, an area of limestone dales and meandering rivers that forms the southern part of the Peak District National Park. The dales – with disused quarries and old railway embankments – provide the perfect habitat for a diverse range of flowers, many of which are at their peak during June and July.

Overcast lighting

These abundant flowers make ideal subjects, whatever the lighting conditions. When moving in closer to subjects such as these, my personal preference is for soft, overcast lighting as this reduces the contrast and brings out the detail, as well as saturating the colours. Close-up macro pictures work extremely well in overcast light in combination with Fuji Velvia film. I also use an 81A colour correction filter in certain situations to increase the warmth of the final image.

Wider shots are best saved for brighter conditions when there is usually a more interesting sky. When I took the main picture shown here, the foreground was lit by weak, diffused sun, while darker clouds bubbled over the barn in the background. This ideal lighting produced good detail and colour in the wild thyme, which was the main focal point of the picture.

By fitting a 55mm wideangle lens onto my Pentax 67 and selecting a low viewpoint I was able to fill the lower portion of the frame with the flowers and include the stone barn as an important element of the background. The choice of a low angle of view produced a more intimate and striking view of the flowers, while the inclusion of the barn conveyed the habitat of this area.

To achieve optimum focus from the flowers to the barn, I stopped down to f/22 and focused the lens one third into the picture. The depth of field provided at f/22 then brought both the closest flowers and the barn into sharp focus. I checked this using the depth of field preview button. The result hints at the wildness of nature which can still be found in the UK. ❖

Opposite page There is a simplicity about blocks of uniform colour that works well photographically. Here, I chose a wideangle lens to include the sky and clouds, thereby adding further interest to the picture *Pentax 67 with 55mm lens, Velvia, 1/15sec at f/16*

Far left This plant uses mimicry to lure bees to land and help pollinate the flowers. I moved in close with a macro lens and filled the frame with two flowers to illustrate this 'bee-like' mimicry *Canon EOS 1n, Tamron 90mm macro lens, Sensia, 1/60sec at f/8*

Below left When selecting an aperture for this type of picture it can be difficult to achieve good focus on the flower head while maintaining a muted background. In this case I compromised and set an aperture of f/8, keeping the front of the flower sharp while making it stand out from the grasses behind *Canon EOS 1n, Tamron 90mm macro lens, Sensia, 1/125sec at f/8*

Planning

Location The White Peak lies approximately between the towns of Buxton, Bakewell, Matlock and Ashbourne in the heart of Derbyshire. Where to visit: Millers Dale Quarry (SK 140731), Lathkill Dale (SK 203665), Chee Dale (SK 120727), the Monsal Trail (SK 186715), Hopton Quarry (SK 262562) and Rose End Meadows (SK 93567) all offer a good range of flowers.
What to shoot Common spotted, fragrant, pyramidal and bee orchid, grass of Parnassus, buttercups, ox-eye daisies, common poppies, wild thyme, bloody cranesbill, yellow rattle, knapweed and dog roses are just a small number of flowers present.
What to take A comfortable rucksack in which to carry your camera gear. A waterproof sheet on which to kneel or lie. Knee-pads can be useful on hard quarry floors.
Time of day Shoot early or late in the day if the sun is shining, or use a diffuser. In overcast conditions you can photograph all day. Mornings are often less windy.
Other times of year Any season is excellent for landscape pictures. Spring is also good for flowers such as cowslips and early purple orchids.
Ordnance Survey map Outdoor Leisure 24
Recommended reading *Wildlife on your Doorstep: A guide to the Nature Reserves managed by the Derbyshire Wildlife Trust* (01332 756610)

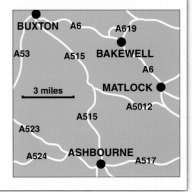

STIRLING

The site of many a bloody battle, historic Stirling is nowadays a more peaceful place but, says **Dave Robertson**, still has plenty to offer the photographer

VISITORS HAVE BEEN coming to Stirling for hundreds of years. English armies sallied over the border many times with the town in their sights. They were met by the likes of Robert the Bruce, King of Scots and, before him, Sir William Wallace. Great battles were fought within sight of Stirling Castle and it is this history that provides superb photo opportunities for today's visitors.

If it is your first visit to Stirling I would recommend starting at the castle which overlooks the town, as from here you can see all the main sites to photograph. To the south is Bannockburn, where Robert the Bruce defeated the English King Edward. The statue there of the Scottish hero King is very powerful and one of my favourite photographs to take while visiting Stirling is a silhouette

Facts about Stirling

Stirling has been at the centre of Scottish history from the time of the Picts. The famous battle (English readers might consider it infamous!) of Bannockburn was fought nearby and Wallace's victory was won nearby to the Auld Brig. Today Stirling is more welcoming to its visitors and is considered to be an ideal base for touring further afield in Scotland.

Tourism is very important to Stirling's economy and has a lot to offer. There are several visitor centres, attractions, walks and many events such as the Beltane Festival and the Highland Games. Stirling Castle has undergone a multi-million pound renovation lasting 25 years and is one of the most popular attractions in Scotland.

of this statue against the setting sun. Looking north from the Castle Esplanade you can see the 'Auld Brig' of Stirling that spans the River Forth and, further on, the Wallace Monument. This view is worth taking at any time of the year, but in October the backdrop of the Ochils creates a vivid patchwork of golden brown and yellow.

Of course, the weather is not always perfect! If outside conditions are not good, take a look inside the Church of the Holy Rude. With permission from the custodian you can picture the fine stain glass windows and with a wideangle lens there is a fine shot to be had of the choir and apse.

Stirling Castle is a superb subject and is best viewed from the King's Knott to the south of the castle. The castle is not sunlit until the afternoon and looks best in the late evening sunshine. Hang on until dark to see the castle illuminated.

Wallace at dawn

As prominent as the castle is the Wallace Monument, which stands on Abbey Craig. In my files I have pictures of the monument taken from every angle, but the main photograph here is the one I like best. It involves an early start to be in position well before dawn at Drumbrae on the hillside above Bridge of Allan. It also involves plenty of warm clothing. There is a car park, but to place the monument above the horizon you will need to walk back down the road, carefully selecting your viewpoint to avoid the telegraph wires. Camera shake ruins any picture so invariably I shoot on a tripod, use my RB67's mirror lock-up facility and a cable release. I used a 360mm lens on my Mamiya RB67, which is equivalent to about 180mm on a 35mm camera.

It was a case of third time lucky for this shot as I saw the expected sunrise was about to materialise. To calculate the exposure I took a spotmeter reading off the sky next to the monument, which read f/8 at one second on Fuji Velvia rated at ISO 50. No filters were necessary. I knew that the monument and Abbey Craig would fall into silhouette but I wanted to retain some detail below the far horizon and in the brighter part of the sky. A quick check with the spotmeter confirmed that the initial reading would produce the picture I was visualising. The speed at which the sky brightens

Above This view from Stirling Castle esplanade overlooks the Auld Brig, the scene of Wallace's victory and his monument on Abbey Craig, behind which he hid his army. Morning light is best for this shot
Mamiya RB67 with 360mm lens, Velvia, 1/15sec at f/22, polarising and 81B filters

always amazes me. Those few brief minutes before sunrise disappeared in a blur of further meter readings, exposure adjustments and firing the shutter. I find that with dawn and dusk shots there is no single correct exposure, so bracketing with a range of exposures will always result in at least one successful image.

Stirling is well worth a visit in its own right – don't just pass through on your way to the north of Scotland! ❖

Below Stirling Castle dominates the town and is best seen from the King's Knott, which was once a formal garden. For a daylight shot the evening sunshine can be dramatic, but it's always worth waiting to see the castle illuminated
Mamiya RB67 with 360mm lens, Velvia, 15 seconds at f/8, tripod

Planning

Location Situated on the River Forth about 30 miles east of Edinburgh.
How to get there By road. Stirling is well signed from Edinburgh, Glasgow and from the north. Public transport: By rail and by coach.
What to shoot The Castle, Wallace Monument, Auld Brig, and the Robert the Bruce statue at Bannockburn. Visit Stirling University for the autumn leaves and the near tame rabbits. The lochs and woods of the Trossachs are only 30 miles away and are best seen in the autumn.
What to take A tripod is a must and there are opportunities to use a wide range of lenses.
Where to stay There is accommodation of all types and to suit all budgets. Contact the Tourist Information Centre (01786 475019).
Nearest pub You are spoilt for choice in Stirling. Try the Golden Lion in King

Street (01786 475351).
Other times of year Stirling has potential at all times of year. In snow the castle looks spectacular, as does the main picture seen here. There is a fireworks display on Hogmanay and the Highland Games in July.
Ordnance Survey map Landranger 57
Essential reading *Around Stirling*, written and published by John M Pearson. For a website, try www.scottish.heartlands.org

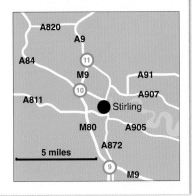

Georgian architecture abounds in East Anglia's Fenland towns, but according to **Lee Frost**, North Brink in Wisbech is about as good as it gets

NORTH BRINK

I'M EMBARRASSED to say it, but having lived in Cambridgeshire for over a decade now, the number of serious photographic excursions I've made in the area could literally be counted on one hand. There's just something about the flat, featureless landscape of the Fens: instead of filling me with inspiration, it leaves me feeling rather numb, and although the area is full of hidden gems I have singularly failed to exploit them.

Until recently, that is. Towards the end of last year I decided it was high time to start exploring my own back

Facts about North Brink

Large-scale draining of the East Anglian Fens during the 17th and 18th centuries created vast tracts of highly fertile farmland and brought great wealth to the region. With much of the produce from the surrounding countryside flowing through its port, Wisbech became a thriving agricultural centre. Evidence of this prosperity can be seen today in the town's Georgian architecture, which was commissioned by wealthy landowners and merchants between 1700-1850. North Brink, on the banks of the River Nene, was described by Pevsner as 'one of the most perfect Georgian streets in England'. Peckover House, in the centre of North Brink, was built in 1722 and belonged to a Quaker banking family – the Peckovers – from the end of the 18th century until 1948 when it was presented to the National Trust. Octavia Hill, a founding member of the National Trust, was born in Wisbech and lived at No 1 South Brink Place. The building has recently opened as a museum in her memory (01945 476358).

yard a little more enthusiastically, and seek out the locations that were worth photographing.

One of the first locations I targeted was the Fenland town of Wisbech. I'd read it had a well-preserved street of Georgian houses along the river and suspected it might have potential. So, when I rose early one autumnal morning last year to be confronted by brilliant sunshine and clear blue skies, I decided there was no time like the present to fulfil my promise.

Arriving on the outskirts of town at around 8.30am, I managed to stumble upon North Brink by chance, mainly because South Brink, the street on the opposite side of the river, is a route into Wisbech town centre. Having located a car park nearby, I then headed back to the riverside with my equipment and started thinking about how to capture the scene on film.

First stop was towards the town end of South Brink, close to Town Bridge, where you get an excellent view along the river and the most interesting section of North Brink. And if the weather is calm, as it was during my visit, vivid reflections of the Georgian houses in the river. I recorded this scene initially with a 55mm wideangle lens on my Pentax 67. The river wall running along South Brink is quite high, and setting up a tripod on the pavement would have meant I recorded the top of the wall in my shot. To avoid this, I placed my LowePro backpack on the wall then rested the camera on top, shooting handheld. A polarising filter was used to boost contrast and colour, and I determined correct exposure by taking an incident reading of light falling onto the scene.

Despite the backpack acting as an excellent support and cushion for my camera, I was still concerned about camera shake. Fortunately, on checking focus I realised that just about everything in the scene was sharp in the viewfinder with focus set to infinity, which meant I didn't need masses of depth-of-field and could set a relatively wide aperture to keep the shutter speed up. In the end I plumped for f/8, which gave me a shutter speed of 1/30sec with the polariser and Velvia.

With this shot in the bag, I switched to a 105mm standard lens and took more shots from the same spot before going for a stroll along the riverside away from the town centre. Fortunately, the further you walk from Town Bridge, the lower the river wall gets so from there on in I was able to use a tripod to support the camera; something I do whenever possible.

Left Use of a telephoto lens for this shot has compressed perspective so the buildings appear crowded together. I like it as much as the main photo, but the effect is completely different *Pentax 67 with 165mm lens and 2x teleconverter, Velvia, 1/2sec at f/16, polariser*

Over the next couple of hours I took a variety of shots from different viewpoints, using a 135mm or 165mm lens on the Pentax, then finally the 165mm with a 2x teleconverter, giving a focal length similar to a 180mm on 35mm format. In each case a polariser was also used. By the end of the morning I had exposed four rolls of 120 film and headed home feeling rather smug. Until that day, Wisbech was the last place on earth I would have thought about photographing, but having done so I can now say, with confidence, that for North Brink alone the town is well worth a visit – and I for one shall certainly be back. ❖

Above As you wander along the riverside, the style of architecture changes, but the scene is no less inviting. For this shot I hopped over the river wall onto the grassy bank to take in much more the North Brink
Pentax 67 with 105mm lens, Velvia, 1/8sec at f/16, polariser

Planning

How to get there Wisbech is located on the A47 approx 20 miles east of Peterborough. As you approach the town centre you will drive along South Brink with the River Nene to your left. North Brink is on the opposite bank. Before reaching the town bridge, turn right onto Somers Road and park in the car park. The walk back to South Brink takes just a minute or two.

Where to stay Try the Hare & Hounds Hotel (01945 583607) and the Phoenix Hotel (01945 474559), both of which are on North Brink.

Nearest pub The Hare & Hounds Hotel – see above.

What to shoot The classic view of North Brink is looking across the River Nene from South Brink, with reflections of the Georgian houses in the river. You could also shoot architectural details or reflections in the river with a telephoto lens. If you're there between March 27th and October 31st, be sure to visit the National Trust's Peckover House on North Brink (01945 583463). The Crescent, off Bridge Street, is also home to more beautiful Georgian buildings.

Best time of day For views across the River Nene to North Brink, arrive during the morning. For shots of Peckover House from the gardens,

visit during the afternoon.

Best time of year I photographed North Brink during early autumn, but any time of year would be suitable in the right weather. A crisp winter's morning with mist rising off the river could be rather special.

What to take A general selection of photo gear including polariser and warm-up filters, lenses from 28-200mm and a tripod. The town centre is a stone's throw away, so you can grab a coffee and a sandwich after a busy morning's photography then head to Peckover House in the afternoon.

Ordnance Survey map Landranger sheet 142 or 143.

Essential Reading *A Breath of East Anglia* by Rod Edwards, which highlights the best subjects and scenery in the region. £12.99 (paperback), Jarrold Publishing, ISBN 0-7117-1026-0.

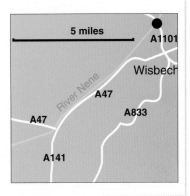

Whoever developed a fishing village in this dip on the North Yorkshire coast must have had photography in mind. **Mike Kipling** tells what makes it so photogenic

ON A CORNER of the North Yorkshire coast, nestled into a tight, curving valley under the lee of massive cliffs, sits the village of Staithes. An unspoilt red roofed fishing community, it is remarkably similar to – though bleaker than – several Cornish villages. Perhaps this is to do with its position, facing out into the North Sea, or perhaps it's because of Boulby Cliffs to the north – the highest in England, towering 660 feet above the sea.

Staithes also attracts fewer visitors than any Cornish fishing village, so commercialisation has not ruined its character. In fact, the young James Cook, who worked in the town as a boy, would probably still recognise the place, while photographs of Staithes by the eminent Victorian photographer Frank Meadow Sutcliffe show little change at all. All this is great for photography. Currently much effort is going into restoration and conservation to protect this unique place and any development is carefully managed.

There are two approaches to photographing Staithes. The first is to scour the village for the wealth of detail. The second, illustrated here, is to show the whole village in its setting. There is a spectacular view from high above the beck at Cowbar Cottages, looking down the valley to the sea. This is the typical view, everybody does it, and a

STAITHES

Facts about Staithes

Staithes is a conservation area located in the North York Moors National Park and on the Cleveland and North Yorkshire Heritage Coast. It is a very sensitive area and should be respected. Do not try to drive down into the village or to Cowbar slipway. The roads are very narrow and there is no parking for non-residents, so park at the car parks provided at the top of the banks.

If you venture on to the beaches beyond the breakwaters check tide times, as it is very easy to be cut off. Stay off the breakwaters in rough weather. Some of the viewpoints I have used are on the cliff tops. Stay away from the edges and do not venture anywhere near cliff edges in windy conditions.

Public access is available through the many alleys and ginnels. Remember people live in the village so don't interfere with their privacy. If you need to go onto private land to take a picture, just ask – most people will give permission.

Left The village and Boulby Cliffs can only be seen together from the slope behind Church Street or from the cliff top. It's a bit of a scramble to get up there, and can get very windy, so take extra care when shooting. This shot was taken during the late afternoon. Cowbar Nab, from where the main shot was taken, is in the centre distance. *Bronica ETRSi with 50mm lens, Provia 100, 1/30sec at f/11; polarising and 81A filters*

seat has even kindly been provided. Despite its popularity, however, it is still worth spending some time on getting the right shot. Early evening is perfect, when the sun gently warms the stone cottages.

Another grand view is from the other side of the village. Climb the slope behind Church Street and look back towards Boulby. It is also worthwhile – if sea and tide conditions permit – to photograph the village from either of the two breakwaters, preferably with boats in the harbour.

For me, the best location is to photograph from Cowbar Nab. The nab is owned by the National Trust and this sweeping promontory protects the village from the ravages of north easterly gales. Access is from the road leading down to Cowbar, a stile has been provided where the road bends. The location for my shot is at the end of the nab looking back over the village. This can be a hard work picture! Because the village faces north it can only be achieved in summer. In order to ensure the lighting is right and the sun is not in your lens or putting the village into shade, it can only be achieved before 6am. To add to the difficulties, not only is good light needed for this shot but it must also be taken when the tide is in and the air is still, to reflect the

buildings in the water. I estimate there is less than one hour of flexibility either side of high tide.

I took the photograph with a 40mm lens on a Bronica ETRSi (equivalent of a 24mm lens on a 35mm camera). The camera was tripod mounted and an exposure of 1/125sec at f/5.6 was used on Fuji Velvia film. I added polarising and 81A filters. The use of a relatively fast shutter speed was necessary because of the many flying seagulls. The cliff at Cowbar Nab is a nesting site and, however careful you are, the gulls will be disturbed and on a long shutter speed a flying gull will leave a white streak on film. ❖

Below Boulby Cliffs' distinctive profile, scarred by the mining of alum, is best seen from Cowbar Nab. In fact, turn around from the location of the main picture and this is the view you see. However, it has to be taken at sunset in summer, leaving all day to explore the village and surrounding area
Bronica ETRSi, 40mm lens, Velvia, 1/30sec at f/11; 0.6 grey grad

Planning

Location Staithes is located on the North Yorkshire coast approximately 15 miles north of Whitby and 20 miles east of Middlesbrough.

How to get there By road, take the A171 from Middlesbrough to Guisborough, then the A173 to Skelton to join the A174. After Loftus, Staithes is six miles. From Whitby take the A174 signposted to Saltburn. There is a rail service to both Middlesbrough and Whitby and a regular bus service to Staithes from both. For walkers, the Cleveland Way long distance footpath passes through the village and along the top of Boulby Cliffs.

What to shoot Vistas of the village and cliff tops. Sunset and dawn over the sea, only possible at this time of year. The narrow ginnels and alleys. Visit on Lifeboat Day, 29 July, if you can. Visit the privately run Staithes Museum on the High Street and talk to Reg who is a font of knowledge on the village and Captain Cook.

What to take Walking shoes for cliff top walks and waterproofs. It can be very exposed if the weather turns bad. Tide timetables. Plenty of film, as

there is nowhere in the village to buy specialist film.

Nearest pub There are several pubs in the village. The Cod and Lobster (01947 840295) on the sea front does excellent local fish and chips and crab sandwiches.

Other times of the year Late autumn and winter when it is frosty and misty. The smoking chimneys, red roofs and low sun can provide the chance for atmospheric photography.

Ordnance Survey map Outdoor Leisure 27, North York Moors Eastern Area

Essential reading 'History and Geology of Staithes' by Jean and Peter Eccleston, the Post Office, High Street, Staithes TS13 5BH, price £7.99.

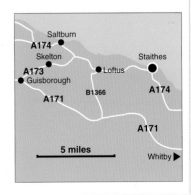

 Brighton's derelict but photogenic West Pier comes alive when thousands of starlings use it as a place to roost. **James Warwick** has witnessed this spectacle

DURING FEBRUARY 1998 I made repeated visits to Brighton's derelict West Pier. Well, it didn't take too much effort on my part because I only live five minutes walk from it. I not only wanted to capture the pier's unique structure protruding into the English Channel, but also the drama of a natural spectacle in the form of a flock of starlings that use the pier as a place to roost. Living so close to my quarry enabled me to be very selective about when I photographed this scene. At this time of year, the lighting conditions are often superb, without the problems of haziness inherent to the summer months.

When starlings mass to roost in winter, they form one of the great natural wonders of the world. The huge flocks can often be millions strong, although I

Above A slow shutter speed, resulting from the low light level and a stopped down aperture that ensured sufficient depth of field, created a strong sense of movement throughout the flock
Nikon F90X with 28-80mm lens, Fujichrome Sensia 100, tripod

would estimate the number of birds in the main picture to be in the tens of thousands. They collect and swirl in one amorphous cloud and as they change direction, seemingly simultaneously (I don't think anyone quite knows how they manage this!), you can hear them clearly as their wings rip through the air. Although they usually choose to roost in reed beds or trees, a manmade structure, particularly a derelict one such as the West Pier, can provide a perfectly secure place for

Facts about the West Pier

The West Pier is widely thought to be England's finest seaside pier and is the only Grade I listed pier in the country. It opened in 1866 and extra buildings were added up until 1916 when the concert hall was completed. Initially it was a place for the Victorian middle classes to socialise and take in the sea air, but by the 1920s it had evolved into a 'pleasure pier', with a great variety of seaside entertainment both indoors and out, such as

paddle steamer excursions and pantomimes.

The pier is unique in that it has largely been unaltered since that time. However, in 1975 it was closed due to financial problems and since then it has been in an ever-increasing state of dereliction. The West Pier Trust was created to save the pier and renovation work (funded privately and by the National Lottery) is to start soon, possibly just in time before it collapses into the sea.

WEST PIER

Above My eye was drawn by the golden reflections in the windows of what was once the pier's concert hall. A slow shutter speed created an almost surreal 'scratching effect' from the birds swirling above the building
Nikon F90X; 70-300mm lens; Fujichrome Sensia 100; tripod

Above The intense colour of the sky in this picture is typical of the winter months on the south coast
Nikon F90X; 28-80mm lens; Sensia 100; tripod

the birds to spend the night.

When I arrived at the water's edge on the evening I took the main picture, I had to rush to set up my tripod, realising the fleeting potential of the scene before me. I carefully positioned the sun in the space underneath the pier and included a small section of pebbles at the bottom of the frame to create a balance. All that remained for me to do then was to leave enough space above the pier for the birds to fill as they 'exploded' from the roof and performed their wondrous display. Although they did this several times before finally settling down for the night, this picture was the first frame of about 10 that I took that evening.

The slow shutter speed, resulting from the low light level and a stopped down aperture that ensured sufficient depth of field, created a strong sense of movement throughout the flock. It also allowed enough time for the swirling shape of the flock to follow that of the pier. With this kind of photography, there's only really so much planning and anticipation you can do – the rest is down to good fortune.

If and when the renovation plans for the West Pier do go ahead, its peace and security will have been broken, and sadly the starlings will have to find somewhere else to show off their breathtaking acrobatic skills. ❖

Above Using a wideangle lens from a reasonably low perspective enabled me to accentuate the different colours and shapes of the pebbles on Brighton beach. In fact, if you look hard enough, you can see a swirl of starlings above the pier in the distance
Nikon F90X with 28-80mm lens; Fujichrome Sensia 100; tripod

Planning

Location The West Pier is close to the border between Brighton and Hove, opposite Regency Square.

How to get there By car from the north, the A23 leads you straight to the coast. Turn right at the roundabout in front of the Brighton Pier (formerly the Palace Pier), and the West Pier is about 1km further west along the coast road. From Brighton railway station, head directly south to the sea and turn right. You can't miss it!

What to shoot When photographing the starlings I think the strongest pictures are those which show the whole spectacle rather than just a zoomed in section of it. But the building itself is a fascinating structure and sometimes close-ups of it can work well, especially when some sea and sky are included.

What to take A range of lenses from 24mm to 300mm would be ideal, particularly if they are zooms, because they allow you to hone your compositions without actually moving yourself. Sunset really is the best time to make dramatic pictures, so a tripod is an absolute necessity with the inevitably slow exposures.

Nearest pub There can't be a wildlife photographic location in the world with more pubs close by than this one! Try any of the seafront bars between the West and Brighton Piers.

Other times of year Photographing here at other times will often lead to disappointing results because it is from November to March when the skies are at their most interesting and the atmosphere at its least hazy.

Ordnance Survey map Landranger 198

Essential reading The novel *Breakfast in Brighton*, by Nigel Richardson, published by Victor Gollancz (ISBN 0 5754 0201 6), is non-essential but helps you to appreciate the town's unique eccentricity before tackling the West Pier, Brighton's most eccentric building!

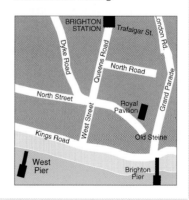

TEESMOUTH

An industrial landscape can be a dramatic and often awe-inspiring combination. **Mike Kipling** takes us to his favourite such location

THE MAJORITY OF my photography is evenly divided between traditional landscape photography of countryside and coast, and photography of strong urban subjects usually in built up areas. Rarely, I find, do both these interests come together. One place, however, where the two combine, is the South Gare area of the Tees estuary, a few miles north of Redcar.

This small, visually exciting area forms the most northerly part of the North Yorkshire coast. There is a steel making complex, a vast stretch of beautiful sandy

beach backed by dunes, a breakwater complete with lighthouse, and a fishing community complete with its own little harbour (delightfully known as Paddy's Hole). And, due to the rare flora and an important bird population, most of the area outside the steelworks is designated a Site of Special Scientific Interest. It is also one of the few areas on the north east coast where the sun sets behind an expanse of water all through the year.

This makes an exciting blend. The blast furnace, higher than St Paul's Cathedral and the largest in Europe

Facts about Teesmouth

Beyond the council depot at Warrenby, the whole area is private land owned by the steel works and the port authority. Access is permitted by car and on foot but under no circumstances try to access the steel plant, which is fenced off. Park on the Gare, but do not try to drive to the lighthouse or obstruct access to the lifeboat. Certain areas may be fenced off due to nesting birds, rare plants or

conservation work. Do not enter these areas. When the sea is rough, the area around the lighthouse can be dangerous due to breaking waves and if you venture onto Bran Sands at low tide take care because this area of the estuary, although shallow, floods fast. As is usual when shooting around salt water and sand, take special care of your equipment.

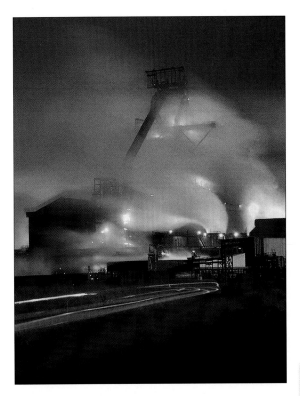

semi silhouette of the steelworks. The main photograph here was taken during the late afternoon. After a shower, the sun glints on the roofs of the huts and is a lucky bonus. Your camera will be pointing south east into the sun, so if the sun is low ensure your lens is properly hooded.

A short telephoto lens is essential for compressing perspective and increasing the apparent scale of the works compared with the huts. I always use a tripod, cable release and lock up the mirror. These three actions are critical to eliminate camera shake – they make a considerable difference to the quality of images, especially with longer lenses. I took a spotmeter reading from the centre of the picture, which gave me an exposure of 1/4sec at f/22 on Fuji Velvia, rated at ISO 40. A polarising filter and 0.3 grey grad was used over the sky area to ensure it did not overexpose. An 81A filter was also used to slightly warm the image.

However, the most important aspect of achieving this picture was timing. The steam plumes from the coke ovens billow out only every 15 minutes or so. I waited until one was vented and released the shutter when it created a frame for the works. Do not wait too long for your perfect shot, though, as the plume dissipates quickly in windy conditions. ❖

Far left One of the great attractions of this area is that the access road runs alongside the blast furnace, allowing relatively close photography of this massive structure. This shot was taken at the cross over light time between daylight and dark, and I spotmetered from just below the top of the furnace. This gave a reading of eight seconds at f/11, so I doubled this to avoid reciprocity failure. Then all I had to do was wait until a car passed to record the tail lights on film.
Bronica ETRSi with 150mm lens, Velvia, 16 seconds at f/11

– together with the coke ovens, gasometers, ore terminal and myriad pipes and chimneys – dominates the landscape. The furnace and coke making plants continually pour steam and smoke into the air and the whole complex is awash with light at night.

Whenever photographing this dramatic scene, I make the steelworks the focus of the photograph, but at the same time capture the environment in which the steelworks are located. The composition looking across the fishermen's huts is one of my favourite viewpoints. It contrasts the scale and might of this industrial giant with the little wooden huts where fishermen while away their time waiting for the tide. It is taken from the access road, which is elevated above the huts. If you are lazy you can just park and shoot!

Any time of the year between July and March is suitable, and the best time of day is between 11am and 4pm to ensure some backlighting of the steam and a

Above High tide and still conditions provide the best opportunity for this shot across Paddy's Hole. Different times of the year provide the opportunity to vary the industrial background, but I find early autumn best. For this shot I spotmetered from the water area above the boats
Bronica ETRSi with 40mm lens, Velvia, 1/2sec at f/11, 0.6 grey grad and 81C filters

Planning

Location North east England. Eight miles east of Middlesbrough, two miles north of Redcar.

How to get there From Middlesbrough take the A66 and A1085 to Redcar. On arriving at Redcar turn left onto Kirkleatham Lane (Arriva Vauxhall Garage on your left). At the roundabout 1/4 mile over the rail bridge turn left and follow this road through Warrenby Industrial estate until you pass the blast furnace on your left. Continue for another mile to park. An alternative for the active is to continue across the roundabout after the rail bridge; in about 1/4 mile alongside the beach you will come to the Majuba Road car park. Park here and walk along the beach and dunes to the Gare, a four to five mile round trip. Although there is a good bus and local rail service to Redcar, there is no public transport to the Gare.

What to shoot The steelworks with a foreground of dunes, the beach, fishermen's huts and fishing boats. Ships entering and leaving the estuary, the lighthouse and numerous details in the huts and boats. Some of the fishermen are characters and will pose if you ask.

What to take The land is flat and exposed and it can be windy and cold, so it is worthwhile taking warm clothes at any time of the year. If you wander over the slag areas the ground can be rough, so stout shoes are useful, and if you wander into the sea to take pictures, as I do, then take your wellies. Take plenty of film, as

the nearest proper camera shops are at Middlesbrough – Cleveland Camera Mart and Jessops. A wide lens is an asset and grey or ND grads are important for balancing the sky with the land. Skies are often essential to successful images in this flat area. There is nowhere on the Gare to buy food or drink so take a picnic.

Nearest Pub There is no pub on the Gare, but there are several in Redcar. The nearest is The Lobster (John Smiths) on Coatham Road (01642 483574).

Other times of the year The great attraction of this area is that it provides exciting photographic opportunities any time of the year, the significant difference is where the sun sets over the estuary.

Ordnance Survey map OS Pathfinder Series Scale 1:250,000, Sheet 591 Billingham and Teesmouth.

Essential reading For an account of what life was like in the Teesside steel industry in the 19th century, read 'At the Works' by Lady Bell, published by Teesside University, Middlesbrough TS1 3BH, price £9.95.

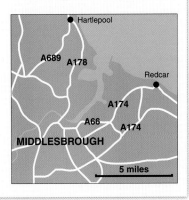

The Lord Mayor's Show and Guy Fawkes mean November in London is a time for photographing fireworks. **Pawel Libera** reveals how he goes about it

LONDON FIREWORKS

AS WE HEAD INTO autumn, we start thinking of the festive season, and at this time of year especially, that means firework displays. These offer enormous photographic opportunities, but also create problems for those trying to record them on film.

An obvious time to take firework pictures is around 5 November when we celebrate Guy Fawkes' Night. Every local park or common ground organises bonfires and has firework displays in the evening.

This season of fireworks lasts for about a week and in my experience, the most spectacular shows are those organised by local authorities in bigger cities. For the past few years I have attended the firework display which closes the City of London's Lord Mayor's Show and takes place on the River Thames on the second Saturday of November. I like this particular event as it gives a lot of opportunities for choosing angles, vantage points and gives plenty of framing options, including a variety of backdrops.

Even the most basic camera can be used for this sort of picture-taking. This is because we only need to use a pre-selected lens aperture and time exposure – either 'B' or 'T'. In the case of using modern electronic cameras, the program mode should be switched to manual. Because fireworks create bursts of light which, surprisingly enough, are quite constant, we only have to adjust the aperture in a similar way as when shooting

with a flashgun. The time for which the shutter remains open will control the number of explosions registered and ambient background light. I use the rule that for film speed of ISO 50 the aperture should be set at f/5.6-8, and for ISO 100 at f/8-11.

The picture shown above, of fireworks bursting over the City of London was taken on the evening of the Lord Mayor's Show. As I had attended many previous displays, I was familiar with the location and my main decision concerned the best place from which to photograph, where I would be able to include nicely lit London landmarks in the background of my picture.

Knowing that the show began at 5pm, I arrived 1½ hours earlier, and decided to position myself on Waterloo Bridge. This gave me some time to finely adjust my viewpoint, as I knew that the fireworks were going to be detonated from the barges moored on the river – although you can never be sure about the height of the bursts until the first few fireworks go off.

I decided to use the 50mm standard lens on my Nikon F5. Because of the lack of any foreground detail, the lens was focused to infinity. It may be a good idea to tape the lens in this position, using a small piece of electrical vinyl tape, to prevent shifting focus when shooting in darkness.

As mentioned earlier I wanted to have an attractive and recognisable backdrop, so decided to include St

Paul's Cathedral and the City of London skyline. My previous shots of St Paul's indicated that optimal exposure was 4-6 seconds at f/8-11, long enough to register about four or five bursts of fireworks.

A sturdy tripod is essential as the wind at this time of year can be pretty strong and, if shooting from a bridge, your position exposed. Not only that, but it's easy to forget that there will be quite a lot of other keen spectators trying to get a good view and knocking into your tripod's legs!

One potential problem which occurs when photographing from bridges is the movement created by moving traffic, and this was certainly the case even on the concrete construction of Waterloo Bridge. I made a point of keeping an eye out for oncoming buses, as these vehicles are the most likely to induce camera shake. To avoid problems, I made sure not to release the shutter when a bus was approaching.

The only control I was bothered with was a fine

adjustment of cropping at the top of the frame after I assessed the height of the explosions. I was also aware of the accumulating effect of smoke following the explosions, which was obscuring the clear view. In fact, I even had to stop taking photographs for a while because the smoke was so thick!. This may be of particular concern on windless and wet nights when smoke will build up after just a few explosions and may prevent you from getting good photographs. ❖

Below A slightly different viewpoint was chosen to put more weight on the fireworks, but still giving a suggestion of location. There may be an alternative shot by close cropping just on the fireworks, but the base created by the line of buildings gives an impression of stability
Nikon F4 with Nikkor lens, Fujichrome Provia, exposed on 'B' for six seconds at f/11

Planning

Location Waterloo Bridge or balconies of National Film Theatre with public access.

How to get there The closest London Underground stations are Waterloo and Embankment, although fireworks can be watched from both banks of the river between Waterloo and Blackfriars Bridge.

What to shoot Make the most of the famous London landmarks, using them as a background when shooting from Waterloo Bridge in the east, or the House of Parliament to the south (from the left bank). Additionally, every large local municipality ground will organise displays within first two weeks of November. To find out times watch billboards and arrive early. The best vantage points tend to be slightly higher. Watch out for people obscuring your view. To avoid this altogether, try to be in the first row or next to the barrier. Include some foreground to illustrate the height of the fireworks, and to give your shot a strong base.

What to take Standard and wideangle lenses of about 28-35mm. You might like to try a short telephoto used to zoom in on the firework explosion alone. Don't forget the tripod! Best film is slow to medium speed, ISO 50-100, warm clothing, and a torch to find your way around the place and the equipment in your bag.

Time of day After dusk, usually between 5pm and 8pm in autumn and winter, about 10-10.30pm in summer.

Time of year The busiest season for fireworks is between November and the new year, although watch out too for summer shows connected with special occasions, such as the summer concerts at Kenwood House, north London, during July.

Nearest pub There is a multitude of pubs and restaurants on both sides of Waterloo Bridge including the South Bank complex on one side and Covent Garden on the other.

Essential reading *Time Out* – for details of major firework displays as well as the *Evening Standard*'s Hot Tickets.

Website www.londontown.com

CONTRIBUTORS' CONTACT DETAILS

Pierino **Algieri** *(see page 40)*

Bry Dedwydd
Penrhiw
Llandoged
Conwy
LL26 0BZ
Tel: 01492 642183
E-mail: sales@algieri-images.pjww.co.uk
Website: www.algieri-images.pjww.co.uk

Philip **Askew** *(see page 10)*

Tel: 01503 264235

Steve **Austin** *(see pages 30 and 94)*

17 Burn Brae
Westhill
Inverness
IV2 5RH
Tel: 01463 790533
E-mail: steveaustin@care4free.net

B. **Baskar** *(see page 84)*

35 Arklow Road
Intake, Doncaster
South Yorkshire
DN2 5LB
Tel: 01302 366 666 (daytime)
E-mail: bskr@btinternet.com

Niall **Benvie** *(see pages 16, 20, 34 and 92)*

24 Park Road
Brechin, Angus
Scotland
DD9 7AP
Tel/fax: 01356 626 128
Mobile: 0780 1067 160
E-mail: niall@niallbenvie.com
Website: www.niallbenvie.com

David **Cantrille** *(see pages 76 and 98)*

High Views, Beach Road
West Bexington, Dorchester
Dorset
DT2 9DG
Tel: 01308 897798
E-mail: david.cantrille@ukgateway.net

Joe **Cornish** *(see pages 2, 12, 24 and 48)*

Derek **Croucher** *(see pages 4, 14, 28, 56 and 66)*

Tel: 01483 211108
Fax: 01483 224922

Steve **Day** *(see pages 58, 62, 72, 88, 104, 106 and 114)*

'Woodcock', 3 Forest Houses,
Farley, Salisbury
Wiltshire
SP5 1AG
Tel: 01722 712713
E-mail: steve@steveday.co.uk

Ruth **Eastham** & Max **Paoli** *(see page 44)*

31 Kerridge Close
Cambridge
CB1 2QW
Tel: 01223 314746
Website: www.wildscapes.co.uk

Guy **Edwardes** *(see page 50)*

'By Ways', St Mary's Lane
Yawl, Uplyme
Lyme Regis
Dorset
DT7 3XH
Tel: 01297 443276
Mobile: 07977 390513
E-mail: guyedwardes@eggconnect.net

Lee **Frost** *(see page 22, 60, 118, 126)*

Tel/Fax: 01733 312266

E-mail: mail@leefrost.demon.co.uk

Steve **Gosling** *(see pages 64, 80 and 116)*

The Red House,
16 St Winifreds Road, Harrogate
North Yorkshire
HG2 8LN
Tel: 01423 881987
Mobile: 0776 996 7933
E-mail: steve.gosling@virgin.net

Gary **Hacon** *(see page 54)*

Tel: 01953 604176

Bill **Hall** *(see page 74)*

13 Alan Avenue
Littleover
Derby
DE23 7RT
Tel: 01332 517878
Mobile: 07775 756 442
E-mail: billhall33@yahoo.co.uk

Mark **Hamblin** *(see pages 86 and 122)*

63 Waller Road
Walkley Bank
Sheffield
S6 5DP
Tel/Fax: 0114 233 3910
E-mail: mark@markhamblin.com
Website: www.markhamblin.com

Granville **Harris** *(see page 78)*

3 Lidgett Grove
Leeds
LS8 1NR
Tel: 0113 2931680

David **Herrod** *(see pages 18 and 32)*

Blencathra House
Mockerkin, Cockermouth,
Cumbria
CA13 0ST
Tel: 01946 861167
E-mail: dherrod@ukgateway.net
Website: www.davidherrod.co.uk

Fred **Hill** *(see page 38)*

64 Holmeriggs Avenue
Penrith
Cumbria
CA11 8NN
Tel: 01768 890711
E-mail: lakeland-landscapes@tinyworld.co.uk

Ross **Hoddinott** *(see pages 6 and 82)*

Higher Broxwater
Kilkhampton, Bude
Cornwall
EX23 9RL
Tel: 01288 321328
E-mail: rosshoddinott@supernet.com
Website: www.rosshoddinott.co.uk

Mike **Kipling** *(see pages 52, 128 and 132)*

1 Weardale
Guisborough
Cleveland
TS14 8JL
Tel: 01287 633665
E-mail: mikipp@ntlworld.com

Pawel **Libera** *(see page 134)*

190 Lionel Road North
Brentford
Middlesex
TW8 9QT
Tel: 020 8560 9819
Fax: 020 8847 2110
E-mail: pawel.libera@btinternet.com

Continued overleaf

Dave **Robertson** *(see page 124)*

35 Strude Mill
Alva
FK12 5JW
Tel: 01259 762901

Geoff **Simpson** *(see page 46)*

'Camberwell'
1 Buxton Road,
New Mills, High Peak,
Derbyshire
SK22 3JS
Tel: 01663 743089
E-mail: info@geoffsimpson.co

Michael **Szarelis** *(see page 68)*

80 Raines Avenue
Worksop
Nottinghamshire
S80 7PB
Tel: 01909 470302

David **Tarn** *(see pages 26, 36, 70 and 102)*

7 Ragworth Place
Norton
Stockton on Tees
TS20 1EL
Tel: 01642 556771
E-mail: david.tarn@virgin.net

Ann & Steve **Toon** *(see page 42)*

6 Lynslack Terrace
Arnside
Cumbria
LA5 0EL
Tel: 01524 762804
E-mail: Sandatoon@aol.com
Website: www.toonphoto.com

Colin **Varndell** *(see pages 8, 90, 96, 100 and 108)*

The Happy Return
Whitecross
Netherbury, Bridport,
Dorset
DT6 5NH
Tel: 01308 488341

James **Warwick** *(see page 130)*

17 Brunswick Square
Hove
BN3 1EH
Tel: 01273 772441
E-mail: james@jameswarwick.co.uk
Website: www.jameswarwick.co.uk

Peter **Watson**

(see page 120, also inside back cover for details of books)

Maythorn Cottage, Buffs Lane
Heswall, Wirral
Merseyside
CH60 2SG
Mobile: 07931 358626
E-mail: peterwatson.lp@virgin.net

Chris **Weston** *(see page 110)*

61 West Street
Lilley
Hertfordshire
LU2 8LH
Tel: 01462 768607
E-mail: chris.weston@naturalphoto.demon.co.uk
Website: www.naturalphoto.demon.co.uk

Keith **Wilson** *(see page 112)*

c/o Outdoor Photography
GMC Publications Ltd, 86 High Street,
Lewes
East Sussex
BN7 1XN
Tel: 01273 477374
E-mail: keithw@thegmcgroup.com

NT IN

DAVID BLAYNEY BROWN

Oil Sketches from Nature

TURNER AND HIS CONTEMPORARIES

TATE GALLERY

cover
J.M.W. Turner
Tivoli, the Cascatelle 1828
detail (cat.no.36)

ISBN 1 85437 075 8
Published by order of the Trustees 1991
for the exhibition of 22 May – 1 September 1991
Copyright © 1991 The Tate Gallery All rights reserved
Designed and published by Tate Gallery Publications,
Millbank, London SW1P 4RG
Photography: Tate Gallery Photographic Department
Typeset in Monophoto Baskerville by Keyspools Ltd, Warrington
Printed and bound in Great Britain by Balding + Mansell plc,
Wisbech, Cambridgeshire on 150gsm Parilux Cream

Contents

FOREWORD

Oil sketching from nature has a long history. For many years enshrined in academic practice as part of an artist's training or as a means of assembling material for subsequent synthesis in the studio, it began to assume a new legitimacy in the Romantic period. In Britain it had no more passionate advocate than Constable. More than any other painter of his generation, he committed himself to the discovery of a new landscape painting, a 'natural painture', through sincere observation on the spot. Turner was more completely a studio painter than Constable, but he too, at certain points in his career, felt the impulse to paint outdoors, and among the many oil sketches in the Turner Bequest are some that were definitely made in the open air. Other British artists of their generation were similarly moved to refresh their imagery or technique through outdoor study in oil, and in recent decades the Tate Gallery has formed a notable collection of their work. The Constable exhibition held here this year seemed to us to present an ideal opportunity for a further display, drawing widely on our collections to survey Turner's activities as an outdoor sketcher and painter alongside works by Constable and other British contemporaries.

Turner is confirmed by this exhibition as only an occasional *plein-airiste*, far more cautious and even ambivalent in his attitude to outdoor painting than Constable. Yet when Turner did embark on campaigns of painting outdoors, he did so to powerful effect. In fact neither Constable nor Turner, nor the other artists shown here, pursued the logic of the open air as far as the Impressionists did, and indeed the mature Constable returned to much the same pictorial values as Turner had always embraced. Yet their work, as seen here, does show an undeniably fresh appreciation of nature and of the possibilities of paint itself. It illuminates the creative tensions between private study and public art, between sketch and finished picture, between the open air and the studio, felt at the beginning of the century that saw the emergence of Impressionism.

To develop these themes, some works not necessarily painted outdoors are juxtaposed with open-air sketches, and the catalogue is prefaced by an essay written across a broad historical and geographical span, relating the exhibits to the artists' wider concerns and to the history and practice of oil sketching from nature in Britain and continental Europe. David Brown would like to record his gratitude for the benefit he has received over the years from conversations with John Gage and Luke Herrmann. He is also most grateful to Peter Galassi and his publishers Yale University Press (especially to John Nicoll and Gillian Malpass in London), for allowing him to see an advance copy of Mr Galassi's book on Corot in Italy and the tradition of oil sketching in Rome (see bibliography). This arrived too late to avoid similarities in the presentation of the historical background in our catalogue; it may be enthusiastically recommended to readers seeking a more comprehensive account than can be provided in the following pages. Thanks are also due to David Hill and to the same publishers, for access to Mr Hill's forthcoming work on Turner's Thames tour of 1805.

Nicholas Serota *Director*

OIL SKETCHING FROM NATURE:
CLAUDE TO THE ROMANTICS

> Open air:– that is the beginning and end of
> the question we are now studying.
> Stéphane Mallarmé

Few of the visual documents of the Romantic period convey so much of the vital spirit of the time as the oil sketch made outdoors from nature. Nowhere is Constable's searching curiosity about the natural world, his unwavering love of the scenery most familiar to him, and his sparkling handling of paint more generously spread before us than in his many oil sketches. Such is their siren beauty that we are tempted to see more of the real man in his brilliantly impromptu impressions of a sunlit Suffolk lane (cat.no.58), the beach at Brighton (cat.no.61) or Hampstead Heath (cat.no.59), or in his even more swiftly caught records of his beloved 'bolder phenomena of nature' (cat.no.60), than in his exhibition pictures composed in the studio. Likewise, Turner's vivid sketches of the wooded banks of the Thames (cat.no.19), yachts skimming the waves off Cowes (cat.no.32), and seas and skies in calm or storm (cat.nos.33, 39) seem to challenge the old barriers between sketch and finished work, private vision and public art.

Yet we should beware. Both Constable and Turner would have vigorously asserted the superiority, aesthetic and moral, of their more considered public statements, while keeping their sketches to themselves; and in this they would have been joined by most of the other painters in Britain and continental Europe who carried their oil colours out-of-doors in the early years of the nineteenth century. There were many of them, and taken together their work seems to proclaim a new empirical spirit in landscape painting. In fact these artists had no particular programme beyond a desire to refer more to the natural world than to other works of art. When it came to picture-making, they had no wish to overturn the established conventions of landscape, or the studio processes that transformed experience into art. Indeed some remained far more slavishly devoted to them than did Constable or Turner. Unlike the Impressionists, they made no special claim for the legitimacy of fleeting effects – those 'differences of minutes' of which Monet declared himself such an 'anxious observer' – and would have offered rather circumspect justifications for their outdoor sketching, considering it a discipline of training and practice like the scales of the concert pianist.

But the fact remains that through isolated but remarkably similar outbreaks of sketching from nature, emerged a recognition that the art of landscape could not remain the same. The old hierarchical structure, descending from ideal and historic compositions designed as vehicles for moral pronouncement to works of descriptive topography, could no longer serve. Direct observation in the open air created its own momentum, bringing painters to a new awareness of the potential of landscape and of painting itself. The naturalistic impulses communicated by their outdoor activities, and the rapid and responsive techniques developed by them, could either be discounted – as they certainly often were – or else demanded fuller acknowledgment. The art of landscape, as Constable realised, must be reconciled to 'the art of seeing nature'.

To bring matters to this point was the particular achievement of the generation of Constable and Turner, though the contributions of those two great landscape painters were very different. Turner's oil sketches are the focus of this exhibition, but it will be seen how much more occasional, and qualified, were his labours in the field than Constable's, and how different were the results in form and function. We claim no very precise connection between the sketching careers of these or other painters, either in Britain or on the Continent. But it is to be hoped that the differences will be as revealing as the similarities; and that a sample of the sketches of Turner, his British predecessors and contemporaries will illuminate the creative tensions of a time when landscape painting stood on the brink of significant change, at the beginning of a road that led inexorably to Barbizon and Ornans, Argenteuil and Pontoise, and the new art of Impressionism.

Early Oil Sketching in Italy and France

Painting outdoors was never easy. Not only were there the hazards of weather to contend with, or the interruptions of curious onlookers, but the materials did not for many years lend themselves to small-scale work in the open. What Lawrence Gowing memorably described as 'the oleous paste in its sticky inconvenience' was impractical enough as a vehicle for spontaneous memoranda, though portable painting boxes were available in Italy at least by the mid 1650s. Until the development of composition surfaces such as millboard, the artist had to carry out with him either paper, which though sized for the purpose was far from ideal as a base for oil, heavier panels of wood, or small pieces of canvas which were not always attached to a stretcher. Unless he resorted to the improvised frames on sticks or folding screens described by various painters, he also needed an easel. A more particular problem was the dazzle of outdoor light, always worse when using oil than watercolour, for apart from anything else the wet pigment reflected it, as Jonathan Skelton found when he tried to paint outdoors in Italy in the 1750s; his oils 'shone so much when they are wet that there is no such thing as seeing what one does'. Even if one could see, the brightness of the light was apt to ruin one's colour sense; Turner found this time and again, as did the Frenchman Karl Robert, who warned that work in open sunshine was impossible without a parasol, for otherwise 'you will make studies that are so dark that you will be totally astonished on returning to the studio, not to be able to see a single detail'. Not surprisingly, the Impressionists and their contemporaries were the most candid on the subject of painting from nature, not only on the practical methods that must be adopted for it, but upon its sheer inconvenience.

For the Impressionists, the practice was central to their philosophy. But it could hardly have become so without the efforts of those painters who had been adventurous or patient enough to persist with an odd, impractical habit in the preceding two centuries. Among the earliest, and the memory to revere, was Claude, whose activities painting outdoors were mentioned by his first biographers, Sandrart and Baldinucci. In fact Sandrart claimed that Claude had adopted the habit on his advice, though his description of Claude's actual practice records not the making of complete landscape designs, but painted records of the gradations of atmospheric tone which he would then assimilate into his finished pictures in the studio. By this account, Claude's habit remarkably anticipates Turner's in his 'colour beginnings' – though Turner's studies of this kind were often made from recent memory rather than on the spot, and more usually in watercolour than oil. But Claude certainly drew outdoors in brush and wash, and his drawings from nature – some of the earliest and loveliest manifestations of pure landscape in the history of art – probably encouraged him to paint it and to attempt a more elaborate representation. Baldinucci describes him painting, outdoors in the Vigna Madama in Rome, a picture which he afterwards kept beside him 'every day to see the variety of trees and foliage'. In any event, whether Claude did or did not paint complete images of landscape outdoors is less important than the fact that later generations believed he did. Constable, who copied the picture sometimes identified as the one described by Baldinucci, the small 'Landscape with Goatherd' in the National Gallery, when it belonged to Sir George Beaumont, considered it a 'Study from Nature', that 'diffuses a life and breezy freshness into the recess of trees which makes it enchanting'. Here then was one of the chief models

Constable had in mind when he himself worked in the fields; it contained 'almost all that I wish to do in landscape'.

Claude's Roman circle was also apparently involved in sketching from nature around the city or in the Campagna. Similar traditions attached to Nicolas Poussin, and to Velazquez during his Roman period, establishing Rome as the undisputed capital of outdoor painting, although the young Salvator Rosa was active in the country around Naples, sketching the sombre and sinister rocks and trees that were to appear in his easel pictures. Thereafter such practices seem to have fallen into disuse, to reappear in more isolated cases at the beginning of the eighteenth century. From Italy the scene shifted to France, where François Desportes, landscapist, animal painter and designer for tapestry and porcelain, began to paint sketches *en plein air* about 1702, and where in 1708 the theorist Roger de Piles recommended oil sketching outdoors in the landscape chapter of his influential book *Cours de peinture par principes* (Constable owned an English edition, and Turner certainly read it). Desportes's son, Claude-François, in a lecture to the French Académie in 1749, gave a graphic description of how and why one artist had set about painting outdoors, and of the materials he used. His father

> had made many of his studies in pencil, but afterwards reflecting on the importance of uniting exactitude of form with precision and truth of local colour, he made it a custom to paint them on a strong paper which was not oiled. What he painted was at first absorbed, thus making it easier to retouch and finish immediately . . . he carried into the fields his brushes and a loaded palette, in metal boxes. He took with him a cane with a long pointed steel tip, to hold it firmly into the ground, and fitted to the head was a small frame of the same metal, to which he attached the portfolio and paper. He never went into the country to visit his friends without taking with him his light baggage, of which he never tired, nor failed to make good use.

Desportes's principal object was to achieve accuracy of natural detail in his finished paintings. Consequently his subjects were often individual trees or plants, or animals and birds, observed from a close viewpoint, but on occasion he was also moved to essay some beautiful studies of more complete views, clumps of trees on a hillside or a flaming sky, that show a more developed landscape sensibility, and a wonderfully fluent handling, as if he were using watercolour rather than oil. His sketches were purely functional, constituting a repertoire of motifs for use in the studio. Yet his painter's eye and sensitive feeling for combinations of sharply observed detail constantly inform them; in the rhythmic fall of slanting tree trunks across a plain page, or in the delicate tracery of flowers and wild plants, his sketches become – like Peter de Wint's remarkably similar plant study of a century later (cat.no.49) – far more than the sum of their parts. Here, as in the sketches of the Romantic painters, we can observe the process, subconscious but inevitable, by which a practical discipline becomes a form of poetry in its own right; there can be little doubt that Desportes had come to feel a real delight in this activity.

The bold and often asymmetric patterns of Desportes's sketches, the quirky repetitions or omissions by which he constructed his *mises-en-page*, show him liberated, as sketchers so often were, from the constraints of convention; in this guise, artists needed to engage only with their subject, and with the eye's perception of it. Theophile Thoré, in 1866, was far from the first to realise that 'to paint in the open air, as one feels and as one sees, without thinking of anyone, either old masters or of the public, is without doubt the way to assure one's own originality'. The difference was simply that originality was not the prime motive of the earlier sketchers; instead they sought only an additional dimension of experience to nourish their art. Yet this particular activity, self-imposed, often awkward but ultimately so rewarding, tended to create a visual language that was, at least potentially, anti-academic. That it should have been undertaken very often as part of academic practice is a paradox; and it is a paradox that became more pronounced as the eighteenth century progressed.

Few oil sketchers have been more objective and free-spirited than the Welshman Thomas Jones, who in 1772 made some remarkable studies of the rolling scenery and wide expanses of sky to be seen from the terrace of his home at Penkerrig, and in 1780 embarked on a still more extraordinary series of studies in Italy. If Skelton had found outdoor painting a nuisance, it was joyous recreation to Jones, the task of 'many a happy hour'. His Italian sketches ranged from an archaeological excavation in Rome – the occasion for a work that comes rather close to conventional picture-making save in its small size and broad handling (cat.no.2) – to the sharp angles and patterns of sunlit walls and roofs seen from the window or roof of his Neapolitan lodgings (cat.no.3). His views of Naples, demanding an abstract and unconventional approach, are like no others in their uncompromising realism, brilliant lighting and expressive brushwork, and above all in their happy coincidence between subject and picture plane. Their 'modernism' is often and rightly stressed, but while Jones surpassed both himself and his century in making them, they had no impact on his art as a whole, nor upon his contemporaries; and his finished paintings are unexceptional exercises in classical landscape.

Jones had been the pupil of Richard Wilson, but this may not alone explain his predilection for outdoor sketching, for Wilson was altogether suspicious of colouring in the open air, in watercolour let alone in oil, believing it a less reliable guide to tonal effect than his memory and the monochrome media of pencil or chalks. Indeed he had advised Jones to draw in a 'middle tint', so that he could learn 'the principles of light and shade without being dazzled by the flutter of colours'. On the other hand, Wilson certainly acknowledged the possibility of easel painting outdoors, for in the corner of a painting by him of Tivoli sits an artist doing just that, and in 1765 another of his pupils, Joseph Farington, drew him painting from nature in Moor Park (Victoria and Albert Museum). Farington also seems to have attempted it himself, for the watercolourist Thomas Hearne made a drawing of him, with Sir George Beaumont, at work on easel pictures beside Lodore Falls in 1777 (Wordsworth Trust), and this, like Farington's drawing of his master, has all the marks of a documentary record. Beaumont had briefly been taught painting by Jones, and also knew Wilson. Colouring from nature may have formed at least a qualified part of Wilson's teaching, but Jones took it to exceptional extremes.

Jones's originality as a sketcher remains difficult to account for, but for Skelton's experiments in Italy in the late 1750s there is a clearer explanation, for in Rome it was already not at all unusual to paint outdoors. Indeed the practice was more established and co-ordinated than is often realised, especially among the many French artists who visited the city. It was in Rome, in the early 1750s, that the distinguished French landscape and marine painter Claude-Joseph Vernet gave to Joshua Reynolds the advice that the recipient later passed on to another marine artist, Nicholas Pocock: 'I would recommend you above all things to paint from nature instead of drawing ... This was the practice of Vernet, whom I knew at Rome; he there showed me his studies in colours, which struck me very much, for that truth which those works only have which are produced while the impression is warm from Nature'. Here was the opposite point of view from Wilson's – though it had been Vernet who confirmed Wilson's decision to devote himself to landscape – and Vernet's nature study had left a powerful impact in Rome. Writing of the artist's Italian period, the connoisseur P. J. Mariette recalled: 'Everywhere he studied nature and her effects, and then rendered them on his canvas with the utmost truth ... It was by studying and working with the greatest application that ... he learned to render with such truth the different effects of light, the effect produced by the vapour in the air'. Ironic indeed that Constable, who knew as we do today only Vernet's public pictures, relegated him to the 'mannerists, who employ themselves in sweeping up the painting rooms of preceding ages . . . men who have lost sight of nature and strayed into the vacant fields of idealism'. In fact Vernet went further than many of his contemporaries in transmitting the results of his nature study into his studio pictures, and it is no accident that anecdotes of it overlap suspiciously with those told of later painters. The famous story of Turner observing a seastorm tied to the mast of a boat has an almost exact prototype with Vernet. For an artist like Skelton, arriving in Rome in 1757, Vernet's outdoor work survived in recent memory as an inspiration; Skelton was thrilled to find himself installed in the very room the Frenchman had occupied in the artist's colony in the Palazzo Zuccari, and eager to begin painting the evening skies from the window.

It is clear from Reynolds's and other remarks that Vernet had specifically recommended the use of oil outdoors – although the handful of very beautiful on-the-spot studies Pocock (usually a conventional and finicky draughtsman) went on to make of trees, plants or a Welsh waterfall, are in watercolour. It was among French artists that the principle of oil sketching from nature was most firmly established as part of academic practice. De Piles had laid down the axiom that the painter should always make a 'lightly coloured sketch' in which he could 'give his fancy free play in the relations between different features and in the general effect' – and preferably in oil on paper as this was 'doubtless the best for drawing nature more particularly' – before progressing to a picture, while a later writer, Dézallier d'Argenville (whose collection of biographies of artists would also feature in Constable's library), declared that the purpose of a sketch was to 'express a single idea forcefully or else to represent in a detailed and in a perfect way separate features which are to take place in some composition'. Defects, he added significantly, could not occur in such private works as normal value judgements did not apply to them.

In France, oil sketching was divided into distinct categories, related to different stages in the preparation of pictures. Landscape sketches from nature were in fact among the least important; they were *études*, on a par with renderings of an individual head, figure or portion of drapery. More significant were *esquisses* and *ébauches*, respectively composition sketches and lay-ins for finished paintings. It was through Reynolds that British students were to learn to build their pictures through painted sketches, but travellers like Jones would not have appreciated the rigid categorisations applied by their Continental colleagues. They were probably well aware of the French habit of making landscape *études*, without realising quite how limited their function was; if taken literally, at their face value, these *études* would have made all the greater impact. Visitors to Rome could hardly have remained unaware of outdoor sketching if they had contact with the artists who gathered around the French Academy in the Villa Medici, where landscape study was particularly encouraged, and tended to assume a more realist bent than it did in Paris. This had been partly due to Nicolas Vleughels, the friend of Watteau and the Academy's Director in the 1720s. Vleughels had encouraged his students to go outdoors and study nature, and one of them, C.J. Natoire, after he succeeded as Director in 1751, was to urge his own distinguished generation of *pensionnaires* to do the same.

French artists were for many decades more enthusiastic oil sketchers than their British counterparts, and exemplify more clearly the divisions long maintained by artists between their sketches and their finished work – if only because the French tended to deal with the theory of landscape in a more structured way, and to submit their work to rigorous academic discipline. This is not to say that landscape was accorded higher status in Paris – or among Frenchmen in Rome – than in London; far from it. Landscape painters were everywhere regarded as a sub-species, and in Paris were not recognised by the Académie Royale. Just as Turner and Constable felt a sense of mission to restore and elevate their art, the one by raising landscape to the status of history and the other by asserting the validity of 'natural painture', so it would have been admitted by most Frenchmen in 1800 that landscape had fallen prey to the greater claims of the history painters. Yet in France it had been possible in the 1780s for one painter, Pierre-Henri de Valenciennes, to proclaim the nobility of landscape by reinventing it in a reformed neo-classic mode that recalled the antique splendour of Poussin and the Carracci, but belonged distinctly to its own age. It was in the work of Valenciennes, most inspired of sketchers, that the divergence of style and purpose between study from nature and public exhibition pictures became most pronounced.

It was perhaps Vernet, the encourager of both Wilson and Reynolds, who taught Valenciennes the advantages of painting outdoors. In Paris in 1781, Vernet gave the younger man some valuable instruction in perspective and its application in painting, and showed him – as he had earlier shown Alexander Cozens (cat.no.1) – the importance of sky and cloud in determining the appearance of landscape, thus anticipating both Turner's colour studies of aerial perspective and Constable's 'skying'. In Italy the following year, Valenciennes began to translate these lessons into a programme of oil sketching from nature, producing a marvellous series of oils on paper of landscape motifs under transient effects of weather and light. Alone among his contemporaries, Valenciennes returned to the same subjects under different conditions, as Turner and

Constable were to do, and developed through his sketches a highly expressive painterly language for rendering atmosphere and climate. To the modern eye, the results are totally satisfying in themselves, proclaiming a vigorously objective naturalism, an openness to things as they are. At the same time, his choice of subjects and viewpoints seems always extraordinarily sure; it is hard to avoid the conclusion that, if only at a subconscious level, a strong pictorial imagination was at work at this supposedly functional level of his production.

Valenciennes himself would not have admitted as much. For him, the sketches were firstly educational, and then served either as raw materials to be adapted and synthesised in his studio pictures, or, after he returned to France and began to teach in his *atelier*, as models for his students to copy. When he came to write his important treatise on landscape painting, published in 1800 – a work devoted in large measure to propagandising historic landscape – he recommended outdoor sketching in the specific contexts of artistic training and the preparation of pictures. The casual, impromptu aspects of the activity were part of the discipline; the painter acquired particular skills and responses through making *études d'après nature*, and so he should concentrate on broad effects rather than detail, finish or composition. It was vital to work quickly; no sketch should occupy more than two hours, and half an hour was as much as should be spent on a transient effect of light such as a sunrise. One wonders if Turner knew of this, and was he thinking of Valenciennes's dictum when, speaking of the oil sketches he made in Devon in 1813, he declared that the best were done in less than half an hour?

It would be tempting to suppose that Jones, at least, knew of Valenciennes's Italian sketching, for there are many parallels between their sketches, and indeed between their finished works – so far removed, in each case, from the vigour and spontaneity of their outdoor production. Yet Valenciennes went further in both aspects of his work, for Jones neither attained the Frenchman's subtle and scientific appreciation of weather and light, nor aspired to so dogmatic and archaising an ideal in his public art. The separation between the two strands of Valenciennes's work is striking indeed, and one that many subsequent painters were unable to sustain. Turner and Constable in Britain, Corot in France, were bound in their different ways to attempt a new synthesis of nature and art, of the lessons of the open air and the mature reflection of the studio.

Up to 1800, outdoor sketching remained as it had begun, a largely Italian, indeed Roman, phenomenon. Nor did it cease to flourish there in the following decades. Corot, who arrived in 1825, was one of the last of a stream of French artists who had come to complete their education in

Italy. Many of them, partly through Valenciennes's influence, were newly committed to landscape – a *Prix de Rome* for *paysage historique* was inaugurated in 1817 – and expected to adopt the practice of outdoor sketching while in Italy. Artists from elsewhere in northern Europe were to make their own distinguished contributions in this field, as we shall see. Cut off for many years by war, the British were unable to join them. There is no Romantic equivalent of Jones; Constable never travelled; and Turner was distinctly reticent in his use of oil when he visited Italy, at first painting little or nothing and then only indoors, thus failing to participate in what had become both a traditional and a commonplace activity. In Britain itself, on the other hand, oil sketching from nature suddenly took off around the turn of the century.

OUTDOOR SKETCHING IN BRITAIN BEFORE TURNER AND CONSTABLE

Between Jones and the Romantic generation there were a few isolated outbreaks, largely among painters who were not primarily landscapists. The animal painter and sculptor George Garrard made during the early 1790s some delightfully uninhibited studies of trees and parkland in and around London, manifestly for his own pleasure (cat.no.5). Some much more distinguished artists also found refreshment in landscape sketching. Reynolds had once or twice painted the sweeping river views that lay outside the windows of his house on Richmond Hill, if not outdoors at least, we may assume, before the motif; and Benjamin West, his successor as President of the Royal Academy, essayed a few rather brighter little studies of the scenery in Windsor Park (cat.no.4), as well as two larger oils on paper, begun outdoors according to Joseph Farington – whom he advised to tackle some similar work – and finished for exhibition at the Academy in 1799. Precisely because landscape lay outside the main scope of his art, and could contribute relatively little to his portraiture and history painting, West could relax when painting it, and Constable, his student at the Academy, found him a sympathetic teacher. West admired some of Constable's early Suffolk studies, declaring that he 'must have loved nature very much', and he helped him to understand that 'light and shadow never stand still'.

But in Britain in the 1790s, the impulse to sketch in oil, or – and this can be an important distinction – to produce works that looked like sketches, often arose from other considerations than those of pure naturalism. If in France or among painters in Italy the motive was practical or academic, in Britain it was mainly stylistic. Nature was not necessarily to be allowed its own voice. A prevailing factor was the fashion for the 'Picturesque', an aesthetic that favoured rough, untidy or random landscape effects drawn from the vocabulary of Dutch seventeenth-century painters or of recent artists like Gainsborough. This taste certainly encouraged painters and connoisseurs to look with new eyes, freed from the rational restraints of the classical tradition, but the result was less a new look at nature than a new idea of what could make a picture. Small pictures were constructed to look like spontaneous impressions of corners of nature, but were in truth full of artifice. When Richard Payne Knight, arbiter of the 'Picturesque', declared a preference for sketches over finished works, he did not mean outdoor sketches of real motifs, but studio assemblages in a calculatedly impromptu technique. The 'sketch as picture' that occupied a number of young artists after 1800 was as much the child of the 'Picturesque' as of its painter's innocent eye, and the 'studies from nature' of trees or buildings that those same painters produced were – as much as those by Desportes or Valenciennes – means to an end. It is the modern eye that sees in them an overwhelming impulse of naturalism. As Constable realised in 1802, the battle for 'natural painture' had still to be fought.

TURNER'S EARLY OIL SKETCHES; KNOCKHOLT AND THE THAMES

It was the 'Picturesque' that first moved Turner to anticipate Constable in the habit of oil sketching, in Kent at the turn of the century. Turner had already painted a few small studies in oil, which either anticipate projected paintings or seem to be essays towards small, cabinet-size 'sketches' of the kind admired by Knight. Their subjects were sometimes historical, but in Kent in 1799 or 1800, he suddenly broke into a freer recording of the autumnal beechwoods near Knockholt and Chevening, in oil or mixed media with oil, on prepared paper (cat.nos.9–12). Several other sketches of the gloomy interior of a cottage (cat.nos.7, 8), and two more developed sketches of gypsies beneath trees, in the Fitzwilliam Museum, proclaim the 'Picturesque' context for this outbreak of sketching, but the tree studies reveal a more open-minded approach to real scenery, and indeed the most direct confrontation with nature in Turner's painted work to date.

What role if any William Frederick Wells, landscapist and drawing master, and Turner's host at Knockholt, played in encouraging all this is not known. Turner could have been inspired by another painter who worked outdoors in oil, William Delamotte, for he visited him at Oxford in 1800, or by the engraver John Raphael Smith, with whom he had worked in the 1790s, for when De Wint was his apprentice, Smith took him along the Thames to experiment with oil sketching while he fished. At all events, after his Kentish work, Turner did not return to the practice again for several years. It remained always an occasional activity for him, limited to a very few places, and was never absorbed into his working pattern. One reason must be the fact that 'natural painture' was never the great mission for Turner that it was for Constable. He could not have endorsed the uncompromising message that Constable sent home to his friend Dunthorne in his famous letter of 1802:

> I shall shortly go home to Bergholt where I shall make some laborious studies from nature – and I shall endeavour to get a pure and unaffected representation of the scenes that may employ me, with respect to colour particularly.

Beside the objectivity announced here, Turner has almost more in common with Valenciennes. This is not to deny Turner's prodigious curiosity as to natural effects; his enquiries into them were as sustained and penetrating as Constable's. But they were conducted for different purposes and in different ways. With the very significant exception of the larger sketches he made a few years later along the Thames valley, Turner's oil sketches from nature were not, as Constable's certainly were, intended to transform the art of landscape through their own messages of immediacy, of transience and of the commonplace and familiar.

Turner was, moreover, evidently less at ease with oils outdoors than Constable. Constable did not immediately achieve the sparkling freshness of his mature sketches, and indeed after his first Suffolk campaign in the summer of 1802, he largely abandoned oil sketching until his Lakeland visit four years later. But thereafter he persevered. Turner had, and kept, his reservations. With one or two brilliant exceptions, the Knockholt sketches had been rather dark in tone, and somewhat heavy in their touch. Clearly Turner had fallen into the trap acknowledged by so many would-be sketchers outdoors – he had failed to compensate for the brightness of the light, or to shield himself from it. Years later he would admit his reluctance to paint outdoors because he 'always got his colours too brown', and dismiss a whole series of sketches on this count. So far from assimilating outdoor painting into his practice, Turner was to make it a general rule *not* to do it, and this reluctance extended more and more, as the years passed, to watercolour or gouache as much as to oil. The many hundreds of studies in watercolour, in which he preserved recollected effects of light or cloud or designed the tonal structure of paintings or drawings, and the smaller number of such studies in oil, were made in the studio, from recollection or from memoranda taken on the spot in pencil.

Yet, like Constable, Turner returned to oil sketching outdoors about the middle of the first decade in the century, and the results this time were marvellous. They were also more ambitious in scale and purpose than anything Constable had yet attempted. By May 1805 Turner had acquired a second home at Isleworth, and later he moved to Upper Mall, Hammersmith. Both these retreats opened up, outside his windows, a gentle world of meadows and shady river banks; Windsor and Eton lay upstream; and nearby also was the more intimately pastoral valley of the Wey. It was a modest, quintessentially English landscape that resisted the self-conscious coarseness of the 'Picturesque' and was wholly unsuited to the histrionics of the 'Sublime'. Turner's imagination could never resist translating observed effects into some appropriate realm of art, and he devoted several sketchbooks to the task of adapting the placid reaches of the Thames into Claudean vistas of seaports and antique cities. But in a series of substantial oil sketches on canvas and mahogany panel, made, as is now thought, during a single trip along the Thames and Wey by boat in the summer and early autumn of 1805, he essayed a more direct approach.

Turner's studio and exhibition pictures were themselves displaying a greater naturalism at this time. The emphasis was shifting from the old masterly machines that had first made his reputation as a painter, to a tranquil, pastoral mode; the familiar scenery of southern England was becoming for Turner, as it was already for Constable, a fit subject for art. The oil sketches must have played a significant part in establishing it as such, for it is striking how consistently they reveal his organising imagination at work in choice of view and play of light. To catch a momentary effect or preserve an incidental detail was not enough for Turner. Even the smallest or most apparently spontaneous of the Thames and Wey sketches were submitted to a pictorial process, and others may have been intended to become pictures themselves. Turner had probably, at this one period of his life, come to terms with the possibility at least of beginning a picture outdoors, bringing together the responses and skills associated with outdoor and studio work, as West had done in his Windsor views exhibited in 1799.

The sketches on mahogany (cat.nos.13–17) range in size from the very small to the more substantial and sometimes employ formats such as a wide and low rectangle that are not yet found elsewhere in Turner's work. They are more developed in handling than their counterparts on canvas, but they are more truly sketches nevertheless; thinly and freely painted, always inventive in the touch of the brush, they have most in common with Turner's use of watercolour. The most compositionally resolved of them display a vivid appreciation of light and tone; others wonderfully capture the pattern and movement of trees and foliage, or of the silvery skies of the Thames valley. Nowhere does Turner seem so close to Constable.

These panels were clearly conceived as a distinct, isolated group, experimental and educative in purpose. The canvases painted at the same time (cat.nos.18,19) were an experiment of a different kind. Turner evidently painted some of them outdoors, yet he was building up compositions of a standard exhibition size. The son of his friend Mr Trimmer, who as a boy had gone fishing with Turner, recalled that the painter kept a boat at Richmond, from which he 'painted on a large canvas direct from nature. Till you have seen these sketches, you know nothing of Turner's powers'. Here Turner was certainly in the vanguard of the Impressionists – of Daubigny, who toured the rivers of France in his studio-boat from 1857, or of Monet who worked from one at Argenteuil. Like them, he probably had pictures as well as sketches in mind, although he did not intend to finish them on the spot. He apparently neither separated nor stretched the canvases he used by the Thames, but kept them rolled, laying the relevant section over a frame while he painted – a method he was to use several times later. The canvas had first been prepared with a dryish white ground, to give brightness and clarity of tone, and, when appropriate, to serve by itself to mark the highlights, just as he was by now leaving areas of paper bare in his watercolours.

The Thames canvases vary greatly in character and finish, being sometimes swiftly or coarsely painted, sometimes more gracefully treated and bearing evidence of reworking in the studio. Everything suggests that Turner was, in effect, beginning pictures outdoors, rather than consciously restricting the work to a level of private study, and it is entirely possible that some of the Thames pastorals that he completed for exhibition at this period were commenced in this way. Yet Turner was never again to work outside in quite this manner. The leap of imagination, conception and technique that he made from his Richmond boat was one from which he retreated in the years ahead.

Turner was not alone in sketching the Thames in the early years of the century, even if he did so on an unprecedented scale. Delamotte's outdoor study of Waterperry near Oxford (cat.no.51), was painted over two days (and carefully annotated as to time and effect) in 1803, the year he moved to Great Marlow to take up a post as drawing master at the Royal Military College. At Twickenham in 1806 and thereabouts, the water-colourist and teacher John Varley took a house and assembled some favourite pupils to put into practice his motto 'go to Nature for everything'. Young painters like William Henry Hunt and John Linnell were dispatched 'into the highways and byeways to make such transcripts as they could'; they busied themselves 'sketching and painting, using oils, and working on millboard'; 'sitting down before any common object, the paling of a cottage garden, a mossy wall, or an old post', they would 'try to imitate it minutely'. Turner, with his own house at Twickenham, must have known of these expeditions, but a study of the results only emphasises the completeness and sophistication of his own vision. His Thames and Wey sketches are studies of whole scenes; he could not avoid the processes of selection and synthesis, the classical or 'Picturesque' intuition, that came so naturally to him. Hunt's tree (cat.no.48), Linnell's river bank (cat.no.45) or indeed De Wint's plants (cat.no.49) – De Wint was a friend and had recently been a London neighbour of Varley – are not pictorial in the way that Turner's sketches are; like Desportes's plants and trees, they are but pieces of the jigsaw, components carefully observed to help the painters understand the whole. Turner did not despise such concentrated study, and indeed attributed to it the generalising genius of Claude. Nothing could account for it, he declared in a lecture in 1811, but 'continual study of parts of nature. Parts, for had he not so studied, we should have found him sooner pleased with simple subjects of nature, and would not have as we now have, pictures made up of bits, but pictures of bits'. But Turner did not choose, or did not feel the need, to study such 'bits' in oil.

Varley's Twickenham nature study also took root in Kensington, in that rather untamed part known as the Gravel Pits where, by 1811, Linnell had moved to share a house with William Mulready, Varley's brother-in-law and the painter he would originally have preferred as a teacher. Nearby lived another young artist, Augustus Callcott, who had emerged as a professional competitor of Turner several years earlier. Together these painters, and the friends who came to visit them or to live nearby, formed something of a Kensington School, devoted to an uncritical naturalism in outdoor work. Mulready had been exhibiting some cottage scenes in which an uncompromising directness almost outweighs the 'Picturesque' subject matter (cat.no.50); Linnell turned a sharp eye towards the Kensington landscape in both oil and watercolour; and Callcott produced some similarly fresh rustic scenes (cat.no.57). Although his later friends the brothers Redgrave asserted that Callcott 'never painted directly from nature', and Callcott himself told Samuel Palmer that 'a picture done out of doors must needs be false, because nature is changing every minute', it is clear that he had quite often painted on the spot. In 1812 he sent three 'studies from nature' to the British Institution; there is in the Kettering Art Gallery an exquisite, signed Italian study from his tour in 1827–8 that is hardly put in the shade by the finished outdoor paintings of French or German artists in Italy in the 1820s; and in his executors' sale in 1845 were what the *Art Union* described as '"sketches" – early sketches exhibiting amazing power, and which afforded a contrast disadvantageous to the later style of the accomplished painter'.

Through artists like Linnell, Mulready and the younger Callcott, Varley's teachings lived on and inspired painters elsewhere to 'go to nature'. It must have been their early exhibited oils (and particularly Mulready's) that encouraged John Sell Cotman, visiting London from Norwich, to essay some similar subjects in oil. Poverty and isolation were to curtail his development as an oil painter, but there are a few small oils, including the beautiful study of trees at Duncombe Park (cat.no.52), that could well have been painted from nature, and attain a solemn and mysterious beauty the equal of anything he did in watercolour and indeed hardly matched since the pastorals of Claude. Here as always, Cotman's vision is uniquely his own and moves far beyond the objectivity that Linnell or Mulready would have recommended in principle. Their advice was certainly not always taken literally; Palmer, when urged by Linnell in 1828 to curb the imaginative excesses of his Shoreham work, responded with some more rationalist drawings but also with the famous avowal, 'I will, God help me, never be a naturalist by profession'. A more faithful interpretation of Linnell's and Mulready's advice may be found in the clear and bright open-air sketches of William Dixon, an elusive portrait and landscape painter who had known them in London before moving to Northumberland around 1816 (see cat.no.56). Picking over his chaotic London lodgings after his death, Linnell found and bought Dixon's 'beautiful studies from nature made for the pictures which came to nothing through double mindedness & infirmity of purpose'.

Linnell's words are perhaps more telling than they seem, for Dixon's problems may have lain not only in an irresolute personality, but in the specific question of how to instil the vigour of his sketches into pictures that could make a mark in the exhibition room. If so, Dixon was far from being alone. Neither painting outdoors, nor fidelity to nature, were to be the predominant characteristics of Linnell, Mulready and their friends. *Pace* Palmer, Linnell was not really a 'naturalist' at all. The motifs he studied so faithfully at Twickenham were those of the 'Picturesque', and his later ambitions were towards 'poetical landscape'. Inspired by his religious beliefs to express divinity in nature, the mature Linnell made his landscapes general and ideal – 'aspects of nature' or selections of 'spiritual artistic facts'. Mulready, for his part, adapted his landscape studies to the service of genre. Yet as these painters' finished pictures changed and their unspoilt paradise in Kensington disappeared beneath stucco or formal gardens, they never abandoned their nature study, and there is something touching, if a little ridiculous, in the stories of their later attempts to obtain verisimilitude – subsequent friends and neighbours like Thomas Creswick 'braving cold and wet, and all other trials incident to painting in the open air', or Thomas Webster catching gout from hours standing 'to study the effect of reflection in the ice' and, undaunted, having himself wheeled back to a frozen pond in a Bath chair. Through such enterprises were the principles of the Varley circle transmitted to the Pre-Raphaelites.

After 1800, then, Constable was by no means the only British artist to assert the importance of outdoor work and inspiration. With hindsight it is easy to sort out those painters for whom the practice was of fundamental importance from those for whom it was merely incidental – or even a matter of presumptuous pride. The landscapist T.C. Hofland, for example, went so far as to claim that he was 'the first who commenced painting in oil colours out of doors' – a statement justified neither by facts nor results. Hardly less strident, but with better reason, was the Reading painter William Havell, whose friendships with Varley and Delamotte had encouraged a propensity for outdoor sketching in both oil and watercolour. It was most probably oil that he chose for a study of 'an old crazy brick wall overgrown with ivy' during a sketching trip to Windsor Forest in 1804 – as W.H. Pyne recalled, Havell 'opening his pictorial budget exhibited a colour scrap'. This subject was obviously related to the rough-and-ready – or perhaps 'Picturesque' – details so meticulously observed in the Varley circle, but his views of Caversham Bridge and Windsor Castle (cat.nos.54, 55), the fruit of Thames tours from 1805, are broad studies of complete scenes, subtly articulated in tone and lighting. Havell, besides, matched Turner in laying pictorial foundations on the spot; his oil on paper, 'Reading Abbey' (Reading Museum and Art Gallery), exhibited at the Royal Academy and British Institution in 1807, was probably begun before the motif and finished in the studio. Havell continued to sketch in oil on paper, card and board for some years, and his notes on one such study, made at Richmond in 1814, are worth quoting for his recipe; 'Painted on the spot in two hours in Copal varnish mixed with sugar of lead to make all the colours dry immediately'.

Havell claimed much of Constable's empirical naturalism for himself, and like Constable, he suffered for it. In 1815 the British Institution rejected a landscape of his in circumstances reported by the wife of the painter Thomas Uwins: 'he has painted sunshine so near to truth that it absolutely makes the eyes ache to look at it. The artists are all alarmed and the patrons stand all aghast . . . the picture was rejected on account of its novelty and originality'. More important than this hyperbole is Havell's own statement of his credo, in an angry letter of protest: 'My first desire as an English Landscape Painter is to represent my own beautiful country without referring to other painters, ancient or modern; my next, is to paint the splendour of daylight and sun-shine, the glory of Art and Nature'. Such had been Constable's wish when in 1802 he had forsworn 'running after pictures' and returned to his native Suffolk, and there can be no better descriptions than Havell's and Constable's of the motives felt by a generation of British painters when they set out to sketch from nature. They were motives too limited for Turner to share.

Even those most committed to a greater naturalism acknowledged the difficulty of it. How to achieve the unity of Art and Nature was a problem that taxed them all. For it would prove time and again that what was simply *there* was not enough. Constable, who travelled furthest down the path of naturalism, also offers the most powerful example of the dilemma. While some of his sketches – whether in pencil in sketchbooks or in oil on board or paper – were translated into finished pictures, there could be no guarantee that spontaneous observation could produce material sufficiently monumental for the purpose. Only once, in 'Boat-Building', 1814–15 (Victoria and Albert Museum), was Constable able to finish a picture outdoors, but even this was not commenced innocently or ad hoc, as his drawings prove; the composition was carefully considered in advance, and Constable prepared himself for the task by studying Claude's technique.

The truth was that finding subjects for pictures outdoors worked best when human interest was added to the landscape. In 1815 the portrait painter George Robert Lewis produced two memorable harvest scenes from nature at Haywood in Herefordshire, and exhibited them the following year with a small series of similar studies, all described as painted on the spot, including the gleaning scene exhibited here (cat.no.53). A friend of Linnell, Lewis had put Varley's principles of truth to nature into practice very successfully, but his scenes of rural labour probably bear additional social or political connotations; the modern eye may be right to sense a heroic quality in Lewis's gleaners, for the painter could well have shared Linnell's belief in human equality and his respect for the working man. If Lewis was painting a manifesto (at a time, it must be remembered, of severe agricultural depression), it was less a manifesto for the art of landscape, in the sense that Constable's pictures were, than for the men who toiled in the field. We may well question just how spontaneous these pictures really were, and it is significant that in one of the larger of Lewis's 1816 exhibits (also in the Tate Gallery), he made a major repaint in one of the workmen at the centre of the composition – just the sort of change that suggests the studio and traditional methods of picture-making. Constable, besides, reverted more and more to these as his aspirations for landscape mounted. He continued to sketch outdoors, both making whole views and, in such studies as his famous skies (see cat.no.60), gathering specific information, but his great 'six-foot' exhibition pictures of the 1820s were prepared through studio sketches to ensure conceptual integrity, so that he could paint with ready facility on the final canvas. No less than Turner, Constable was sufficiently the child of his time to feel the need to unite his love of real nature with more universal messages, and his remarks about sketches made after other pictures would also have held for those made from nature; the sketch, he declared in 1823, 'will not serve to drink at again & again – in a sketch there is but the one state of mind – that which you were in at the time'. Turner would have taken such considerations for granted.

TURNER'S LATER SKETCHES: DEVON, COWES, ITALY

Turner never again attempted his Thames-side experiments, and studio sketches largely supplanted colour study from nature. Apart from an isolated sketch or two (cat.nos.20–2), he did not take his oils outdoors again until 1813, and then only on a friend's persuasive advice. Staying in Devon that summer – in glorious weather and surrounded by the abundance of the last good harvest for several years – he was induced to some sketching by a local painter, Ambrose Johns, who provided him with 'a small portable painting-box, containing some prepared paper for oil sketches as well as the other necessary materials'. Thus equipped, Turner went to work with confidence and speed – and without his usual reserve, proudly emphasising the short time ('less than half an hour') he had spent on some of the best sketches and even showing them around at a picnic, 'perhaps to verify them'. He was readier than usual to record simple truths, but even here he took liberties for compositional effect.

Today the Devon sketches seem brilliantly fresh, but for Turner they were not in the end a success. The problem was partly one of colour, for he later dismissed them as 'worthless, in consequence, as he supposed of some defects in the preparation of the paper; all the grey tints, he observed, had nearly disappeared'. But there was more. Years later he sent Johns, in gratitude for his help and hospitality, a small oil sketch *not* made from nature, thus probably betraying his deeper reservations. By their very immediacy the Devon sketches were doomed to a conceptual vacuum. When he barked at a colleague, 'What, do you not know yet, at your age, that you ought to paint your impressions', he was recommending an approach entirely the opposite of the Impressionists' – not the largely impartial reporting exemplified in his own Devon sketches, but the tranquil and considered recollection, in Ruskin's words the 'arrangement of remembrance', manifested in the great picture that came out of the Devon tour, the 1815 'Crossing the Brook'.

After 1813, Turner very rarely worked in oil outdoors again. His first impressions, the raw materials of his art, were gathered in pencil in his sketchbooks, and his ideas of tone and colour were most often explored through studio sketches in both oil and watercolour. The more eager he was to gather information, the less likely he was to work in colour at all, and what was perhaps his last campaign of painting before the motif, on the Isle of Wight in 1827, occurred in a specialised context. Invited that summer to stay with the architect John Nash at East Cowes Castle, Turner planned to paint the Cowes Regatta and some associated events, using the sort of large rolls of canvas he had apparently employed for his earlier Thames studies. Writing to his father, he asked him to order one or two pieces of unstretched canvas for despatch to Cowes. He received one 6 by 4 feet, and on this, cut into two strips, he painted a series of vivid sketches of racing yachts, placid harbour scenes and gatherings of people by the water's edge. Not all these were necessarily painted entirely before the motif, for there is little evidence of the kind of changes and uncertainty that might be expected had Turner been working only from what presented itself, moment by moment, and the Regatta subjects, by definition, portray rapid movement. But even if Turner made some of these sketches back at the castle, others have a powerful feeling of immediacy and it is hard to discount some direct reporting. Turner's vantage point was probably aboard a naval vessel moored offshore, perhaps the position between decks looking through a gun-port that is the subject of one of the sketches. A secure pitch on a substantial ship, out of the sun, would have overcome the dazzle, reflection and other difficulties encountered by Berthe Morisot when she attempted to paint from a smaller boat off Cowes in 1857: 'Everything sways, there is an infernal lapping of water; one has the sun and the wind to cope with, the boats change position every minute'.

The Cowes sketches served for a finished picture painted for Nash, but such impressions of transience and swift movement had little to contribute to the kind of grand and historicising pictures Turner planned as his tributes to Italy. His apparent abstinence from oil painting in Italy in 1819, and his decision when there again in 1828–9 to confine his painting activities mainly to the studio, stand out as all the more deliberate when one considers the long history of outdoor sketching in Rome, and the recent upsurge of it both there and in Naples. Rome by now served as a vast open-air studio to an international community of artists. The French remained among the most active of sketchers. The year of Turner's arrival, 1819, also saw the departure of one of the most distinguished of them, F. M. Granet, mainly a history painter but the author of many splendid Roman sketches. From 1818 until 1821, Italy was the home of one of Valenciennes's pupils, Achille Michallon – later, briefly, the teacher of Corot – who was also a prolific and effective sketcher. Corot's own marvellous Italian sketches, made between 1825 and 1828, owed much to Michallon's example and were in turn very influential.

In the tradition of Valenciennes, the Frenchmen saw their sketching as part of their academic training, and generally adhered in their finished works to classical and ideal types; the spontaneous, *trouvé* aspect of their outdoor work was not intended to modify their conceptual approach to landscape, although in Corot such a process certainly did occur, and it must be added that most of these artists tended to produce not only pure sketches but also small, more finished works that were probably intended to be read as *plein air* 'pictures'; like Constable at Flatford, they were experimenting with finishing outdoors. The same observation may be made of some of the Roman paintings of the Dane, C. W. Eckersberg, who had trained with David in Paris and was in Italy for three years from 1813, before returning to teach other Scandinavians who were to gather and sketch in Rome in the 1830s. Almost as numerous as the French were the Germans and Austrians – J. A. Koch, F. L. Catel, Joseph Rebell, Georg von Dillis, Ernst Fries, Carl Blechen, J. C. Reinhart, J. M. von

Rohden, the architect painters Leo von Klenze and Karl Schinkel – whose output ran the gamut from classicising or medievalising works to coolly observed open-air studies. Nor was outdoor work confined to Rome and the Campagna. The Norwegian, J. C. Dahl, arrived in Naples in 1820 to paint some very robust sketches of the Bay, and Catel, Rebell and Corot were among the painters who spent time in the city and became associated with the 'Scuola di Posillipo', a group of artists gathered around the expatriate Dutchman, A. S. Pitloo, who was devoted to the resurgence of landscape in Naples and to the practice of oil sketching – though in a markedly looser, more plastic manner than the sharp, bright style particularly associated with painters based in Rome.

The majority of these painters were not unknown to Turner, and in 1819 he listed many of their names. Then, and on his subsequent visit to Italy, he could have met them through his friend and host, Charles Eastlake, most sociable of painters and himself no mean outdoor sketcher. Yet Turner had no wish to emulate them. In 1819 he remained wedded to his pencil and his sketchbook, and when he coloured at all, in his room in the evening, it was in watercolour. He was no less impressed than his fellow visitors from the north by the clarity of the air and the brilliance of the light, but above all he stored these in his memory. There was too little time, too much to learn, to permit the use of oil. The son of his friend John Soane wrote home to his father:

> Turner is in the neighbourhood of Naples making rough pencil
> sketches to the astonishment of the Fashionables, who wonder of what
> use these rough drafts can be – simple souls! At Rome a sucking blade
> of the brush made the request of going out with pig Turner to colour –
> he grunted for answer that it would take up too much time to colour
> in the open air – he could make 15 or 16 pencil sketches to one
> coloured, and then grunted his way home.

When he returned to Italy in 1828, Turner did paint, but almost entirely in the studio he set up in Rome. One or two small oils breathe an outdoor freshness (cat.no.35), but they are exceptional. Apart from the large paintings he made and exhibited in the city, his more private oils from this visit, on rolls of canvas or small millboard panels, were studio studies of classical compositions (cat.nos.36,37), and they can only very occasionally be associated with actual places. Whereas sketchers from Valenciennes to Corot sought the specific, Turner was already creating a more universal language, forming his art through studies of form, tone and colour. His studio sketches in oil – like his studies in watercolour –

look astonishingly modern in their economy and abstraction, but are in fact old fashioned in design and concept.

There is very little evidence that Turner sketched in oil outdoors in the 1830s and 40s, and perhaps nothing better illustrates his retreat from the practice than his apparent failure to pursue it at Petworth. Nowhere, after all, did he feel more at home at this time in his life. Constable, always most prolific in the places he knew best, would have reacted very differently; and what better stimulus could there be than the great expanse of park and lake, spread beneath a spacious sky, so conveniently seen from the terrace at the back of the house? Yet we know that the paintings Turner made at Petworth – all substantial works – were made behind a locked door in his temporary studio in the Old Library, and there are no records of him painting in the grounds. As we have seen, Constable's own attitudes to picture-making, if not to sketching *per se*, had changed by this time, and the preparation of Turner's pictures of Petworth and Sussex subjects for Lord Egremont's dining room through the medium of studio sketches on the same scale for once exactly matched Constable's methods when developing his 'six-footers'. In neither case did painting from nature have anything to do with the pictorial process.

Yet towards the end of his life, Turner devoted himself to making a number of paintings, evidently for his own interest and pleasure rather than with any public purpose or serious intention to finish, which at least conveyed the powerful impression of a direct response to nature, and adopted the painterly language of the sketch. Turner's late studies of seas and beaches can seem as immediate and concentrated as Constable's sketches (cat.nos.39–44). But the sheer size of some of Turner's canvases of marine subjects is sufficient evidence that they were studio meditations on favourite themes (cat.no.39), while a distinctive group of small millboard panels carry beach scenes of such extraordinary minimalism that the images of boats or figures seem to be suggested by the movement of the paint beneath the brush rather than by things observed (cat.nos.40–4). These works are best seen as recurrent considerations of elements and episodes that Turner now saw so often that they could readily be summoned before his mind's eye. Staying at Margate in the 1830s and early 1840s with his mistress Mrs Booth, in her house overlooking the harbour, he had constant access to the beach and the sea in all its moods. To explore ways of marking its motions and colours in paint, to synthesise natural and painterly energy, became for him a compulsion. He was obsessive, too, in stressing the impact of personal experience and observation upon effects presented in his exhibition pictures – effects which observers tended to dismiss as fantastic or merely incompetent ('soapsuds and whitewash') in execution. Even as he had abandoned methodical painting from nature, he insisted as never before on profound naturalism in his art. But it was a naturalism that sprang from long experience rather than from a single act of looking. Indeed it was the quality of an experience of nature that Turner was recreating: and now more than ever, to paraphrase Ruskin, he was arranging remembrance.

Epilogue: Towards Impressionism

Both Turner and Constable played a vital part in confirming, if not actually stimulating, Continental painters to a fresh approach to nature and the outdoors. So too did Richard Parkes Bonington, who made some marvellous open-air sketches in France and Italy from the early 1820s. Bonington's brief Continental career helped to draw together threads in British and French painting, by promoting the breadth of handling associated with British artists among young Frenchmen alienated by the formalism and high finish of their elders in the *Salons*. As a student in Paris Bonington had talked 'ceaselessly' of Turner to his fellow student Paul Huet, and his own work, in and out of the exhibitions, shone as a beacon of light and painterly freedom. At the *Salon* of 1824, the conservative critic Auguste Jal felt himself attracted, but against his better judgement, for Bonington's small pictures could not, should not, be the stuff of a public exhibition: 'His paintings are, from a distance of several feet, the accent of Nature, but they are, in truth, only sketches'. Yet the impulse towards nature, and a more animated handling – or rather the recognition that the two aspects were connected – was by now irresistible, for this was the famous *Salon des Anglais* in which Constable and other British painters scored such a palpable hit. They had sent, of course, exhibition pictures – Constable's 'The Hay-Wain' is hardly a sketch – but their bold execution, high colour key and open response to the natural world were sufficient to inspire younger painters – Huet, Corot, Delacroix and Théodore Rousseau – to try to combine aspects of their academic discipline of nature study with their final intentions.

But the time was not yet ripe to attempt a complete match of private study and public art, of outdoor sketch and finished picture, by exchanging the studio for the open air. Such a synthesis required a radical rethinking of what landscape painting should be about. Turner knew this from the first, and never attempted such a revision. For him landscape was complex and many-layered, a compound of vision and memory, of ideas and associations. His art was not about immediate impulses or sensations, and he could never have departed the studio for the field. Constable, having assimilated outdoor sketching furthest of all his contemporaries, came round to the same position. Like Turner's, the works to which he attached greatest importance were anything but spontaneous, and even as his eye became more acutely trained, its innocence yielded to vaunting intellectual ambition. In 1812, after a successful summer's sketching, he had stood at a watershed:

> How much real delight have I had with the study of landscape this summer [;] either I am myself much improved in "the art of seeing Nature" (which Sir Joshua Reynolds calls painting) or Nature has unveiled her beauties to me with a less fastidious hand – perhaps there may be something of both.

Yet there was already a sense that 'art' would win, as it did also with Corot, whose later *Salon* pictures with their dreamy equivocations and tremulous touch are a world away from the clean confidence and tonal clarity of his early sketches, and with Rousseau whose large canvases can be as highly wrought as Constable's 'six-footers'. Baudelaire's verdict on Rousseau – that he was 'a naturalist, ceaselessly swept towards the ideal' – could speak for them all. But not for Turner, an idealist from first to last.

What then did a later generation see in these Romantics, so alike and sometimes so different, that confirmed them in their commitment to forge a new painting, and to do so in the open air? Certainly a greater naturalism than had appeared before, and when Eugène Fromentin came to number 'a sincere passion for rural things' among the special features of the art of his time, he had no doubt that 'the first impulse came to us from English painting'. But that 'sincere passion' was not alone sufficient to drive artists outdoors; nor can it explain Impressionism, so often an urban art. Just as the *Salon* audience of 1824 must have realised that 'The Hay-Wain' was not really a transcript from nature, so the Impressionists did not discount the relative artificiality of Turner; Pissarro on occasion analysed his colour harmonies unfavourably, and Monet went so far as to declare him 'antipathetic' on account of 'the exuberant romanticism of his fancy'. Yet they added their names to a letter praising Turner's 'scrupulously exact observation of nature', his 'rendering of forms in movement' and 'fleeting phenomena of light'. These were the qualities they could identify with, just as their predecessors had been stirred by the spirit and agitation of Constable's paint – the chief survival from his sketches into his studio work and proof indeed that he 'did not see *handling* in nature'. Recollected though they often were, Turner's magnificent visions of light and air, of flux and change, Constable's own portrayal of animate nature, his billowing skies and his trees sparkling at the fickle touch of the sun, opened a world of possibilities.

We may think it ironic that the later painters knew nothing of the really private sketches of Turner and Constable, only their exhibition work or the more developed studies that were included in the early displays of the Turner Bequest. But even these were enough to provide a spur. In the end it did not matter that very little if any of the work they knew was painted outdoors, any more than it mattered that Claude had probably painted outdoors much less than his legend suggested. Just as Constable had admired Claude's 'life and breezy freshness', and Turner his unrivalled appreciation of 'ambient vapour', so later painters felt in their work still more powerful and suggestive qualities of the same kind. Even the Impressionists, once they had trained their eyes and liberated their handling of paint, were to return to their studios. Yet for a time in the 1870s it seemed that they could only realise the possibilities inherent in painting by taking it outdoors, by submitting themselves to the air and light that Turner and Constable had carried into their work. Monet, after a lesson in *plein air* painting from Eugène Boudin, felt 'a veil had suddenly been torn from my eyes. I understood. I grasped what painting was capable of being', and for a few years the logic of the open air seemed inescapable. For more than two centuries, it had been details and motifs that artists had sought to master through painting outdoors, but it was not these, nor even their subjects, that lived on as an inspiration in their work, but what Manet, that great *plein-airiste*, called 'the vibrations of the atmosphere'. As Mallarmé wrote in the essay on Manet with which we began:

> The search after truth, peculiar to modern artists, which enables them to see nature and reproduce her, such as she appears to just and pure eyes, must lead them to adopt air almost exclusively as their medium, or at all events to habituate themselves to work in it freely and without restraint; there should at least be in the revival of such a medium, if nothing more, an incentive to a new manner of painting. This is the result of our reasoning, and the end I wish to establish.

3 Thomas Jones **Naples: the Capella Nuova outside
the Porta di Chiaja** 1782

8 J.M.W. Turner **The Kitchen of Wells's Cottage,
Knockholt** c.1801

9 J.M.W. Turner **Chevening Park** *c.*1801

14 J.M.W. Turner **Guildford from
the Banks of the Wey** 1805

19 J.M.W. Turner **Willows beside a Stream** 1805

28 J.M.W. Turner **A Quarry, Perhaps at Saltram** 1813

33 J.M.W. Turner **Shipping off East Cowes
Headland** 1827

32 J.M.W. Turner **Sketch for 'East Cowes Castle,
the Regatta Beating to Windward' No.2** 1827

35 J.M.W. Turner **Hill Town on the Edge of the Campagna** ?1828

36 J.M.W. Turner **Tivoli, the Cascatelle** 1828

46 John Linnell **Study of Buildings
('Study from Nature')** 1806

58 John Constable **Stoke-by-Nayland** *c*.1810–11

53 George Robert Lewis **Harvest Field with
Gleaners, Haywood, Herefordshire** 1815

57 Augustus Wall Callcott **A Road
Leading to a Village** *c.*1812

41 J.M.W. Turner **Two Figures on a
Beach with a Boat** *c.*1840–5

61 John Constable **The Sea near Brighton** 1826

CATALOGUE

Measurements are given in millimetres followed by inches in brackets; height before width. Works illustrated in colour are marked *

Abbreviations

B&J   Martin Butlin and Evelyn Joll, *The Paintings of J.M.W. Turner*, 2 vols., 1984 (revised edition)

TB   A. J. Finberg, *A Complete Inventory of the Drawings of the Turner Bequest*, 2 vols., 1909

PREDECESSORS

Oil Sketching in Britain before Turner and Constable

Since at least the mid seventeenth century, artists had painted in oil in the open air, either attempting complete views of landscape or studying particular motifs from nature. The practice was commonest in Italy, especially among the international artistic community in Rome, and in France where oil study from nature was, during the eighteenth century, established as part of artistic training and of the process of preparing pictures. In Britain the earliest attempts were made by artists who travelled to Italy, like Jonathan Skelton, although the most remarkable of British oil sketchers, Thomas Jones, made some powerful studies of his native Penkerrig before his Italian visit. Benjamin West also painted some outdoor landscapes and even on occasion began works for exhibition in the open, before the motif – a precocious acknowledgment of the possibility of picture-making outdoors which even Constable and the Romantics treated with reserve. On the whole oil sketching outdoors remained a private activity, pursued for study or enjoyment. Jones's sketches were not intended to be seen and contributed little or nothing to his finished work. The animal painter George Garrard occasionally referred to his landscape sketches for a background motif, but their freshness and charm sprang mainly from the fact that he was off-duty when he painted them. The same may be said of West. Yet West proved a benign tutor to both Constable and John Linnell, and the tenor of his advice shows that his own investigations of nature had fostered some apprehension of the possibilities of pure landscape and of observed effects of light and atmosphere.

ALEXANDER COZENS 1717–1786

I   **Before Storm** *c.*1770
Oil on paper
241 × 314 ($9\frac{1}{2}$ × $12\frac{3}{8}$)
Inscribed on verso of the mount 'Before Storm'
T01949

Romantic artists often made oil sketches of the sky. Alexander Cozens's small painting is an example of an interest that, in Britain, reached a peak with Constable's intensive campaign of 'skying' at Hampstead in 1821–2. Cozens, a landscapist and drawing master who only occasionally painted in oils, is principally remembered for his various systems for the invention of landscape composition. His own landscapes were usually invented according to fixed principles of design, and intended to convey the moods and associations he connected with particular natural forms or climatic effects. An appreciation of natural phenomena was thoroughly assimilated into his ideal and conceptual art, nowhere more powerfully than in his various studies of skies. In Rome in 1746 he had regularly visited the studio of C.-J. Vernet, whose oil studies from nature – praised by Reynolds but now lost (see p.12) – no doubt included sky or cloud subjects. Cozens's painting, made during his later years in England, was not a direct outdoor study, although it looks remarkably like the open-air studies made a few years later in Italy by P.-H. de Valenciennes. Cozens intended it to indicate a typical rather than a fleeting effect, and one that could convey a particular mood. Its purpose was emotive and instructive – just as Valenciennes subsequently made his own sketches available to his pupils when he brought them back to his *atelier* in France. 'Before a Storm' was one of twenty-seven 'Circumstances' affecting landscape that formed part of a series of characteristic types and incidents that Cozens seems to have prepared for a publication to be known as *The Various Species of Landscape, &c, in Nature*. Sixteen landscape etchings in the British Museum, and a title page in a private collection, relate to this project, as do twenty-three numbered pencil drawings and several more developed versions, washed and varnished, in an album in a private collection. Among these last is the foundation drawing for the Tate Gallery oil. The subject presumably conforms to no.20 of the 'Circumstances', 'Before a Storm', but may also be related to the first type of 'Composition' in the *Various Species*, 'The edge of a hill, or mountain, near the eye'. Two other oil studies by Cozens of sky effects related to the 'Circumstances' are in the Yale Center for British Art, New Haven, and the Stanford University Art Gallery, Palo Alto. Though far from spontaneous, Cozens's schema did much to stimulate the Romantics to more direct study of the sky. Constable knew of the 'Circumstances' through Sir George Beaumont, a pupil of Cozens's at Eton; made various copies of Cozens's cloud renderings; and followed him in his appreciation of the sky as a prime 'organ of sentiment'.

THOMAS JONES 1742–1803

2 **An Excavation of an Antique Building in a Cava in the Villa Negroni, Rome** 1779
Oil over black chalk on paper
406 × 552 ($16\frac{1}{16}$ × $21\frac{3}{4}$)
Inscribed lower left 'T. JONES', and on verso 'No.2 [corrected from '1']. An Antique Building discovered in a *Cava*/in the Villa Negroni at Rome in y^e Year 1779/T. Jones'
T03544

Jones had already painted 'a number of Studies in Oil on thick primed paper after Nature' in Wales by the 1770s, but his finest sketches were made during his years in Italy, 1776–83. According to his *Memoirs*, he visited the excavations at the Villa Negroni on 5 July 1777; the date of 1779 may have been added later from memory. The grounds of the villa lay to the south-east of the Baths of Diocletian, in the part of Rome now covered by the Stazione Termini: the building in the left distance may be the convent of S. Eusebio, and in the foreground is one of the excavations which were taking place for much of the second half of the eighteenth century and were a magnet for visitors and Grand Tourists. The surrounding gardens, unkempt but deliciously shady and full of echoes of antiquity, were described a few years later by William Beckford, for whom his accompanying draughtsman, J.R. Cozens, made a drawing: 'thickets of jasmine, and wild spots overgrown with bay; long alleys of cypress totally neglected, and almost impassable through the luxuriance of the vegetation; on every side, antique fragments, vases, sarcophagi, and altars, sacred to the Muses ... The forlorn air of this garden, with its high and reverend shades, make me imagine it as old as the baths of Dioclesian which peep over one of its walls'. Jones's teacher Richard Wilson had made some drawings of trees in the gardens, and Jones was treading a familiar path in recording this scene; although he has almost certainly followed his own instinct in painting this sketch in the open, he has still produced what is in effect a small picture, very much in Wilson's manner even to the inclusion of some judiciously placed staffage figures. He has yet to exchange established pictorial values for unprejudiced scrutiny of a particular motif, as he would do so astonishingly in Naples. If anything the Roman sketch marks a regression from the unfettered realism of his first Welsh sketches, as if the burden of association of what Jones himself called 'classic ground' had for once restrained him as much in private as it did in his public pictures.

outcrops of vegetation growing from stone and tile. Planes of light and shade are laid down with absolute confidence. In some of his Neapolitan sketches, Jones treats a flat wall, laid across almost the whole of his small picture space, as if it were the picture itself. Yet a tightly cropped glimpse of sky, a window or a shaft of dark shadow is always there to set the context. Jones's contemporary, Valenciennes, also made oil sketches of roofs and buildings from unpicturesque angles, but they are by no means as forthright. Neither Jones nor Valenciennes carried any of the implications of their private work into their studio pictures.

THOMAS JONES 1742–1803

3 **Naples: the Capella Nuova outside the Porta di Chiaja*** 1782
Oil on paper
200×232 $(7\frac{7}{8} \times 9\frac{1}{8})$
Inscribed on verso 'The Capella nuova fuori della porta di – /Chiaja Naploi /May 1782/ TJ'
T03545

Jones's most remarkable oil sketches were made during his second stay in Naples from 1780. In May 1782 he moved into lodgings in the Convent of the Capella Vecchia, near the Palace of Sir William Hamilton. In his *Memoirs* he recalled: 'The room which I was in possession of at the Convent, was large and commodious for such a place, and as it was on the ground floor and vaulted above, very cool and pleasant at this Season of the Year – The only window it had, looked into a Small Garden, and over a part of the Suburbs, particularly the Capella nouva, another Convent, the Porta di Chaja, Palace of Villa Franca, and part of the Hill of Pusilippo, with the Castle of S. Elmo and Convent of S. Martini &c. all of which Objects, I did not omit making finished studies in Oil upon primed paper'. The originality of Jones's Neapolitan works lies in his readiness to accept these predetermined window and roofscapes, with their powerful contrasts of light and shade and eccentric combinations of shape, as the limits of his vision. In a city hardly matched in Europe for its 'views', Jones chose to spend his leisure hours studying the parts that made up the whole. Here the planes and angles of walls and the dome make up an uncompromising image a world away from the language of the contemporary *vedutista*: yet how Jones revels in the brilliance of the sky, in the dry and crumbly texture of the masonry, and the

BENJAMIN WEST 1738–1820

4 **View from the Terrace at Windsor** ?1792
Oil on canvas
283×371 $(11\frac{1}{8} \times 14\frac{5}{8})$
Inscribed lower left 'B.West/Windsor/[?] 1792'
N05310

Although mainly devoted to portraiture and history painting, West was an occasional landscapist. He sometimes painted from nature, notably in the Great Park and elsewhere in Windsor, where he owned a house. This small canvas may well have been painted in the open, as it is particularly bright in colour and loose in its brushwork. It is taken from the East Terrace of Windsor Castle, looking over the Home Park towards Datchet. The inscribed date is hard to read. A rather larger and more animated oil sketch on paper, of a view from the opposite direction looking towards Eton College Chapel, in the Museum of Fine Art, Boston, is clearly dated 1798. This latter is notable for its vivid sky, seen clearing after a storm, and double rainbow – an anticipation of Constable's sketches and an insight into the impressionable sensitivity in West's private persona that made him so sympathetic to early nature studies shown to him by Constable: indeed West advised Constable, 'Always remember, Sir, that light and shadow *never stand still*'. The Tate Gallery's sketch displays very effectively the broken cloud and silvery light so characteristic of the upper Thames valley in summer, and calls to mind West's more particular advice to Constable: 'In your skies ... always aim at *brightness*, although there are states of the atmosphere in which the sky itself is not bright. I do not mean that you are not to paint solemn or lowering skies, but even in the darkest effects there should be brightness. Your darks should look like the darks of silver, not of lead or of slate'.

West's more ambitious attempts to assimilate open-air work into the process of picture-making may be seen in a larger view of Windsor from Snow Hill in the Tate Galley, one of two oils on paper exhibited at the Royal Academy in 1799. On 1 January 1799, Joseph Farington visited West and found him 'washing up in oil colours 2 landscape sketches on paper – made in Windsor Park'. West was evidently not going as far as to paint the pictures wholly out-of-doors, but his wish to build nature study and direct observation into picture-making constitutes an interesting step in this direction. No less significant is his apparent willingness to leave the constructive process of the picture visible. West was later to condemn Turner's Thames paintings or sketches as 'vicious' and 'crude blotches' (see preliminary notes to cat.nos.13–19) but his own work can be seen to be breaking new ground here. West probably felt more able to experiment in this way from a secure academic base and because his reputation did not depend on his landscapes. Nevertheless, he recommended at least one landscape painter, Farington, to adopt the same practice of commencing his pictures before the motif and advised his pupils, including the young John Linnell, to study direct from nature.

portrait exhibited at the Royal Academy in 1797, they served no very important part in building his art, but are, perhaps, so precociously fresh precisely because of this. At times his sketches achieve a clarity of vision and animated handling almost worthy of Constable. They are strikingly free of the conventions and contrivances of the 'Picturesque', and ignore the cottages and fences so beloved of that taste in favour of trees and open fields. A later inscription on the backboard dated this sketch to 1794 but if the date beneath the image – presumably the artist's own – is correct, this would be the earliest such sketch known by Garrard. The subject is perhaps Coombe Hill to the south of Richmond Park.

BRITISH SCHOOL

6 **Dedham Vale** *c.*1795–1800
Oil on canvas
215×266 $(8\frac{7}{16} \times 10\frac{7}{16})$
TB LXX V
D04173
B&J 551a

This little oil, on canvas but quite probably painted from nature, may be dated to the end of the eighteenth century. It belongs to the Turner Bequest, but is clearly not by Turner himself, and its presence there is unexplained. Its style is rather problematic, combining reminiscences of Richard Wilson in the creamily painted distances and of Alexander and J.R. Cozens in the fir trees on the left, with a more advanced looseness of touch and brightness of tone. As the subject is definitely Dedham, seen from Langham with the Stour estuary in the distance, and has some affinities with Constable's early work – for example the upright 'Dedham Vale' painted in 1802 in the first flush of the artist's 'natural painture' – it would be tempting to

GEORGE GARRARD 1760–1826

5 **Coombe Hill** 1791
Oil on card
137×184 $(5\frac{3}{8} \times 7\frac{1}{4})$
Inscribed 'Coomb Hill 1791'
T03299

Garrard was chiefly an animal painter and sculptor and his oil sketches of landscape subjects in and around London, painted in the 1790s, were usually made for his own pleasure, or at the most to develop technical facility. Although one of a barn at Marlow (private collection) was used for the background of a cattle

attribute the picture to Constable himself but this would not be justified on present evidence (unless it were an early experiment corrected by another hand). It probably predates Constable's development of a truly personal style, rather than being a more cautious derivation from it. The attribution remains an open question. A recent suggestion of Constable's early friend Ramsay Richard Reinagle cannot be confirmed, nor is the handling particularly close to that of Sir George Beaumont, though this talented amateur and sometime painter in the open air might otherwise be a possibility as he was a frequent visitor to Dedham, where his mother had lived for some time and where he first met Constable. In view of Beaumont's prolonged hostility to Turner's work, it would be ironic if Turner had possessed an example of the baronet's; this is most unlikely, but there remains the possibility that 'Dedham' is the work of one of the numerous artists who visited Beaumont and advised him on his own painting. At the end of the century J.C. Ibbetson and S.W. Reynolds were his predominant influences, but neither is a candidate. Whatever its authorship, this picture may well have served to remind Turner of the characteristic imagery that a great contemporary drew direct from nature. Perhaps he even thought it *was* by Constable; perhaps, also, it helped to inspire some of his own occasional efforts at painting on a small scale from nature.

OIL SKETCHES BY TURNER

Kent Sketches, *c.*1799–1801

Turner's first attempt to paint a group of sketches in oil before the motif took place in Kent at the turn of the century. Nine early sketches in oil and mixed media by Turner are recorded, of which five, all in the Turner Bequest, bear inscriptions linking them with Knockholt and other Kent subjects. The remaining four, including examples in the Fitzwilliam and Fogg Art Museums, are clearly from the same series on grounds of subject matter and general treatment, although they are distinctive in being brighter in colour and, in the case of the Fitzwilliam pair, more like small pictures in their own right, with the addition of figures. The subjects are chiefly of woodland scenery, or of cottage interiors. On 30 October 1799 Farington recorded in his diary a visit from Turner who 'Has been in Kent painting from Beech Trees'; this would seem to be the earliest record of Turner painting from nature outdoors. The Fitzwilliam sketches certainly portray beechwoods in autumn, but a watercolour version of one of them may date from a year or two later. Turner's sketches of Knockholt and nearby Chevening Park have usually been associated *en bloc* with his visits to his friend William Frederick Wells, who had a cottage at Knockholt, and the kitchen interior exhibited (cat.no.8) is inscribed as being a study of Wells's cottage. But Wells did not move into it until 1801, leaving earlier work by Turner in or around the village open to some other explanation; Wells may have been a visitor to the area before acquiring his own property, or Turner's contact and host could have been another local acquaintance, Henry Fly, curate of the village church of St Katharine's.

The Kent sketches are experimental in character. They are generally executed in mixed media over sized paper. Exhibited with them here is a sized sheet on which Turner had only drawn in chalks, but which may be one of the Kent woodland scenes left unfinished (cat.no.12). It is included as an example of the prepared surfaces used for the Knockholt sketches. The use of combination media is consistent with Turner's practice about 1799–1800, and the interest in shadowy rustic domestic interiors (cat.nos.7, 8), and the gypsy motifs in the Fitzwilliam sketches, are in line with aspects of fashionable 'Picturesque' taste. By contrast, the studies of trees against light, although sometimes more subdued in colour than the Fitzwilliam examples, present a more unaffected view of pastoral nature that anticipates the Thames sketches in oil and watercolour of about five years later (cat.nos.13–19), while perhaps showing some reminiscence of the woodland subjects of Gainsborough, whose drawings Wells collected and engraved.

Turner's friend W.F. Wells. Although Turner may well have visited the area earlier, Wells did not move into his cottage until 1801. Turner's interest in dark and shadowy interiors, which appears also in watercolour about this time, may be connected with 'Picturesque' taste and also with his early interest in Rembrandt.

7 **Interior of a Cottage** *c.*1801
Oil, perhaps with watercolour and ink on paper
277×384 ($10\frac{7}{8} \times 15\frac{1}{8}$); painted surface 275×370 ($10\frac{3}{4} \times 14\frac{1}{2}$)
Inscribed on verso: '103 Interior of a Cottage, Kent'
TB XCV(a) C
D05956
B&J 35f

9 **Chevening Park*** *c.*1801
Oil, perhaps with watercolour, and size on paper
270×375 ($10\frac{5}{4} \times 14\frac{9}{16}$)
Inscribed on verso: '104 Chevening Park'
TB XCV(a) D
D05957
B&J 35g

8 **The Kitchen of Wells's Cottage, Knockholt*** *c.*1801
Oil, perhaps with watercolour and ink on paper
276×369 ($10\frac{3}{4} \times 14\frac{1}{2}$)
Inscribed on verso: '101 Wells' Kitchen Knockholt'
TB XCV(a) A
D05954
B&J 35e

With cat.no.7, one of two oil sketches of rustic kitchen interiors associated with the Knockholt cottage of

10 **Chevening Park** *c*.1801
Oil, perhaps with watercolour, and size on paper
279 × 376 ($10\frac{15}{16}$ × $14\frac{7}{8}$)
Inscribed on verso: '102 Chevening Park Kent'
TB XCV(a) B
D05955
B&J 35h

11 **'An Evening Effect': Trees at Knockholt** *c*.1801
Oil, perhaps with watercolour, and size on paper
262 × 187 ($10\frac{3}{8}$ × $7\frac{3}{8}$); painted surface 240 × 165
($9\frac{1}{2}$ × $6\frac{1}{2}$)
Inscribed on verso: '106 Knockholt Kent'
TB XCV(a) E
D05958
B&J 35i

Whereas most of the Kentish woodland sketches portray general effects, this concentrates on the more particular motif of a fractured tree-stump – though this also may be as much a gesture to 'Picturesque' vocabulary as a direct response to observed fact.

12 **Trees at Knockholt or Chevening** *c*.1799–1800
Pencil and white chalk on sized paper
374 × 271 ($14\frac{3}{4}$ × $10\frac{5}{8}$)
TB CXIX U
D08208

Hitherto kept among miscellaneous drawings in the Turner Bequest, this sheet may be convincingly placed

with the group of Kentish sketches in oil and other media on paper. Its size conforms closely to the larger of these, and would also match the much smaller ones on the assumption that some sheets were cut in half. The tree types and the rhythmic Gainsborough-like drawing style is directly comparable to the drawing visible beneath the pigment in the coloured Kentish sketches, and the size used to prepare the paper appears to be the same. Most probably this was another sheet from this group, which Turner never got around to colouring; it is shown as an example of the way he sized the paper in readiness for painting.

Thames and Wey Valley Sketches, 1805

Turner's next significant campaign of oil sketching outdoors took place in 1805. That year he moved into Sion Ferry House at Isleworth, and took an extended holiday in the summer and early autumn, exploring the Thames and its tributary the Wey, mostly by boat. Although he was off-duty in the sense that he had cut himself off from his London studio and from the production of exhibition pictures and finished watercolours, this was very much a working holiday. He had with him five sketchbooks, some canvas on a roll, which had first been prepared with a chalky white ground, and some small panels of mahogany veneer of various sizes, together with his watercolours and oils. From the work he did in various media, we can reconstruct a tour that took him upstream from Isleworth to Windsor, then along the Wey – a river that had been adapted into a navigation system for barges – to Godalming and Guildford, back to the Thames and further upstream to

Oxford. There Turner seems to have turned about and returned down river through London and out into the Estuary, perhaps continuing as far round the coast as the North Foreland and Margate.

The 1805 tour yielded a substantial body of work in pencil, watercolour and oil that addressed scenery that Turner knew from boyhood, and now appreciated both as potentially classical and Arcadian, the basis for pictures in the tradition of Claude, and as quintessentially English and pastoral, worthy of scrupulous investigation for itself. His watercolours and paintings of 1805 amount to the most sustained campaign of pure naturalism in all his work, and include the largest number of works painted directly from nature. The watercolours made this year, notably those in the 'Thames from Reading to Walton' sketchbook (TB XCV), are exceptional in his production so far – sparkling and pellucid but quite developed, evidently made for his own pleasure and instruction rather than as studies specifically directed towards other works. The oil sketches are still more remarkable, painted it seems for the most part outdoors, from Turner's boat (see the young Trimmer's account on p.20), and approaching as close as Turner ever came to the verve and immediacy of Constable's open-air sketching.

The oils fall into two distinct groups, with very different functions. One group, evidently begun first, consists of eighteen sketches on mahogany (of which five are exhibited). Turner began painting these when he reached the Windsor area (cat.no.13), and continued making them during his trip along the Wey (cat.no.14). The subjects are closely related to drawings in the 'Wey, Guildford' sketchbook (TB XCVIII). Turner used panels of various sizes – perhaps he had obtained some off cuts from a cabinet-maker – some of which he primed with a chalky material and some of which he painted on direct. All the panels were very absorbent, obliging him to work very quickly, deciding his compositional structures and chromatic patterns either beforehand or literally as he worked. He can be seen to have worked the paint with his fingers as well as with his brush, and to have rubbed and scratched at the paint while still wet to indicate features or highlights, just as he did in his watercolours. These sketches are in every sense private works, made perhaps as a deliberate experiment in the open-air painting that he knew was becoming fashionable among his contemporaries – although his vision was always general and pictorial and refused to settle on the kind of foreground details that were studied by artists like Linnell (see cat.nos.45–7).

The second group of oil studies from 1805 were painted on canvas, on unstretched sheets prepared with a dryish white or off-white ground, and carried rolled or folded; while Turner worked on them he probably tacked them over a frame or board. Fifteen show Thames subjects, made it seems between Richmond and Oxford and in tandem with drawings in the 'Thames from Reading to Walton' sketchbook. The handling of oil in the canvases is very similar to the bright and broken wash of these beautiful watercolours. These canvases too were probably painted or at least started out-of-doors, since they must be the works referred to by Trimmer as done on the boat. Their function is clearly different from that of the panels. The subjects were painted to one of Turner's standard exhibition sizes, and, however lightly brushed in, are thoroughly resolved in compositional terms. Rather than making sketches, Turner was probably experimenting with beginning pictures in the open air; the canvases may be seen as 'lay-ins' (or *ébauches*, in French parlance), with the potential for completion. Indeed it is possible that some of the finished and exhibited Thames subjects shown at Turner's Gallery in 1807 and 1808 could have begun in this way. Perhaps also these unfinished works were shown near them to make the process of their evolution, and their basis in direct observation, plain – and thus also accounting for Benjamin West's reaction as expressed to Farington, that he was 'disgusted with what he found there; views on the Thames, crude blotches, nothing could be more vicious'.

13 **Windsor Castle from the Meadows** 1805
Oil on mahogany veneer
222 × 556 ($8\frac{3}{4} \times 21\frac{7}{8}$)
N02308
B&J 179

This exceptionally freely handled sketch – especially bold in the bursts of dark paint in the trees at right – is one of three oils on the same wide, low format in which the castle is observed from distant viewpoints beyond meadows and trees, and beneath animated skies. The castle is seen from the west, lit by bright sunshine. A similar view was elaborated on a larger scale and with a wider area of water in the foreground in the sketch on canvas (cat.no.18).

15 Godalming from the South 1805
Oil on mahogany veneer
203 × 349 (8 × 13¾)
N02304
B&J 190

This panoramic treatment of the valley and winding course of the Wey, with Godalming church at left and St Catherine's Hill and chapel in the distance at centre, in evening light, anticipates the breadth of some of Turner's Devon sketches of 1813 (cat.nos.23–31). The facility and adaptability of Turner's handling is seen in the rounded modelling of the trees in the foreground, in the use of his fingers to rub in the paint in the sky, and in the hatched and cursive scratching out with the brush-handle – a habit taken over from his watercolour practice.

14 Guildford from the Banks of the Wey* 1805
Oil on mahogany veneer
254 × 197 (10 × 7¾)
N02310
B&J 188

This very freely brushed sketch shows Guildford Castle and the eighteenth-century brick tower of Trinity church from the banks of the Wey near St Catherine's chapel, in sunset light. Chalk quarries are indicated by the touches of white to right. The strongly pictorial vision that Turner maintained in even his smallest and most vigorous oil sketches is well displayed here in the upright format and essentially Claudean symmetry of the composition.

16 Walton Reach 1805
Oil on mahogany veneer
368 × 737 (14½ × 29)
N02681
B&J 185

One of two oil sketches of the Thames on wide, horizontal panels that serve to emphasise the breadth of the river. Both sketches show exceptionally mature articulation of tonal relationships and an absolutely confident concentration on essentials; their handling is correspondingly direct, the paint being laid thinly straight onto the wood, without a preparatory ground. Both sketches have sometimes been dated later than others in the Thames series, but there seems no reason to dissociate them from the campaign of sketching and drawing in 1805 that led to the two paintings of Walton Bridge probably exhibited in 1806 and 1807 (the Loyd Collection, and National Gallery of Victoria, Melbourne). The compositions are not directly related, however, and this sketch, unlike its companion, does not show Walton Bridge nor indeed any other feature specific to this stretch of the river.

17 **Sunset on the River** 1805
   Oil on mahogany veneer
   156×187 $(6\frac{1}{16} \times 7\frac{5}{16})$
   N02311
   B&J 194

While Constable was to become, in the 1820s, an assiduous sketcher of skies in oil on paper or panel, Turner's sky studies were usually made in watercolour or bodycolour. Unlike Constable's on-the-spot records, they were coloured from recollection, based either on memory or swift pencil memoranda annotated with colour notes. This sketch, made thinly and swiftly with lateral strokes of the brush, is not primarily devoted to the sky but to recording the river at evening beneath its pervasive glow; it is as likely as the other Thames sketches to have been painted in the open but its effect is one of calm rather than of a fleeting transience.

18 **A Thames Backwater with Windsor Castle in the Distance** 1805
   Oil on canvas
   867×1210 $(34\frac{1}{8} \times 47\frac{5}{8})$
   N02691
   B&J 163

One of the seventeen sketches or unfinished pictures in the Turner Bequest that seem to have been painted alongside the Thames, sometimes from an open boat, on to a roll of unstretched canvas prepared with a chalky white ground. Related to the very similar view on panel (cat.no.13) this may be the study or 'lay-in' for a projected picture, similar to the pastoral Thames subjects Turner exhibited at his own gallery between 1806 and 1809; in its unfinished state it displays a fluent and liquid handling and a bold exploitation of the ground colours, to provide clarity of tone and, where it remains exposed, to mark highlights, that is closely related to Turner's watercolour techniques. The sketch anticipates an effect of strong and enveloping light, and, through its inclusion of figures and animals and its rhythmic disposition of trees, the compositional order required for a completed work.

19 **Willows beside a Stream*** 1805
   Oil on canvas
   860×1162 $(33\frac{7}{8} \times 45\frac{3}{4})$
   N02706
   B&J 172

One of several of the large Thames sketches on unstretched canvas devoted to recording the graceful configurations of trees along the banks of the river and its tributaries. The pictorial breadth of studies like the Windsor views (cat.nos.13, 18), is balanced here by a more intimate engagement with the forms of nature –

although Turner's eye was by no means as tightly focused on specific details as Linnell's or De Wint's in their tree and plant studies (cat.nos.47, 49). The similarities to Turner's watercolour methods, observed in other Thames oils, are nowhere more marked than in this canvas. The bursts of white and brown paint in the left foreground may anticipate some narrative addition to the composition.

Occasional Sketches, *c.*1805–1815

20 **Tabley House** *c.*1808
Oil and gum arabic on paper
226 × 295 (9 × 11¾)
TB CIII 18
D06848
B&J 208

Unusually, this sketch was painted on a page of a sketchbook, the 'Tabley' book used when staying with Sir John Leicester there in the summer of 1808; it was based on the pencil drawing on pp.15 verso and 16 of the sketchbook. The sketch was cut from the book and bears signs of having been folded into four as if for despatch by post – perhaps to Sir John himself in connection with the two paintings of Tabley Turner exhibited in 1809. Turner did not normally prepare samples of this kind, but the sketch was evidently made for a practical purpose rather than from nature.

21 **English Landscape** *c.*1810
Oil on paper
192 × 268 (7⁹⁄₁₆ × 10½)
Inscribed on verso '9'

TB CXXI P
D08272
B&J 211a

More finished and darker in colour than the Devon sketches of 1813, this sketch is probably earlier. It shows a broad, rolling landscape, arranged in simple planes differentiated by tone and light with little indication of specific detail save for trees and shrubs. Although no such building appears, Finberg's association of the style and topography with the two views of Lowther Castle Turner exhibited in 1810 may well be correct.

22 **A Mountain Stream, perhaps Bolton Glen** *c.*1810-15
Mixed media over pencil on paper
445 × 590 (17⅝ × 23¼)
Watermark: 'WHATMAN 1801'
A00910
B&J 212

In subject and technique this large sketch has often been associated with the watercolours of Yorkshire scenes

Turner made for Walker Fawkes *c.*1809–18. The branches of the trees beyond the stream are indicated by drawing with the handle of the brush in wet paint, as often occurs in Turner's watercolours. The medium seems not to be pure oil but a resinous compound. Unusually among Turner's sketches in oil or related media, this was included in the 1857 display of the Turner Bequest at Marlborough House and may be one of two mountain stream subjects described in the catalogue as 'from' or 'evidently from' nature.

Devon Sketches, 1813

In the high summer of 1813 Turner paid his second visit to Devon, and was persuaded by a local landscape painter, Ambrose Johns, to make some oil sketches of the Plymouth area. Turner had almost completely ceased to sketch outdoors since his Thames and Wey studies; cat.nos.20–2 are occasional examples from the intervening years. Charles Eastlake, who was another of Turner's companions that summer, later recalled that when Turner

> returned to Plymouth, in the neighbourhood of which he remained some weeks, Mr. Johns fitted up a small portable painting-box, containing some prepared paper for oil sketches, as well as the other necessary materials. When Turner halted at a scene and seemed inclined to sketch it, Johns produced the inviting box, and the great artist, finding everything ready to his hand, immediately began to work. As he sometimes wanted assistance in the use of the box, the presence of Johns was indispensible, and after a few days he made his oil sketches freely in our presence. Johns accompanied him always; I was only with them occasionally. Turner seemed pleased when the rapidity with which those sketches were done was talked of; for, departing from his habitual reserve in the instance of his pencil sketches, he made no difficulty of showing them. On one occasion, when … the day's work was shown, he himself remarked that one of the sketches (and perhaps the best) was done in less than half an hour.
>
> When he left Plymouth, he carried off all the results. We had reckoned that Johns who had provided all the materials, and had waited upon him devotedly, would at least have had a present of one or two of the sketches. This was not the case; but long afterwards, the great painter sent Johns in a letter a small oil sketch, not painted from nature, as a return for his kindness and assistance. On my inquiring afterwards what had become of those

sketches, Turner replied that they were worthless, in consequence, as he supposed of some defects in the preparation of the paper; all the grey tints, he observed, had nearly disappeared. Although I did not implicitly rely on that statement, I do not remember to have seen any of them afterwards.

Twelve of these sketches are in the Turner Bequest. Another is in the Leeds City Art Galleries, and two are in private collections in the USA. It seems that a number of others once existed; they were probably removed or sold from Turner's studio after his death, and before being registered for his Bequest.

One sketch was made on an unprimed surface composed of at least two sheets of strong paper, one of which had belonged to a printed prospectus for *The British Gallery of Pictures,* by William Young Ottley and Henry Tresham, published in 1808. Others were painted on ordinary thick wrapping paper, probably originally of a pale blue colour. The buff-grey that appears today in the unpainted areas of the sketches is probably the result of changes in the ground applied to prepare the papers for painting; this was probably a grey oil base, made with a proportion of indigo. Johns was evidently responsible for this preparation, and it was unusual for Turner not to use surfaces prepared either by himself or by his father. His remarks about subsequent tonal changes must have applied to the ground colour rather than to his own pigments in the painted areas, for these remain vivid and bright even today. Despite his later disillusionment, he was at first pleased with the results, and another Devon friend, the journalist Cyrus Redding, reported him in uncharacteristically forthcoming mood at a picnic at Mount Edgcumbe; 'Turner showed the ladies some of his sketches in oil, which he had brought with him, perhaps to verify them'.

Redding's remark suggests a no less unusual emphasis on topographical accuracy, although in fact the sketches – most particularly those of panoramic views – take some of Turner's usual liberties with scenic truth for pictorial effect. Redding's account differs significantly from Eastlake's in its description of Turner's method; according to him Turner 'would only make a few outlines on paper, scarcely intelligible to others. The next day or days after he would have the sketch filled up in oil upon millboard, not much larger than a sheet of letter-paper, still confused to the unpractised eye'. None of the Devon sketches now known are on millboard. All are on prepared paper, painted over black chalk outlines to varying degrees of finish. It has been suggested that Turner made a second set after the failure of the first, in 1813 or 1814, but the deterioration he described to Eastlake probably occurred some time later.

23 On the Plym Estuary near Crabtree 1813
Oil over black chalk on prepared paper
158×257 ($6\frac{5}{16} \times 10\frac{1}{8}$); painted surface 150×235
($6 \times 9\frac{1}{4}$)
TB CXXX J
D09216
B&J 222

Turner's subject is the limekilns at Crabtree, below Plympton's Long Bridge, near the east entrance of Saltram Park.

25 Milton Combe 1813
Oil over black chalk on prepared paper
165×240 ($6\frac{1}{2} \times 9\frac{1}{2}$); painted surface 150×235
($6 \times 9\frac{1}{4}$)
TB CXXX A
D09207
B&J 213

Perhaps a view of Milton Combe from the elevated field now known as Donkey's Platt.

24 Shaugh Bridge, near Plymouth 1813
Oil on prepared paper
158×266 ($6\frac{1}{4} \times 10\frac{1}{2}$)
TB CXXX I
D09215
B&J 221

Shaugh Bridge lies at the confluence of the Plym and the Meavy, six miles north of Plymouth. Together with the eminence known as Dewerstone Rock, seen beyond the bridge in the right distance, this was a popular sketching spot. Cyrus Redding recalled Turner having a picnic 'on the romantic banks of the Plym' at a point about three miles from here, towards the end of his Devon tour in 1813.

26 Plympton 1813
Oil over black chalk on prepared paper
148×255 ($5\frac{13}{16} \times 10\frac{1}{16}$); painted surface 140×235
($5\frac{1}{2} \times 9\frac{1}{4}$)
TB CXXX B
D09208
B&J 214

The birthplace of Joshua Reynolds, Plympton was also the home of the father of Turner's friend Charles Eastlake. Eastlake recalled that Turner made a 'sketching ramble' to the house, St Mary's Hill, which stood very near this vantage point. The mound in the left-distance is Dorsmouth Rock; the bridge in the foreground crosses the Tory Brook. There is another landscape study on the back of this sheet.

27 **Hamoaze from St John, Cornwall** 1813
Oil on prepared paper
164 × 257 ($6\frac{7}{16}$ × $10\frac{1}{8}$); painted surface 160 × 235
($6\frac{1}{4}$ × $9\frac{1}{4}$)
TB CXXX C
D09209
B&J 215

St John looks towards the Hamoaze and Plymouth Dock (now Devonport). A line of men-of-war appears there at anchor. Cyrus Redding observed the ships during a boat-trip with Turner along the St German's River, an inlet opening into St John's Lake, seen here in the middle distance. Turner's view is taken from the popular beauty spot of Wolsdon Hill.

29 **A Bridge with a Cottage and Trees beyond** 1813
Oil over black chalk on prepared paper
159 × 261 ($6\frac{5}{16}$ × $10\frac{1}{4}$); painted surface 150 × 235
($5\frac{7}{8}$ × $9\frac{1}{4}$)
TB CXXX F
D09212
B&J 218

This is the less finished of two sketches in the Turner Bequest apparently showing the same unidentified bridge from different sides.

28 **A Quarry, Perhaps at Saltram*** 1813
Oil on prepared paper
144 × 257 ($5\frac{11}{16}$ × $10\frac{1}{8}$); painted surface 135 × 235
($5\frac{1}{4}$ × $9\frac{1}{4}$)
TB CXXX D
D09210
B&J 216

Turner's subject, a slate quarry of which a number existed around Saltram, provides an opportunity for a working landscape of the type sketched by other artists like John Linnell and G.R. Lewis (cat.no.53).

30 **Plymouth from Stonehouse** 1813
Oil on prepared paper
156 × 258 ($6\frac{1}{8}$ × $10\frac{1}{8}$); painted surface 145 × 235
($5\frac{3}{4}$ × $9\frac{1}{4}$)
TB CXXX G
D09213
B&J 219

A view of Plymouth from Stonehouse Creek, to the west of the town. Plymouth citadel probably appears veiled in mist in the right distance while the tower of St Andrew's church, and the spire of Charles church may be seen to left of centre.

31 **The Plym Estuary from the North** 1813
Oil on prepared paper
155 × 257 ($6\frac{1}{8}$ × $10\frac{1}{8}$); painted surface 145 × 235
($5\frac{3}{4}$ × $9\frac{1}{4}$)
TB CXXX add L
D40028
B&J 224

A view from Lipson Hill, looking along the old Laira road to the estuary and the woods of Saltram House at night. Clarke's Battery is seen on the top of a hill at left, and beyond it the edges of Dartmoor. This particular area was admired for its fine views and Turner has responded with an expansive sketch in which he is fully alert to 'Picturesque' pictorial possibilities.

Isle of Wight Sketches, 1827

In July and August 1827 Turner stayed with the architect John Nash at East Cowes Castle. A group of oil sketches on canvas belongs to this visit. For these Turner employed the sort of rolls of canvas he had probably used for his earlier Thames and Wey sketches. He asked his father to send him one or two pieces of unstretched canvas, either a piece 6 feet by 4 feet or a 'whole length'. He received the former, and cut it into two strips, on which he painted the nine sketches in the Bequest, five on one and four on the other. These rolls were rediscovered at the National Gallery in 1905 and separated.

Three sketches of yachts racing in the Solent and the Medina river served for each of two pictures painted for Nash, and exhibited at the Royal Academy in 1829, 'East Cowes Castle, the Regetta Beating to Windward' (Indianapolis Museum of Art) and 'East Cowes Castle, the Regatta Starting from their Moorings' (Victoria and Albert Museum). The Cowes Regatta had only been inaugurated the previous year, 1826, so was both a dramatic and a highly topical subject. It is uncertain whether or not Turner painted his sketches of it in the open – the practical difficulties of handling a fairly bulky roll of canvas on the water or even near the shore, and the constant movement of the yachts in the strong breeze, might well seem insuperable, but there is an outdoor immediacy and freshness of colour about the sketches that seems to suggest spontaneous response. Some of the sketches may have been taken from the secure vantage point of a naval vessel at anchor; one sketch not exhibited shows a scene between decks looking towards an open gun-port – perhaps Turner's chosen viewpoint.

Besides the sketches definitely associated with East Cowes and the Regatta, and known to have been on the rolls of canvas, there are some other small oils on canvas of marine subjects taken near the coast which could be of the same date and record impressions from Turner's stay on the Isle of Wight. They are more likely to be studio works, sketched perhaps in the painting room Turner used at East Cowes Castle, to organise his observations and memories into pictorial matter much as he did in his oil sketches painted in Italy (cat.nos.36–8). Comparison with such generalised ideas serves to emphasise the vivid actuality of the core group of Cowes sketches – evidently the result of concentrated observation and specific experience, painted while the impression was still very fresh if not always wholly before the motif.

32 **Sketch for 'East Cowes Castle, the Regatta Beating to Windward' No.2*** 1827
Oil on canvas
457 × 610 (18 × $24\frac{1}{16}$)
NO1994
B&J 261

One of four sketches painted on the second of two rolls of canvas that Turner used at Cowes in 1827, and one of three spirited impressions of the Regatta used in the preparation of the picture painted for Turner's host on the Isle of Wight, the architect John Nash, and exhibited at the Royal Academy in 1828 (Indianapolis Museum of Art, Indiana). The sketches are swiftly painted, with considerable impasto. They may combine some rapid notations taken on the spot from a ship, with further work added back at East Cowes Castle.

33 **Shipping off East Cowes Headland*** 1827
Oil on canvas
460 × 603 ($18\frac{1}{8}$ × $23\frac{7}{8}$)
NO1999
B&J 267

With the Regatta subject also exhibited, this was one of four oil sketches made on the second of two rolls of canvas that Turner used at Cowes in 1827. It records a scene of almost transcendental calm, in contrast to the breezy movement of the Regatta sketches, and might therefore be a more likely candidate for a sketch begun outdoors, perhaps from a boat. The view is taken looking directly towards East Cowes headland.

34 **Three Seascapes** *c.*1827
Oil on canvas
908 × 603 ($35\frac{5}{8}$ × $23\frac{5}{8}$)
NO5491
B&J 271

Turner's Cowes sketches in 1827 had included, on the first of his two canvas rolls, an economical but evocative study of a choppy sea beneath a wide field of sky, taken from a point looking towards the distant coastline. A group of similar marine studies, cursory in handling and abstracted in composition, exists in the Bequest. These

sketches may also be dated to the later 1820s, and might have been painted while at East Cowes, or worked up in the studio from the recollections of Turner's stay there: at the same time they look forward to the many meditations on marine and coastal themes Turner painted in the late 1830s and early 1840s. None of these marine sketches is likely to have been painted before the motif, but this canvas is included to show how Turner used his rolls of canvas, and how the Cowes sketches must have looked before they were separated. The canvas bears three sketches of sea and sky, one of which was painted upside down so that one sky serves for two subjects if the canvas is turned. It is exhibited here with two seascapes the right way up.

Roman Sketches, 1828

While painting in oil apparently played little or no part in Turner's activities during his first visit to Italy in 1819, he undertook a considerable body of work in oil when back in Rome in 1828. Besides some large and finished canvases, he made a number of oil sketches. Seven were painted on one large roll of canvas, which was divided in 1913–14; with nine similar sketches, these compositions are surrounded by tack holes, indicating that Turner pinned them over a frame or board while he painted them. As at Cowes, it would have been convenient to transport canvas rolled. Turner also painted some ten sketches on small panels of millboard, covered in most cases with muslin.

Italy, and especially Rome, had long been a centre for oil painting and sketching in the open air (see the introductory essay), and this activity had reached a peak in the 1820s, chiefly among the northern European painters who congregated in the city. Charles Eastlake, Turner's companion during his sketching holiday in Devon in 1813 (see p.52), and now his co-resident in Rome at 12 Piazza Mignanelli, took part in such activities himself and seems to have helped to introduce Turner to a number of other participants. Given Turner's well-established habits of work while on tour – pencil sketching on the spot and making watercolours back in his lodgings – the sheer quantity of material to study in Italy, and his ambitious commitment to studio pictures while in Rome, it is understandable that he did not yield to any pressure that may have been applied to join in; he was also presumably well aware that sketching from nature in oil was widely perceived by the Continental artists as part of the learning process, and must have felt rather above it. He had made his views about open-air painting plain enough in 1819, and there is no evidence that he had substantially changed his mind. The small millboard panels, however, could easily have been taken outdoors, and one at least (cat.no.35) is as fresh and direct as anything by the Romantic *plein-airistes*. But the majority bear subjects of a very non-specific kind – composition studies, exercises in Claudean design, or investigations of atmospheric and aerial perspective. While some convey the synoptic effect of an ideal Italy, others like the desolate marine with a burning hulk (cat.no.38) need not be Mediterranean at all.

The canvases are likewise mainly studio meditations, again on Claudean themes of seaports or idyllic pastorals, rather than direct impressions from nature. One has always been recognised as a study for a picture, 'Ulysses deriding Polyphemus' of 1829 (National Gallery), while another surely served as a basis for 'The Parting of Hero and Leander' of 1837. The entire group is best read as a body of composition studies laid down as a reserve for future reference. However, unlike the millboards the canvases also embody powerful atmospheric and lighting effects, so that the ideal and conceptual is modified by the real and observed. As in his studies in watercolour, there are strong, indeed deliberately exaggerated contrasts of tone in these canvases; the compositions are worked out in broadly brushed areas of flat colour and emphasised by passages of robust impasto.

In such schematic and idealising designs it is vain to

search for topographical sources, although the canvas of the Cascatelle at Tivoli (cat.no.36), with another of Lake Nemi, shows that Turner had – like his contemporary Corot in his own Roman work – assimilated not only the universal compositional conventions of classical landscape, but also the particular Italian sites most hallowed by a long artistic tradition. One sketch from this group, the so-called 'Park' (cat.no.37), may be of special interest in the context of this exhibition, for it is tempting to identify the subject as the rambling and umbrageous gardens of the Villa Borghese or Villa Negroni, both beloved haunts of open-air painters. But its very broad and diffuse treatment serves only to demonstrate how far Turner stood apart from their sharply focused observations.

35 **Hill Town on the Edge of the Campagna*** ?1828
Oil on millboard
410 × 594 ($16\frac{1}{8}$ × $23\frac{3}{8}$)
N05526
B&J 318

Perhaps a study near Rome, with the river Tiber or Aniene. Painted directly on to the millboard, this of all the small oils associated with Turner's Roman stay in 1828 is the most likely to have been painted from nature. Turner's concern is not with details of topography, but with laying down broad bands of tone to match effects of aerial perspective, rather as he did in his studies in watercolour. If painted outdoors, this exercise in recording a chromatic match for atmospheric gradations would correspond closely to the type of open-air painting that Claude was said to have practised (see p.9).

36 **Tivoli, the Cascatelle*** 1828

Oil on canvas

607 × 777 ($23\frac{7}{8} × 30\frac{1}{2}$)

N03388

B&J 311

With a view of Lake Nemi, one of two of the series of oils on canvas painted in 1828 that certainly show particular places. Both Lake Nemi and Tivoli had long been celebrated beauty spots and favourite subjects for painters. As a youth Turner had copied paintings by Richard Wilson of both places, and in 1818, a year before he visited Tivoli for the first time, he exhibited a large watercolour, 'Landscape: Composition of Tivoli' at the Royal Academy. As rich in historical association as in scenic beauty, Tivoli claimed Turner's prolonged attention in 1819 and occupied almost two whole sketchbooks. Turner presumably revisited Tivoli in 1828. In common with the other oils on canvas of 1828, this was most probably painted in the Roman studio rather than in the open; however, it is particularly robust in handling, painted thinly over a pale ground and enlivened by bursts of impasto.

37 **A Park** 1828

Oil on canvas

603 × 987 ($23\frac{3}{4} × 38\frac{7}{8}$)

N03384

B&J 315

Turner's chief interest here is in strong contrasts of light and shade, and in the pattern of trees against a powerful light. Though, like the other Italian canvases of 1828, this was probably not painted out-of-doors, it anticipates exactly the kind of studies of figures that the Impressionists painted in the open air so as to absorb their subjects in what Manet called 'the vibrations of the atmosphere'. The idyllic setting of this painting has not been identified, but is perhaps a shady corner of the garden of the Villa Borghese or Villa Negroni in Rome, where many artists loved to paint.

38 **Seascape with Burning Hulk** ?1828

Oil on muslin mounted on millboard

241 × 416 ($9\frac{1}{2} × 16\frac{3}{8}$)

N05535

B&J 325

The cold lighting and mood of lonely melancholy in this very broadly handled sketch looks forward to the marine sketches of the 1830s and early 1840s, whose subjects were most probably suggested by Turner's experiences during his frequent visits to Margate (cat.nos.39–44). The sketch gives particular attention to the sky, whose changing moods Turner usually chose to preserve in the more fluid medium of watercolour. The motif of the burning hulk may be related to Turner's interest in marine conflagrations, developed in his painting 'Fire at Sea' and in drawings in his 'Fire at Sea' sketchbook (TB CCLXXXII), usually dated to the mid 1830s. There are two similar sketches in oil on muslin in the Bequest, of beaches, seas and skies without specific incident. All three might appear to belong to the 1830s, but the present example was apparently on the same piece of millboard as a very Italianate composition, which must certainly belong to the group of millboard sketches generally assigned to 1828. This sketch was more probably a studio recollection than an impression from nature.

Late Coast Sketches

Turner's studio contained large numbers of oils of beaches and coastal seascapes observed in changing but often stormy conditions. Most were included in the Turner Bequest although some were dispersed after his death. They included both large studies on canvas of the size Turner used for exhibition pictures, and smaller sketches on canvas and board. They are most probably to be associated with the frequent visits Turner paid in later life to Margate, where he stayed with his landlady and mistress Mrs Booth in her house overlooking the harbour. As many portray stormy and rainy effects, these could hardly have been painted in the open air even if Turner's withdrawal from outdoor painting were not by now complete. Nevertheless they are among the most powerful impressions of fugitive natural effects in all Romantic painting, conveying a sense of the artist's total absorption in his subject, and of his by now complete confidence in matching his materials, both in colour and handling, to the experiences he is painting. The truth and understanding that is felt so strongly in the late sea paintings is the result of more than a single observation; it stems from years of looking, learning and remembering. Turner's marine storms may seem as legitimate an investigation of natural phenomena as Constable's skies, but they do not offer us a precise record, rather an overwhelming sense of what it is like to experience such conditions, drenched, blown about, but invigorated.

These canvases may have been painted near to nature, in the sense that they were presumably mainly painted in the Margate house with its marine views, but they were probably meditated over a longer period than the limited attention span of the sketch from nature. Perhaps, like the Thames canvases of 1805, some were laid aside for future elaboration, with ships or figures, into exhibitable pictures, but more probably they were painted for Turner's own interest and pleasure. As with Constable's skies of the early 1820s (see cat.no.60), their purpose must remain rather mysterious. They could be seen partly as a development of his Thames work of 1805 – not made like those studies outdoors, but nevertheless painted near the motif, and from a position of strong emotional involvement. In both scale and

power of feeling, the late marines transcend the limits of the traditional oil sketch from nature.

No less remarkable is a group of small oils on millboard that address similar subjects of beaches, waves and isolated figures or ships, in a manner more abstract and perfunctory than anything he ever painted in oil. These are often little more than studies in tonal relationships, comparable only to the sketches he had long made in watercolour, although a dab or two of a darker colour serves to hint at the life of beach and sea. These too cannot be sketches made outdoors, for Turner seems to have entered into the very spray and surge of the breakers as they crash on the shore. Rather he is recreating the experience of his walks on the sands, from memory and, perhaps, inspired by the movement of paint itself. We may imagine him toying with his brush and using up old pieces of board to amuse himself, perhaps on returning from a walk on the beach. Even if not painted amid the elements they describe, few of his painted sketches convey more sense of the open air.

39 **Breakers on a Flat Beach** *c.*1830–5
Oil on canvas
902 × 1210 ($35\frac{1}{2}$ × $47\frac{5}{8}$)
N01987
B&J 456

One of the more coherent of the larger sketches on canvas of sea and sky painted by Turner during the 1830s and early 40s, this may date from earlier rather than later in the period. Although it is handled with the boldness and nervous energy of a sketch from nature, it is, like the other late marines, almost certainly a studio canvas – or at least one painted indoors. If painted at Margate, on the other hand, these pictures were probably made within sight of the subjects they describe, by the windows of Mrs Booth's house overlooking the harbour, so that they were informed by observation and experience. Rather like Alexander Cozens's sky study, 'Before Storm' (cat.no.1), paintings like these were probably made to present typical effects, suggestive of certain moods rather than particular moments – though unlike Cozens, Turner did not intend them for publication. Such fleeting and fugitive effects as these clouds and breakers are of course impossible to freeze in a single moment, save in a photograph, but as had been the case with Cozens, Turner derived these typical effects from long hours of watching the elements at work, and, as in the famous story of how he had himself tied to a mast to observe a storm at sea, he was at pains to stress their accuracy. Laid aside in the studio, such canvases preserved essential truths about the natural world, and different levels of emotional pitch. They could perhaps have been elaborated with figures or shipping, for sale or exhibition if required.

41 **Two Figures on a Beach with a Boat*** *c.*1840–5
Oil on millboard
245 × 347 ($9\frac{5}{8}$ × $13\frac{5}{8}$)
D36681
B&J 499

40 **Shore Scene with Waves and Breakwater** *c.*1835
Oil on millboard
230 × 305 (9 × 12)
D36680
B&J 486

42 **Sunset Seen from a Beach with Breakwater** *c.*1840–5
Oil on millboard
258 × 300 ($9\frac{3}{4}$ × $11\frac{7}{8}$)
D36679
B&J 497

43 **Riders on a Beach** *c.*1835
Oil on millboard
230 × 305 (9 × 12)
D36675
B&J 485

With cat.no.40, whose restricted palette of yellow, pink, brown and white it shares, this sketch is executed on a smoother and thicker millboard than the others of similar subjects, and is probably rather earlier.

44 **Coast Scene with Buildings** *c.*1840–5
Oil on millboard
305 × 475 (12 × 18¾)
D36678
B&J 487

The most compositionally developed of the group of late coast sketches, this transforms an English beach into the ghost of a classical seaport.

TURNER'S CONTEMPORARIES

Naturalism and the 'Picturesque'

Study from nature and a selective aesthetic like the 'Picturesque' may seem contradictions in terms, yet the former need not imply a quest for naturalism alone. Eighteenth-century painters operating entirely within established traditions and academic discipline had made marvellous studies in oil of individual motifs, without ever intending to take them at their face value in their finished work. Such study was part of an artist's training; as Ruskin was to put it, the duty of the young artist was 'neither to choose nor compose, nor imagine, nor experimentalise but be humble and earnest in following the steps of nature and tracing the finger of God'. But it remained an open question whether such tracings could really make a picture.

The 'Picturesque', meanwhile, had given a spur to nature study by encouraging interest in wild and uncultivated things; its emphasis on the rough and haphazard, contrasts of texture and light and what Fuseli called 'the meanest things in nature' carried with it the idea of spontaneity, but gave the lie to a truly impartial approach. The 'Picturesque' was as selective a taste as the classical ideal to which it constituted so appealing an antithesis. John Varley, whose own work tended to adhere to classical forms, taught his pupils to 'go to Nature for everything', but they responded with studies of features that corresponded exactly to fashionable 'Picturesque' vocabulary, and later incorporated the results into pictures that were not at all to be compared to Constable's 'natural painture'. Mulready, whom Linnell regarded as the most rigorous empiricist of his generation, painted some pictures of cottages and barns that struck some contemporaries as uncompromisingly direct – indeed they seemed hardly 'pictures' at all – but now appear to be textbook expositions of the 'Picturesque'; and he later abandoned even these for genre subjects in which landscape is certainly sensitively observed, but was not the main point. It was in fact Linnell who was most intellectually committed to a greater naturalism, if only as an expression of his religious faith which – especially after his Baptist conversion in 1811, and his reading of William Paley's *Natural Theology* – saw landscape and its proper human cultivation as symbolic of Creation and worship, and his art as an act of witness. If the natural world was the manifestation of the divine, it followed that it should be enough to paint it as it was – and in the field whenever possible. Linnell did in fact relinquish the 'Picturesque' details of his early work in favour of a broader vision of the countryside, but so far from discovering a greater naturalism, moved towards more overt use of typological symbols and sometimes to specific religious or historical narrative, writing of these to a dealer; 'When such subjects are attempted with sincerity I think the painter observes and brings out higher and more impressive qualities of nature than when treating the merely natural'.

Linnell's later work is often highly wrought, and aspires to High Art. Turner's, of course, always had, and Constable too turned towards a more synoptic and elevated view of the natural world than the 'pure and unaffected representation' he had sought in Suffolk in 1802. Such a view inevitably involved a return to more traditional methods of picture-making, and to the processes of synthesis and adaptation associated with the studio. The spontaneity of the landscape sketched outdoors, and the particularity of specific motifs studied from nature, could not alone produce what Linnell called 'poetical landscape' – or Pissarro, after his own return to the studio, the 'true poem of the countryside'.

weather permitted, painting in oil on millboard from nature'. These little oils focus closely on specific details and show a propensity towards the ramshackle and untidy. In these sketches, an impulse towards naturalism is likely to be the chief appeal today, but for the artists it was combined with an interest in the pictorial language of the 'Picturesque'.

JOHN LINNELL 1792–1882

46 **Study of Buildings ('Study from Nature')*** 1806
Oil on board
165 × 254 (6½ × 10)
Inscribed on verso: 'No 9 Study from Nature (1806) in Oil John Linnell'
T00935

This tightly concentrated study of a decrepit barn, reminiscent perhaps of Jones's investigations of Neapolitan walls (cat.no.3), must be another of Linnell's Twickenham studies. Tumbledown farm buildings and cottages were key elements in the 'Picturesque' vocabulary and form the subjects of early paintings by Linnell's friend Mulready (cat.no.50). Linnell often recycled his early material in his mature work, and as late as 1831 he repeated this motif verbatim in his painting 'Milking Time' (Victoria and Albert Museum). Despite a tendency towards highly wrought effects in his later landscape painting, Linnell continued to value a sound basis of nature study, and in 1828 advised Samuel Palmer to modify the personal vision of his work at Shoreham in favour of a more objective approach.

JOHN LINNELL 1792–1882

45 **Study from Nature: At Twickenham** 1806
Oil on board
165 × 254 (6½ × 10)
Inscribed on verso: 'By J. Linnell 1806 at Twickenham'
T00934

Linnell was first instructed by Benjamin West (see cat.no.4), who encouraged him to study from nature. Later he was taught by John Varley. With the two following, this sketch was evidently made during Linnell's year of apprenticeship to Varley, when, aged fourteen, he, W.H. Hunt (cat.no.48) and other pupils were taken to work in oil from nature at Twickenham. Linnell later recalled: 'Hunt and I were always out,

JOHN LINNELL 1792–1882

47 Study of a Tree ('Study from Nature') 1806
Oil on board
324 × 168 ($12\frac{3}{4} \times 6\frac{5}{8}$)
T01490

To be compared to Hunt's tree study (cat.no.48), doubtless made the same summer.

WILLIAM HENRY HUNT 1790–1864

48 Study from Nature at Twickenham *c*.1806
Oil on board
330 × 168 ($13 \times 6\frac{5}{8}$)
Inscribed on verso 'Study from Nature at Twickenham by Hunt about 1806'
T01154

Like Linnell, Hunt was apprenticed to John Varley in 1806, and joined him in expeditions oil sketching at Twickenham. In this sketch he has discovered an unaffected mode almost identical to Linnell's (cat.no.47) and added to it a more fluid, painterly handling. The asymmetric placing of the tree and the use of only part of the board reminds one of Desportes's studies of trees and plants. Hunt's subsequent career as a watercolourist was to lead him into a different branch of naturalism; his studies of flowers, still life, and his very popular birds' nests convey a Pre-Raphaelite intensity of detail far removed from the impromptu feeling of this sketch.

PETER DE WINT 1784–1849

49 Study of Burdock and Other Plants *c*.1806–12
Oil on board
262 × 335 ($10\frac{3}{8} \times 13\frac{1}{4}$)
T03669

Although De Wint was best known as a watercolourist, he had always had ambitions as a professional oil painter, and was first apprenticed to John Raphael Smith for training in engraving and portraiture. In 1806 he was released from his indentures on condition that, besides a group of watercolours, he should paint nine pictures in oil, all landscapes. Smith fostered De Wint's lifelong concern for open-air study by taking him on expeditions by the Thames oil sketching while he fished; and this concern would have been nurtured by De Wint's friendship with John Varley, who was his London neighbour early in the century. The small group of beautiful oil studies of grasses and weeds to which this sketch belongs was surely the result of a campaign of painting from nature. These oils may have been made for Smith, or perhaps De Wint even joined Varley's pupils in their Twickenham expeditions, for they are very close in spirit to the nature studies of Linnell and Hunt (cat.nos.47, 48). Although he generally sought very broad effects, De Wint referred to similarly closely observed studies of flowers and foliage in watercolour – most of which are generally dated *c*.1812 – for the foreground details of his finished works.

the same way as they painted their sketches, working outdoors or *alla prima*. Turner's apparent attempt in 1805 to begin full-scale pictures of the Thames from his boat was an exceptionally adventurous endeavour in this direction, and it was one he never repeated; his smaller oils on wood panel from the same year, although thoroughly pictorial in composition, were not intended to be seen, and cannot be compared to the exhibited 'sketches' of his contemporaries. Constable meanwhile maintained a clear distinction between his sketches and finished works, only once finishing a picture in the open before the motif and in fact disparaging the work of Mulready and Linnell. He thought the artificial overwhelmed the natural in their small rustic 'Picturesque' pictures, and likened his sensations before them to being 'smothered in a privy'.

The Sketch as Picture

Oil sketching from nature had traditionally served purely private purposes. The details and effects that the painter preserved in this way were gathered for his education or pleasure, or were laid down as a stock of reference material for his paintings. It was not envisaged that they could become works of art in themselves; nor was the spontaneity of a sketch, however necessary in training a painter's perceptions, considered appropriate for a picture. But at least for a few years, from the close of the eighteenth century, the ethos of the 'Picturesque' tended to modify this view. The random and untidy natural features, the rough textures of surface, both of subject and paint, the strong contrasts of light and shade, that arbiters of the 'Picturesque' like Richard Payne Knight so admired, matched the qualities found in rapid sketches caught on the spot but were now thought desirable in pictures also. Knight made a point of expressing a preference for sketches over finished pictures, and besides giving a fillip to 'naturalism' by encouraging intense study of the individual landscape features that it favoured most, the 'Picturesque' encouraged the production of small works that were thoroughly pictorial in arrangement, but retained the zest and impromptu quality of a sketch. Small oils by Delamotte, Mulready, Callcott, G.R. Lewis, Cotman or Havell can be seen to create a new genre, the sketch as picture. Such works were not necessarily, but probably most often were, painted mainly outdoors; and they were sometimes exhibited as 'studies from nature' or 'painted on the spot'. In brightness and freshness of colour and freedom of handling they mark a new departure, but it is important to recognise their background and to appreciate that their motivation was not simply naturalistic. Nor did the sketch as picture imply that artists were ready to paint pictures in

WILLIAM MULREADY 1786–1863

50 **Cottage and Figures** exh.1807
Oil on paper laid on board
397 × 333 ($15\frac{5}{8}$ × $13\frac{1}{8}$)
T01746

This small oil was exhibited at the Royal Academy in 1807. Like Linnell in his early paintings and oil sketches, Mulready's work of the first decade of the century shows a synthesis of 'Picturesque' motifs and naturalistic observation. Linnell, who wished him to have been his teacher, considered his method the most vigorously objective of any artist of his generation; indeed he was the only one who 'endeavoured by copying beautiful nature faithfully to do as the Greeks had done – to produce something that was not second hand but from enlightened original perceptions'. But if Mulready's practice was naturalistic, his vocabulary also remained distinctly 'Picturesque', its language owing much to Dutch painting. Like Gainsborough, whose art was formed on Dutch examples, Mulready and Linnell set up models of landscape on a table-top scale, made up of 'carefully chosen picturesque specimens', and by 'carefully copying all the beautiful varieties of tint and texture . . . we learnt to see beauty in everything'. They simply applied the same objectivity to what they studied and painted outdoors. Samuel Palmer also stressed the educative, disciplinary, aspect of Mulready's practice, recalling him as a 'disciple of exactness' who advocated 'copying sometimes objects which were not beautiful, to cut away the adventitious aid of association', and adding an eccentric personal note to prove the value of the exercise; 'when I have gone to school to a potato . . . I have found it difficult to make it unmistakably like'.

It may well seem, then, that the nature sketching of Mulready and Linnell differed little in purpose from that of the eighteenth century painters. But the results *were* different. The 'Picturesque' aesthetic that informed their work enabled them to transmit more of their studies into pictures, and to display pictures that had the feel of sketches, creating, whether they precisely intended it or not, a naturalistic imperative. This process was especially evident in Mulready's early pictures like this study of a near-ruined cottage with St Albans' Abbey in the distance – a classic exposition of the 'Picturesque', handled with the formal and tonal abstraction of a sketch, but presented for exhibition. The delight in contrasted textures and broken patterns seen in Linnell's sketch of a barn (cat.no.46) is developed by Mulready in what is in effect a finished picture on a cabinet scale. Mulready reached something of a watershed in his career when, in answer to a commission obtained on his behalf by Callcott from a Mr Horley, he produced two very direct paintings of the mall at Kensington Gravel Pits (Victoria and Albert Museum). They stand as the climax of his early naturalistic 'Picturesque', and almost certainly embody a degree of open-air work. They were apparently rejected by the Royal Academy, and according to F.G. Stephens in 1867, both the patron and Callcott himself reneged on the commission: 'His patrons were not "educated" enough to admit, still less to admire, anything so literal . . . the one refusing to recognise them as pictures, the other as not fulfilling the commissions he had given'. Mulready's mature work developed, to great effect, the genre elements discreetly present in these early pictures.

WILLIAM DELAMOTTE 1775–1863

51 **Waterperry, Oxfordshire** 1803
Oil on board
324 × 489 (12¾ × 19¼)
Inscribed on verso: July 1st: Waterperry. Oxon. 1803 Wm. DelaMotte 1st day. Cloudy, & likely to rain w. Thunder storms – 2d Day. Weather clearing. w. cloud'
TO1050

An early example of a group of oil sketches on prepared panel made in the Thames valley early in Delamotte's tenure as drawing master at the Royal Military Academy at Great Marlow. Two other similarly bright and broadly handled sketches of Waterperry near Oxford with the Isis flowing in the foreground, are at the Yale Center for British Art, New Haven. They are dated to July 1805 – the same year as Turner was exploring the Thames as far as Oxford from his boat. Delamotte, who had known Turner since at least 1800, may have helped to encourage him to sketch from nature at Knockholt at the turn of the century; it is tantalising to speculate on further contact in 1805.

Delamotte's sketches are, however, more finished than Turner's; they have the gloss and clarity of small pictures. This example is perhaps the closest in spirit to the early oils of Mulready and Callcott, developing similarly 'Picturesque' rustic features.

JOHN SELL COTMAN 1782–1842

52 **Duncombe Park, Yorkshire** *c.*1806–8
Oil on paper laid on canvas
416 × 279 (16⅜ × 11)
N03572

Cotman was only an occasional oil painter; the medium
was often too expensive for him, and the small landscapes in oil that he began to paint on returning to his
native Norwich in 1806 after failing to make any great
success in London, were not well received. Late in his
career, motivated by financial exigencies and by his
predilection as a colourist for earthy and warm effects,
he developed a 'paste' medium of his own. His finest
works in pure oil are from the first decade. They
combine the very personal vision, the superlative gift for
pattern-making, seen in his watercolours, with the
density of texture and tonal resonance of oil to splendid
effect. How much Cotman painted in oil outdoors is
open to question, as too little is known of his approach to
oil painting in general. His early oils, like Mulready's
which may well have influenced him, display 'Picturesque' sensibility as much as a drive to naturalism; they
function as both pictures and sketches. This rhythmic
study of trees against light has both a spontaneous feel
and a profound sense of place, but Cotman achieves this
by the mystery of art rather than by the description of
details. Our sense of recognition springs from a collec-
tive memory of walks in shady woods, and does not
depend on topographical knowledge. Alas Cotman's
contemporaries could not always appreciate this, as he
found in the case of another view of Duncombe Park
included in his series of *Miscellaneous Etchings*: Francis

Cholmeley, in 1811, told Cotman that people 'did not
like the view … because it might have been *anywhere*.
Two-thirds of mankind, you know, mind more *what* is
represented than *how* it is done'. Here Cotman may
simply have chosen, as outdoor sketchers so often do, a
corner of the woods at random, and worked them into
this elegant design; but it is hard to discount other
elements at work on his mind – Rubens's forest
landscapes, perhaps, or Claude's rustic pastorals. 'Duncombe Park', if a sketch from nature at all, is a very
complex one. Its date must be quite early, for the
sombre tonality and almost monochrome palette relates
to his watercolours of *c.*1805–6, and the graceful play of
trees particularly to drawings made at Brandsby, also in
Yorkshire, in 1805. Cotman visited the Cholmeleys at
Brandsby in 1803, 1804 and 1805 and it was in this last
year that he wrote to his patron Dawson Turner that his
'chief Study has been colouring from Nature'. Although
Cotman's first oil is generally dated to the autumn of
1806, it would be tempting to associate this with his
Yorkshire visit the previous year.

GEORGE ROBERT LEWIS 1782–1871

53 **Harvest Field with Gleaners, Haywood,
Herefordshire*** 1815
Oil on canvas
143 × 195 (5⁹⁄₁₆ × 17¹¹⁄₁₆)
Inscribed 'Dynedor Hill Herefordshire/ George
Robert Lewis/ [?B]' on stretcher
T03234

Lewis was a friend of Linnell and toured Wales with him
in 1813. He made a brief showing as a landscape painter
but after 1820 concentrated on portraits. The 'Harvest
Field' is one of a group of four scenes at Haywood in
Herefordshire in the Tate Gallery, and with a subject of

reapers of almost exactly the same size and clearly its companion, and two larger oils of similar views, it formed part of a series of twelve Haywood subjects shown at the Society of Painters in Oil and Water Colours in 1816; the gleaning and reaping scenes were probably shown together, as part of several groups of small subjects arranged three to a frame. All these pictures, including the larger ones, were described in the accompanying catalogue as 'Painted on the Spot' and related to times of day. Haywood is a few miles south-west of Hereford, and Lewis's views are taken looking approximately eastwards, towards Dinedor Hill. We do not know what brought Lewis to work there in harvest-time in 1815, but the painstaking and respectful approach he took to the landscape – and especially to the workers in the field – almost certainly reflects the influence of Linnell, whose early pictures had often included prominent workmen and whose religious beliefs inclined him to a particular interest in subjects like the harvest. In 1828 Linnell would write to Palmer: 'Pray inform me ... if the harvest is begun in your part yet for I should like to see something of that glorious type of the everlasting harvest of spirits, the gathering of the saints'.

Whether or not Lewis shared Linnell's tendency to endow his subjects with a degree of typological symbolism, he must have been powerfully inspired at least by the pictorial possibilities of the harvest, and perhaps also by a political dimension. In 1815 the Corn Law was passed, which protected the landowners at the expense of the farm workers, and when Lewis exhibited his pictures, a severe winter had produced a poor harvest and an agricultural crisis. The introduction of farming machinery had meanwhile created unemployment on the land, and in 1816 there was an outbreak of Luddite machine-breaking by farm labourers – though mainly in the eastern counties. Against this background there may be elements of nostalgia and propaganda in Lewis's apparently unaffected vision of a traditional harvest. His interest in social issues was later evident in a pamphlet on education, published at Hereford in 1838.

WILLIAM HAVELL 1782–1857

54 **Caversham Bridge** 1805
Oil on paper laid on wood
276 × 219 ($10\frac{7}{8}$ × $8\frac{5}{8}$)
Inscribed on verso: 'Caversham Bridge over the Thames near Reading, Berks. by W. Havell 1805'
T01095

A native of the Thames valley, and brought up near Reading, Havell painted a number of views of it in oil and watercolour from 1805, working often in the open air. This sketch is among his earliest Thames subjects, painted in the same year as Turner's Thames campaign of outdoor sketching from his boat. Like some of Turner's small sketches on mahogany, this sketch establishes within a very small compass the essential structure of a classical composition with overhanging trees and bridge in the middle distance. Its spontaneity is thus modified by a pictorial imagination, and the existence of an outline sketch in pen over pencil of a very similar composition on horizontal landscape format (private collection) may indicate that Havell worked up the oil in his studio. In the coming years Havell developed a more unaffected vision in sketches like the following in which greater emphasis is given to bright outdoor lighting.

WILLIAM HAVELL 1782–1857

55 **Windsor Castle** *c.*1807
Oil on card
117×219 ($4\frac{9}{16} \times 8\frac{5}{8}$)
Inscribed on verso 'Windsor – /31/ Windsor Castle/
in the distance/ W Havell'
T03394

Evidently a sketch from nature in view of its small size, broad handling and simplified tonal patterns, this probably dates from about the same time as Havell was preparing watercolours of Windsor Castle for the Society of Painters in Water Colours exhibitions of 1806, 1807 and 1808. It may be compared to Turner's Thames sketches of 1805, and to those of their mutual friend Delamotte (cat.no.51). Another oil sketch, 'On the Kennet, Reading', in a similar technique and on card of the same size, is in the Yale Center for British Art.

WILLIAM DIXON ?1784 or 5–*c.*1834

56 **Cottages near a Track**
Oil on paper laid on paper and canvas
163×202 ($6\frac{7}{16} \times 8$)
T03855

Until recently little has been known of Dixon and his work has been confused with that of his friend and mentor Linnell. According to Linnell's 'Autobiographical Notes', Dixon was a protégé of Mulready and also drew at the Royal Academy. By 1816 he was living in Newcastle and he exhibited portraits and landscapes there in the 1820s. He retained a London address and the friendship of Mulready and Linnell. After his death Linnell bought his 'scetches from nature and studies for Pictures', including this bright and bold study of a rural track. The handling is markedly looser and the architecture of the cottages less painstakingly described than in the early sketches of Linnell (see cat.no.46), although the interest in rustic buildings may be traced back to Mulready's 'Picturesque' cottages and Linnell's Twickenham exercises under the tuition of John Varley, whom Dixon also seems to have known. Linnell regretfully observed that Dixon made no use of his 'beautiful studies from nature' and had kept them in disorder that 'defies description'; he added that his pictures 'came to nothing through double mindedness and infirmity of purpose'. Perhaps Dixon could not solve the problem of translating the freshness of his sketches into works for exhibition. In 1824 he wrote to Linnell, in connection with a portrait that he planned to submit to the Royal Academy, that he had been 'so irregularly connected with the arts & never having exhibited that I have no confidence at all in myself'.

Dixon's subject is perhaps in Northumberland, and might have been painted after *c.*1816; an oil sketch by him of Cullercoats, on the Northumberland coast, is extant. The Tate Gallery also owns Dixon's only signed oil sketch so far discovered, a vivid study of a group of hop-pickers – evidence perhaps of visits to Kent and even through Linnell and another mutual friend, Francis Oliver Finch, of some contact with Samuel Palmer at Shoreham.

AUGUSTUS WALL CALLCOTT 1779–1844

57 **A Road Leading to a Village*** *c.*1812
Oil on panel
197 × 260 (7¾ × 10¾)
T05470

Callcott was born, and lived all his life, in the area of West London known as Kensington Gravel Pits (near what is now Notting Hill Gate). In his youth the district was undeveloped and rustic, and with its dry, sandy soil and ramshackle buildings constituted a veritable lexicon of the 'Picturesque'. Like Mulready, who arrived there to live, and Linnell who came to stay, Callcott made a practice of studying and painting outdoors. Although he later cut himself off from the continued outdoor activities of Kensington artists, and maintained that he never painted in the open air, pictures 'Painted from Nature' were among his early exhibits, and a few small and very fresh oils are known by him, of subjects by the Thames or in the Thames valley, of which this is presumably one. Like Mulready's or Delamotte's, they are crisply handled and bright and crystalline in their tone and lighting; and they must have been intended as small pictures that combined the qualities of sketches and finished pictures within the context of 'Picturesque' taste.

Constable's Oil Sketches

Constable is among the very greatest masters of the oil sketch from nature, unmatched in Britain and perhaps only rivalled by Corot on the Continent. Both Corot and Constable made exceptional use of their sketches; in their hands painting outdoors was transformed from an occasional or escapist activity, or one associated only with study or training, into an essential ingredient in their working pattern. Yet their approaches were very different, for Corot, like Turner, consistently submitted his open-air work to the lessons of the studio, both selecting and composing, and constructing subjects according to appropriate pictorial conventions even as he worked on the spot. Constable, on the other hand, went further than any painter of his generation in finding his own pictorial language through open-air sketching. The 'natural painture' that he set himself to discover in his native Stour valley in 1802 was to be found from nature, and from his own domestic landscape.

Constable did not expect such a fresh vision to come easily. Through 'laborious studies from nature' he would search for a 'pure and unaffected representation'. At this point he singled out the need to find a realistic palette and to work independently of artistic tradition; he had tired of 'running after pictures' seeking 'truth at second hand', but it is clear that he was rejecting received techniques rather than compositional values, for his vision that summer was still formed in large part by Claude. His first attempts at outdoor painting in his own way were tentative and show little obvious pleasure in the paint. Only later did he relax, and it was in 1811, back on the banks of the Stour, that he first displayed the bravura spirit that informed his painting for the rest of his life.

Constable apparently only once finished an exhibition picture in the open air, 'Boat-Building', shown in 1815 (Victoria and Albert Museum), and his oil sketches were not made with a public in mind. But no painter made more use of them in his finished work. For a few years in mid career, he was lucky enough to find a series of near-complete subjects in his first outdoor sketches, both in oil and pencil. Moreover, the verve and immediacy of handling caught in his oil sketches was successfully carried into his studio canvases, and when in the 1820s he began to prepare large-scale sketches for his exhibited 'six-footers', this was less to conform to traditional studio practice than to fix both the composition and that sparkle and instantaneity that he achieved in outdoor work, so that he could transmit it to the final canvas without apparent strain. For Constable 'natural painture' came to mean as much a vivid and varied handling as an earthy, indigenous language of landscape. He did not 'see *handling* in nature', and his own techniques were calculated as the antithesis of traditional painting.

Constable's use of his oil sketches was not consistent throughout his career. For a time the crucible of his art, they were later relegated to a more subordinate role. His very commitment to landscape as Art led him inexorably towards the monumental, and away from spontaneous conception. But although he reverted to traditional methods of picture-making for the more ambitious work of his later years, he never lost the dynamic touch that he had found and developed through his oil sketching, nor ceased to sketch. The sky studies of the early 1820s represent a return to traditional methods of gathering reference material, but they are as vividly painted as any he had ever made.

later concern with the 'chiaroscuro of nature', and indeed the composition of this and related Stoke-by-Nayland subjects was chosen for inclusion in the series of mezzotints of *English Landscape Scenery*, in which this concept was given fullest expression. The Tate's oil sketch displays Constable's natural gift for picture-making, and it was in sketches like this that he was now to discover the subjects of a series of finished pictures. However, it was not until 1835 and 1836 that he contemplated a picture of a similar view, of which a canvas in the Art Institute of Chicago may be all that remains, having perhaps been left unfinished by the artist and worked over by another hand.

John Constable 1776–1837

58 **Stoke-by-Nayland*** *c.*1810–11
   Oil on canvas
   181 × 264 ($7\frac{1}{8}$ × 10$\frac{3}{8}$)
   N01819

Constable frequently drew the church at Stoke-by-Nayland, on the north side of the Stour valley west of East Bergholt and Dedham, in his sketchbooks of 1810–14. Oil sketches closely related to the Tate Gallery's are in the Victoria and Albert Museum, and the Metropolitan Museum of Art, New York. The Tate sketch belongs to that period about 1810 and 1811 when Constable first displayed full maturity as an oil painter; the bold, even agitated handling, with its unusual brushing from left to right in downward sweeps, shows to powerful effect his new confidence with the medium and creates a breezy, fresh effect in contrast to the lack of plasticity found in some oil sketches from earlier in the decade. Constable has fixed a vivid effect of contrasted sunshine and shadow at midday that anticipates his

John Constable 1776–1837

59 **A Bank on Hampstead Heath** *c.*1820–2
   Oil on canvas
   206 × 254 ($8\frac{1}{8}$ × 9$\frac{15}{16}$)
   N02658

After 1819, when he first took a house at Hampstead, Constable made many oil sketches of the surrounding landscape and skies. Constable's handling in his oil sketches is infinitely varied, and this example, which combines his interest in sky effects and in the foreground circumstances of a sandy bank and its surface vegetation, is relatively highly finished. Constable's view is very closely focused on the bank itself, and affords only a glimpse of distant horizon with winding paths and figures on the skyline. The bank is a feature reminiscent of the 'Picturesque' interests of artists like Mulready and Linnell some years earlier (cat.nos.45–50).

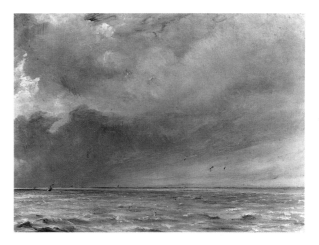

John Constable 1776–1837

60 **Cloud Study** 1822
  Oil on paper laid on board
  476 × 575 ($18\frac{11}{16} × 22\frac{5}{8}$)
  Inscribed in pencil on the original backing paper,
  '27 augt 11 o clock Noon looking Eastward large
  silvery [?Clouds] wind Gentle at S.West'
  N06065

By the early 1820s Constable's personal aspirations had
mounted, and he was seeking a more monumental art.
His oil sketches now played a greater part in furnishing
circumstantial detail and vividness of handling, than in
providing in themselves the inception of a picture. Thus
they were put to a rather more conventional use than in
the previous decade, but Constable's commitment to
the practice of sketching remained as sincere as ever
while the enquiries he pursued through them became if
anything more precise and scientific. Within his exceptional production as a sketcher, his sky studies constitute
a self-contained and extraordinary group. Made at
Hampstead in 1821 and 1822, they include a number of
studies almost entirely of sky with only a hint of trees or
buildings below, and others like this of sky alone. Their
inscriptions of time and prevailing conditions emphasise the spirit of rational inquiry behind Constable's
'skying'; it was an activity he did not maintain for long,
and none of the sky studies was apparently used for a
particular painting, but like Valenciennes before him,
or indeed Turner in his much more vaguely documen-
ted studies of sea and sky, he was now evidently
satisfying personal curiosity while amassing a body of
source material which could be absorbed into his
artistic conception generally, if not literally. Constable
had long appreciated the value of skies in affecting the
tone and character of landscape, considering them the
'chief "organ of sentiment" '.

John Constable 1776–1837

61 **The Sea near Brighton*** 1826
  Oil on paper laid on card
  175 × 238 ($6\frac{13}{16} × 9\frac{3}{8}$)
  Inscribed on a label on the old backing board
  'Brighton. Sunday, Jan.ʸ 1ˢᵗ: 1826 From 12 till 2
  P.M. Fresh breeze from S.S.W' (the hand is that of
  Charles Golding Constable, the artist's son, who
  has presumably copied the artist's inscription from
  the back of the paper)
  N02656

In New Year, 1826, Constable joined his wife and
family at Brighton, and stayed a fortnight. During this
visit he worked on a painting of Gillingham Mill,
Dorset, to be exhibited at the Royal Academy later that
year (Yale Center for British Art), and made this bold
study of sea and sky – apparently his only other work
from this stay in Brighton, and one of the very few oil
sketches he made outdoors in winter. Constable had, on
an earlier visit to Brighton in 1824, found only 'the
magnificence of the sea' to admire; there was 'nothing
here for a painter but the breakers and the sky, which
have been lovely indeed', and he had sketched them, as
he must have done again here, 'in the lid of my box on
my knees'.

£4.95 8b (1972b) —

SELECT BIBLIOGRAPHY

D. Bomford, J. Kirby, J. Leighton and A. Roy, *Impressionism: Art in the Making*, exh. cat., National Gallery, London, 1991

A. Bowness and A. Callen, *The Impressionists in London*, exh. cat., Hayward Gallery, London, 1973

D.B. Brown, *Augustus Wall Callcott*, exh. cat., Tate Gallery, London, 1981

D.B. Brown, *Turner and the Channel; Themes and Variations c.1845*, exh. cat., Tate Gallery, London, 1987

D. Chittock, 'Detective Work at Knockholt', *Turner News*, no.5, March 1977, pp.92–4

M. Clarke, *Lighting up the Landscape: French Impressionism and its Origins*, exh. cat., National Gallery of Scotland, Edinburgh, 1986

P. Conisbee, 'Pre-Romantic *Plein-Air* Painting', *Art History*, vol.2, no.4, 1979, pp.413–28

M. Cormack, *Oil on Water: Oil Sketches by British Watercolourists*, exh. cat., Yale Center for British Art, New Haven, 1986

R. Edwards, *Thomas Jones (1742–1803)*, exh. cat., Marble Hill, Twickenham and National Museum of Wales, Cardiff, 1970

I. Fleming-Williams, L. Parris and C. Shields, *Constable: Paintings, Watercolours and Drawings*, exh. cat., Tate Gallery, London, 1976

J. Gage, *A Decade of English Naturalism 1810–1820*, exh. cat., Castle Museum, Norwich and Victoria and Albert Museum, London, 1969–70

P. Galassi, *Corot in Italy: Open-Air Painting and the Classical Landscape Tradition*, 1991

L. Gowing and P. Conisbee, *Painting from Nature: the Tradition of Open-Air Oil Sketching from the 17th to the 19th Centuries*, exh. cat., Fitzwilliam Museum, Cambridge and Royal Academy, London, 1980–1

L. Gowing, *The Originality of Thomas Jones*, 1985

C.S. Moffett *et al.*, *The New Painting: Impressionism 1874–1886*, exh. cat., National Gallery, Washington and Fine Art Museums of San Francisco, 1986

L. Parris, 'New Light on English Landscape Painting 1800–1820', *Tate Gallery Report*, 1968–70, pp.37–41

L. Parris, *The Tate Gallery Constable Collection*, 1981

L. Parris and C. Shields, *Landscape in Britain c.1750–1850*, exh. cat., Tate Gallery, London, 1973

M. Pointon, *William Mulready 1786–1863*, exh. cat., Victoria and Albert Museum, London, National Gallery of Ireland, Dublin and Ulster Museum, Belfast, 1986–87

C. Powell, *Turner in the South: Rome, Naples, Florence*, 1987

P.R. Radisich, 'Eighteenth Century *Plein-Air* Painting and the Sketches of Pierre Henri de Valenciennes', *Art Bulletin*, 64, 1982, pp.98–104

M. Rajnai, 'Two recently discovered oil sketches' [by Turner], *Turner Studies*, vol.2, no.2, 1983, pp.58–9

S. Smiles, 'Turner in Devon: some additional information concerning his visits in the 1810s', *Turner Studies*, vol.7, no.1, 1987, pp.11–13

S. Smiles, 'The Devonshire Oil Sketches [by Turner] of 1813', *Turner Studies*, vol.9, no.1, 1989, pp.10–26

A.T. Story, *The Life of John Linnell*, 1982

A. Wintermute (ed.), *Claude to Corot: the Development of Landscape Painting in France*, exh. cat., Colnaghi, New York, 1990